Oglethorpe in
Perspective

Oglethorpe
in Perspective
Georgia's Founder after
Two Hundred Years

Edited by
Phinizy Spalding and
Harvey H. Jackson

The University of Alabama Press
Tuscaloosa • London

Library of Congress Cataloging-in-Publication Data

Oglethorpe in perspective.

Bibliography: p.
Includes index.
1. Oglethorpe, James Edward, 1696–1785.   2. Georgia—
Governors—Biography.   3. Georgia—History—Colonial
period, ca. 1600–1775.   I. Spalding, Phinizy.
II. Jackson, Harvey H.
F289.037037   1988   975.8'02'0924 [B]   87-19121
ISBN 0-8173-0386-3

British Library Cataloguing-in-Publication Data available

Contents

Oglethorpe in
Perspective

Introduction

The signs all seemed propitious. The neighbor Carolinians were happy
—in fact had pitched in and helped with the move. James Edward
Oglethorpe, the paterfamilias, was concerned, experienced, a known
quantity. So what if the Spanish were upset by the newcomers? They
would learn to accept change just as everyone did. As for the natives
who preceded the newcomers on the site, their attitudes were certainly
important, but they too seemed pleased. The weather was good, the
spot healthy—and it was almost springtime. Life was good; God most
assuredly was British.

Such were the reports initially to come from the colony of Georgia
when, on February 1, 1733, James Edward Oglethorpe and his feisty
"first forty" families clambered up Yamacraw Bluff to the plain that was
the site of Savannah. Governor Robert Johnson and South Carolina
had generously provided the settlers with supplies and encouragement;
the tiny, weak, isolated tribe of Yamacraw Indians, headed by the venerable Tomochichi—an Englishman's Indian if ever there was one—
had given its permission to let these interlopers make a permanent
settlement near their own meager town. Mary and John Musgrove, an
Anglicized half-breed and her Indian trader husband, helped see to
that. And although the Spaniards made a great noise in formal diplomatic circles to register their rage at this intrusion into their old mission
province of Guale, Spain's all but moribund buffer colony of Florida was
in no position to fight. The French, of course, were another matter,
but their advances into the backcountry had been checked and they

now seemed satisfied to hold on to what they had near Mobile and the immediately adjacent areas drained by the Alabama River system. Oglethorpe had reason to be confident as he approached the Yamacraw Indians for a parlay.

The province of Georgia had, in fact, been a long time in the making. By November 1732, when the *Anne* began her slow progress down the Thames on her way to the New World, most of England knew of the colony. And England applauded. The vision and the drive that its early backers showed reminded English society that it was the Age of Reason and the time of the Enlightenment. Encapsulated in this one movement were many of the reform impulses that stirred Britain during the first three decades of the eighteenth century: the desire to bring the word of Anglican Christianity to the native Americans, the concern that foreign Protestants be offered a refuge from their Catholic persecutors, the sentiment that the new colony would be a place to which the English poor might go to remake their lives and contribute to the well-being of the empire, the anxiety abroad in Britain that gin and other hard liquors were sapping the strength of the nation, and the first dawnings of what was later to become a massive protest against the institution of slavery. All these impulses and more motivated the originators of the Georgia Plan. Surely there was never a colony so widely based in its foundation; surely no province ever had the general acceptance that Georgia did in its infancy.

At the center of all these movements stood James Oglethorpe. In his middle thirties, he was at the peak of his powers. From his father Theophilus, he inherited determination and principle; from his mother, Eleanor Wall, he took his temper, high spirits, and unquestioned dash. Ever since his youth, when he lived on the Continent with his Jacobite parents, to his young adulthood, when he fought against the Turks in eastern Europe, to the day when he returned to Britain and secured election to Parliament from Haslemere, he was a man of influence. In his public and private life Oglethorpe incorporated many of the aspects of the philanthropy abroad in English society at the time. Although by no means a radical, and far from being a revolutionary in any sense of the word, James Oglethorpe was still very much his own man. In his independence of party and in the clarity of his thinking he probably resembled more closely the concept of a seventeenth-century English liberal than anything else. He was a man to be watched.

Although never in command of large numbers of political followers—
he would have been suspicious had such been the case—he was widely
admired and would not be gainsaid. His egoism, self-confidence, and
touchiness made some critical of him; his family's ardent Jacobitism
made others wonder about his loyalties. But now his mettle was to
be tested in the New World. Georgia was a reflection of the reformist
trends in eighteenth-century Great Britain, but would this man—the
associate of such enlightened English figures as Stephen Hales, Thomas
Coram, Thomas Bray, and Sir Hans Sloane—succeed in alien responsibilities under the pressures of a new physical, political, and economic
environment?

The essays that follow in this book attempt to answer some of the
questions that continually come to the surface when Oglethorpe's name
is mentioned. These nine contributions represent the latest research
on America's least known founding father. With typical American impatience, historians of the prerevolutionary years have hurried through
the early decades of the eighteenth century in order to get to the crises
that beset the British Empire from the 1760s on. In their haste, tran-
sitional figures such as Oglethorpe are glossed over, and the value of
examining England's most ambitious colonial experiment in the century of revolution is lost. Oglethorpe dealt with many of the basic
problems that all founders faced—plus more. But to some who viewed
him critically, Oglethorpe was a posing, prancing whirligig bent only
toward self-gratification, while to others he was simply the most recent
in a long line of imperialists who schemed to expand John Bull's empire
at the expense of Spain, France, and the native Americans. His philosophy of colonization was empty rhetoric, said others, full of sound
and fury signifying nothing.

But it is hoped that this volume of essays will provide a sense of what
the man Oglethorpe really was about. Emerging from these articles and
from earlier writings—much of them done by these same contributors
—is a new and more decisive Oglethorpe. In these pages he will be seen
dealing effectively and frequently with the basic issues of southern colonial life: who was to do the decision making and why; what comprised
the nature of the Indian trade and what were its stakes; how political decisions affected cultural and social factors; how to treat with the
native Americans within Georgia's borders; where and how to expand
at the expense of Britain's enemies; and how slavery might be excluded

—along with rum and large landholding—from the southern experience. Oglethorpe was no dilettante who sought to manipulate colonial
situations from London; he came to America strong-willed and determined, from the beginning, to make his personal impression on the
land. His solid self-confidence caused him to meet most outstanding
colonial questions eye to eye; in fact a strong case can be made that in
his enthusiasm and optimism he tackled more issues head-on than any
other southern colonizer, or any American colonizer for that matter.
And when he was finished with the American phase of his career he
was still looking for challenges. So in his middle age, he returned to
the European continent to fight the hated French.

Throughout his career James Oglethorpe, like Georgia's most noted
colonial governor, James Wright, was a builder. In many ways ahead
of his time, he could not succeed in such issues as antislavery, but
in the areas where he made his mark—prison reform, sailors' rights,
establishing a successful colony and giving it its rules—Oglethorpe's
contributions are clear. Only now, after two hundred years, is history
beginning to appreciate his full importance.

Circles in the Sand
Perspectives on the Southern Frontier
at the Arrival of James Oglethorpe

Peter H. Wood

In this opening essay, Peter Wood notes that the long-standing Anglocentrism and northeastern bias of colonial American historians has caused scholars to neglect, and therefore fail to appreciate, the complexity of the southeastern frontier from which James Oglethorpe would carve Georgia. Thus it is often forgotten that the Southeast was an "old" frontier and one whose native population had been greatly altered by nearly two centuries of epidemics and exploitation. Moreover, the Southeast was a large frontier, stretching from the Atlantic Ocean to some point beyond the Mississippi River and including within its limits European outposts, traders, and of course the Indians. This frontier was what James Oglethorpe faced when he landed in 1733, and Wood's analysis provides an ideal point to begin this new look at Georgia's founding father. —Editors

Southern history is almost a virgin field and one of the richest in the world for results. The history of the United States has been written by Boston, and largely written wrong. It must be written anew before it reaches its final form of truth. And for that work . . . the South must do its part in preparation. New England has already over done its part. There have been antiquarians and chroniclers at work in the Southern field, but few historians—few thinkers—and thought is the all-essential. I have only begun to dabble in the edge of it; but the results are quite surprising. A study of the Old South from the inside readily

5

shows an immense number of errors of interpretation by the old school of historians.[1]

Although this blunt statement may still sound contemporary to some, it is not. It was written in 1903 at the University of Wisconsin, where Frederick Jackson Turner and others were doing so much to modernize, and de–New Englandize, the study of American history. The author was a twenty-six-year-old scholar with a bachelor's degree from the University of Georgia and a doctorate from Columbia. He had been born in the town of La Grange, in west-central Georgia, in 1877 and been christened Ulysses Bonnell after the doctor who had delivered him. But as a boy he learned enough Confederate history to know that Ulysses had dubious connotations for an aspiring white lad in the post-Reconstruction South, and he bargained successfully with his parents to change his name to Ulrich.[2] In 1909, as a professor at Tulane, Ulrich Bonnell Phillips published a book of documents on the colonial and antebellum South entitled *Plantation and Frontier*, and he went on to become an influential historian of the region.[3]

The dominant views of U. B. Phillips and his contemporaries regarding "the southern plantation" and their appraisals of racial enslavement as a benign institution have been drastically revised over the last decades. But what about reinterpretations of "the southern frontier"? They have progressed far less rapidly. Turner himself, the pioneer of frontier historians, was geographically most interested in the North and Midwest, and chronologically he was most concerned with the century after European settlers began pouring through Cumberland Gap in the 1770s. He had little to say about the colonial Southeast. One of his students, another midwesterner named Verner W. Crane, had a great deal to say, but Crane's path-breaking study of *The Southern Frontier* (Ann Arbor, 1929) ended tantalizingly in 1732 on the eve of Georgia colonization. And rather than pressing ahead to write a sequel on borderland matters that were of little interest to most colonial historians, Crane returned to the northern fold and became a noted expert on the life of Benjamin Franklin.[4]

Even during the last twenty-five years, with the exception of important scholars and lay experts within the state, professionals and public alike have remained relatively uninformed about early Georgia and its frontiers. I can recall that at Harvard during the early 1960s the post in southern history—a field then known as "mint juleps" in the student vernacular—had gone unfilled for a decade, and the founding of Georgia was scarcely mentioned in my colonial history course. In the Northeast, professors of early America deemed the colonial South as consisting solely of Virginia, and it is still viewed that way to a remarkable degree. If one looks up "Georgia" in the index to a recent collection of essays on colonial British America, the entry says simply, "*See* Lower South colonies." And when one searches for "Oglethorpe, James," one finds no entry between "Occupational specialization, in cities" and "Oligarchy, as form of colonial politics." The leading scholars who contributed to this volume were full of ideas about slavery and plantations, as they labored to consolidate several decades of lively scholarship, but regarding the frontiers of the Southeast they had almost nothing to say. One wonders whether historian Clarence Ver Steeg was off base, or simply farsighted, when he wrote in 1966: "The eighteenth-century southern frontier will certainly be the center of emerging new interpretations."[5]

Truly fresh interpretations do not emerge overnight; they depend upon years and even generations of careful work by many people, and numerous impediments must be overcome. The northeastern bias about which Phillips complained, broadened now to embrace the middle colonies and the Chesapeake, still persists. Hence Francis Jennings's provocative intercultural history from 1975, *The Invasion of America*, and William Cronon's suggestive ecological book from 1983, *Changes in the Land*, deal almost exclusively with New England.[6] They are part of a small renaissance of revisionist studies for the northeastern and middle Atlantic frontiers that as yet has no clear equivalent in the colonial South.

Moreover, this regional bias is couched within a larger cultural bias in favor of the English over the French or the Spanish, the Indians or the Africans. Because the English came late to the South, and then only to one edge of it in any great numbers, this perspective has had a constricting effect on our study of the subject. It is suggestive that some of the best contributions in recent years have been made by historians with a background in Spanish or French colonial materials and by scholars with experience in other disciplines such as geography or anthropology.[7] But for the most part colonial scholars who escape the hoary geographic magnet of the northeastern seaboard still find themselves, like Verner Crane sixty years ago, caught in the wider and less obvious magnetic field of enduring Anglocentrism.[8]

Therefore, even where such Anglocentrism appears most appropriate—as in a study of James Oglethorpe—it seems healthy to fortify ourselves with the tonic of other perspectives, and it falls to me to dispense a few such mild stimulants at the outset lest any large portions of English mutton on the ensuing menu should inadvertently narrow our arteries or our horizons. I shall offer my relativistic cordial in the form of two toasts regarding the southern frontier at the time of Oglethorpe's arrival:

1.   My initial salute will be "*to the venerable age of that frontier*"— it was more than two centuries old when the passengers of the galley *Anne* debarked.
2.   And my second toast is "*to the enormous geographical scope of that frontier*"—far from being a sharp line at the edge of a clearing, the eighteenth-century southern frontier is best understood as a vast and varied zone of political, cultural, and economic interaction stretching from the Atlantic to East Texas and from the Ohio River to the Gulf.

There is no better way to begin exploring these neglected dimensions of the southern frontier—its venerable age and its enormous geographic scope—than to contemplate the familiar "View of Savannah" by local magistrate Peter Gordon. March 29, 1734, the date given for the drawing, was scarcely a year after Oglethorpe ceremoniously drove the initial nail for the town's first house, on March 1, 1733. But already a symmetrical little settlement had sprung up, with scores of identical huts in neat rows. To heighten the picture's dramatic perspective, or perhaps to whet the appetites of investors, Gordon included the precise outlines of future house plots. Days after he completed the picture, Gordon returned to London, where his drawing was presented to the Georgia Trustees and made into a popular engraving by P. Fourdrinier.[9] (See Figure 3-1.)

This view has been featured in books and articles and used on endpapers and dustjackets ever since. Indeed, it has become a veritable icon of Georgia colonization, allowing each succeeding generation to stare south-southwest across the river at the newly laid out and startlingly rectilinear town of Savannah. Along the eastern, downriver edge of the clearing, the artist indicated the beginnings of a palisade that was intended to extend around to meet the bluff again on the other side of town. In the middle of the waterfront, at the center of the picture, he showed Oglethorpe's large command tent. When Philipp von Reck, his mind no doubt prepared somewhat by Gordon's picture, arrived at Savannah with the Salzburgers in 1736, he confirmed that the new town "is built regularly, and is divided into four wards. In each of these an extensive square park has been left for holding markets or for being used for other common good. The region is pleasant, the streets are wide and laid in straight lines. The houses are all of one style and are placed with symmetry and proportion." The German immigrant further reported: "Discord and disorder are prevented by good order and a night watch, which provides the tired workers a restful sleep, although in the midst of the wilderness."[10]

Artist Gordon made this surrounding wilderness clearly evident. Stretching off in the distance on every side he suggested the dense pine forest of Georgia's coastal plain. But numerous generations, glancing repeatedly over the years at the curtain of trees that form the backdrop for Gordon's picture, have tended to ignore the true nature and dimensions of this colonial "frontier." How far backward in time, how far outward over the horizon, did it actually extend from Oglethorpe's tent? Brief answers to these questions can be tied to two small anecdotes from Oglethorpe's own Georgia career: an incident with an ancient Yamacraw chief upon Oglethorpe's first arrival from England, and an encounter with a Chickasaw delegation three years later.

In February 1733, the first Georgia colonists had not yet started to build their town. Indeed, they had not even purchased rights of settlement from the local Yamacraw Indians—a splinter group of the Creek Confederacy that had returned to its ancestral homeland near the coast several years before. While still appraising the English newcomers, the tribe's elderly leader, Tomochichi, showed the colonists a burial mound on Yamacraw Bluff overlooking the Savannah River just east of the projected town site.[11] A generation later the engineer William De Brahm noted this "Indian Hill" on his "Plan of the City of Savannah and Fortification." De Brahm recorded the story that on this site:

(as Thamachaychee the last Jamacraw King related to General Oglethorp at his Arrival) one of the Jamacraw Kings had entertained a great white Man with a red Beard, who had entered the Port of Savannah Stream with a very large Vessel, and himself came up in his Barge to Jamacraw, and had expressed great Affection to the Indians, from which he hath had the Return of as much. The white Man with his red Beard, intending to present the King with a Piece of Curiosity he had on board his Vessel, for which he signified: some Indians might go down to receive it from his Lieutenant on board, to Whom he wrote a Note, which he desired the Indians would deliver to this Officer, who (pursuant to the Order in the Note) delivered what was demanded, and the Indians brought it up to Jamacraw, at which their King was greatly surprised, but more so, that this white Man could send his Thoughts to so great a Distance upon a white Leaf, which surpassing their Conception, they were ready to believe this white to be more than a Man, as the Indians have no other way to express times passed or to come than by rising and setting of the Sun, by New Moons, by Sprouting of the Trees, and the Number of their Ancestors.[12]

According to De Brahm, General Oglethorpe, "by the nearest Computation and comparing History with Chronology, concluded the Person to have been Admiral Sir Walter Raleigh, who probably entered the Savannah Port in 1584, when on his Navigation up this Coast."[13] But the friendly sixteenth-century visitor with the distinctive red beard was not Raleigh, for the Elizabethan admiral never visited the Southeast in 1584 or any other time. Instead, it was apparently the French captain, Jean Ribault, who had first explored this coast more than two decades earlier, in 1562, and who, according to his Huguenot colleague, René Laudonnière, "was easie to be knowen by reason of the great bearde which he weare." And if the distinctive visitor was Ribault, then his Indian counterpart must have been the local chief Audusta, remote predecessor of Tomochichi, known from the documents to have shown great friendship and generosity toward the ill-fated Frenchmen in the 1560s.[14]

When explaining the mound to the English in the eighteenth century, the Indians, according to an account from 1733, "informed Mr. Oglethorpe that the [ancient] King [had] desired before he died, that he might be buried on the spot where he talk'd with that great good Man" with the red beard. A generation later the colonists confirmed by an excavation that this "high Mount of Earth" was indeed a burial mound. According to the engineer De Brahm, a portion of this hill "was dug through" in 1760, "whereby a Stratum was opened near the Plane of the City filled with human bones; this confirmed the History of this Mount, which had traduced it to be an ancient Indian Burying Ground."[15]

Around this hallowed tomb stretched ten acres of open ground, cleared in an earlier time and therefore known to the English as "Indian Old Fields."[16] Oglethorpe "had an avenue cut through the forest" to this nearby tract from the town's east gate and laid out a large experimental garden. "It lies on the river," von Reck reported in 1736, "and has been put in such good condition that one already finds there a lovely nursery of orange, olive, white mulberry, fig and peach trees, a great quantity of curious foreign plants and herbs, to say nothing of European fruits, plants, cabbage, peas, &c., all of which thrive well." But Oglethorpe seems to have ignored the garden's central "artificial hill," which the Indians said "was raised up over the body of one of their earliest emperors."[17] When Tomochichi died in 1739, the General saw to it that his ally was given a European funeral and buried with military fanfare at the center of a square near the town's south rampart.[18]

The Indians' story of their encounter with a bearded man on Yamacraw Bluff, at a site just off the edge of Gordon's picture and scarcely half a mile from Oglethorpe's tent, is of only passing interest in itself, until we begin to fathom all that transpired in the Deep South between the birth of Audusta in the early sixteenth century and the death of Tomochichi near the middle of the eighteenth century. We are socialized to think of frontier contact in North America as a passing phase—whether tragic or triumphant—something that took place in a lifetime and that can be summarized in a ninety-minute movie. But when the Georgia colony was founded, contacts between native Americans and newcomers in the Southeast already spanned seven or eight generations. To put it another way, Oglethorpe was as remote from Ponce de León as we are from the Stamp Act Crisis, and one could argue that in certain respects the South he entered had changed as much since the arrival of the Spaniards as the South we know now has changed since the American Revolution.[19]

Oglethorpe himself was scarcely aware of the vast changes wrought by two hundred years of intermittent exploration and settlement by rival European powers. And until recently historians have remained largely oblivious to those long-term shifts, centering around drastic demographic change. Because we underestimated the size of precontact Indian populations in the southeastern region, we underestimated the scope of the decline in numbers caused by the introduction of new diseases from abroad. Or perhaps it was the other way around: because we did not fathom the decimation caused by strange epidemics, we could not imagine the size of the precolonial—one might even say presmallpox—societies. Either way, only in recent decades have we begun to comprehend in the Southeast, as elsewhere, how large the precontact cultures were and therefore how awesomely steep their demographic drop must have been.[20]

Predictably, Florida sustained the first blows. The so-called carrying capacity of the area could have supported more than 700,000 persons, and the Timucuan-speaking population that dominated the peninsula *may* even have approached that number prior to 1515, at least according to one controversial recent estimate. A century later (fifty years after the founding of Saint Augustine but still before the *Mayflower* reached Plymouth Rock), repeated pandemics of smallpox, measles, influenza, and bubonic plague had reduced the Timucuans to a small fraction—perhaps less than one-tenth—of their previous size. Moreover, these devastating new diseases had begun to appear throughout the Southeast due to the incursions of sixteenth-century Spanish explorers such as Ayllon, Narváez, De Soto, De Luna, Pardo, and González, combined with patterns of extensive contact through trade and warfare among the various southern tribes themselves. When La Salle descended the Mississippi for the French in 1682 he doubted that it was the same river in which De Soto had been interred almost five generations before, because the local populations seemed so much smaller than those described by the Spaniards.[21]

The beginnings of inland trade by the English from Virginia and Carolina in the 1670s and 1680s, accompanied by wholesale distribution of rum and the purchase of many hundreds of Indian captives as slaves, compounded the problems of interior nations that had endured the earlier onslaughts. In 1697 a smallpox epidemic devastated Creek and Cherokee villages some five hundred miles inland, and John Lawson, who explored Carolina after 1700, described comparable desolation among piedmont cultures.

The Small-Pox has been fatal to them; they do not often escape, when they are seiz'd with that Distemper, which is a contrary Fever to what they ever knew. Most certain, it had never visited *America*, before the Discovery thereof by the Christians. Their running into the Water, in the Extremity of this Disease, strikes it in, and kills all that use it. Now they are become a little wiser; but formerly it destroy'd whole Towns, without leaving one *Indian* alive in the Village. . . . The Small-Pox and Rum, have made such a Destruction amongst them, that, on good grounds, I do believe, there is not the sixth Savage living within two hundred Miles of all our Settlements, as there were fifty Years ago. These poor Creatures have so many Enemies to destroy them, that it's a wonder one of them is left alive near us.[22]

Lawson clarified the means by which epidemics could spread to the mountain societies when he related, regarding rum, that these coastal and piedmont Indians "carry it back to the Westward *Indians*, who never knew what it was, till within very few Years. Now they have it brought them by the *Tuskeruro's*, and other Neighbour-*Indians*, but the *Tuskeruro's* chiefly, who carry it in Rundlets several hundred Miles, amongst other *Indians*." Furthermore, Lawson added,

when they happen to carry it safe, (which is seldom, without drinking some part of it, and filling it up with Water) and come to an *Indian* Town, those that buy Rum of them have so many Mouthfuls for a Buck-Skin, they never using any other Measure; and for this purpose, the Buyer always makes Choice of his Man, which is one that has the greatest Mouth, whom he brings to the Market with a Bowl to put it in. The Seller looks narrowly to the Man's Mouth that measures it, and if he happens to swallow any down, either through Wilfulness or otherwise, the Merchant or some of his Party, does not scruple to knock the Fellow down, exclaiming against him for false Measure. Thereupon, the Buyer finds another Mouthpiece to measure the Rum by.[23]

The smallest coastal groups, some of which had resisted the Spanish missionaries as far back as the 1590s, were all but gone by the 1730s, their remnants absorbed into new colonial settlements or heterogeneous inland tribes.[24] And these nations too—the Creeks, Cherokees, Cataw-bas, Choctaws, and Chickasaws—suffered enormous cultural disloca-tions that are only now being documented fully by ethnohistorians.[25] A minister speaking with Indians in South Carolina in 1710 reported their lament that "they have forgot most of their traditions since the Establishment of this Colony." He noted local tribes still "keep their Festivals," yet they "can tell but little of the reasons: their Old Men are dead."[26]

One such festival, combining the traditional and the new, was witnessed by Philipp von Reck in 1736. Whether a war dance or a busk (green corn ceremony), this event apparently took place at Yuchi Town north of Pallachocolas. Von Reck's painting shows evidence of ongoing Indian-European contact, such as the half-dozen rifles hanging in the background. He depicted brightly colored loincloths, probably made from the red and blue material distributed by Oglethorpe when he and von Reck attended an earlier busk at Frederica. Von Reck could not easily imagine the degree of change that had taken place in recent generations, though he did state that "Their age, I have been told, does not nearly attain that of their ancestors. For after strong drink and drunkenness were introduced among them, many died a sudden death."[27]

It is impossible to pinpoint a single critical moment in the long-term demographic and social upheaval of the southern frontier. The social fabric of divergent Indian societies did not unravel all at once but frayed separately at different times, in diverse ways, and to varying degrees. Yet if one examines the broad region from South Carolina, Georgia, and Florida across to East Texas, it seems clear that the early eighteenth century marked a huge and unique turning point for the history of the Deep South as a whole. Available figures, which are far more complete than one might first expect, suggest that the total human population of the Deep South region in 1680 exceeded 190,000, *more than 98 percent of whom were native American*. A half century later, although there were more than 25,000 Africans and 14,000 Europeans on the fringes of this area, the tenfold increase in non-Indians by no means offset the continuing decline in Indian numbers. According to my calculations, Indian losses outstripped colonial gains by three to one, and as a result the region's total population reached its all-time historical low of scarcely more than 100,000 inhabitants in the years between 1710 and 1730. From this low ebb the tide turned quickly and of course changed color as well. Native American losses leveled off, and the new arrivals from Africa and Europe—many of them early Georgians—multiplied rapidly. Fifty years later, by the time of the Siege of Savannah, the population for the entire Deep South had nearly tripled and was approaching 300,000.[28]

Certainly one conclusion, among many we might draw, is that this longer time frame helps explain the seemingly contradictory Indian support and resistance encountered by the first generation of Georgia colonists. For many weary Indian elders, such as Tomochichi of the Yamacraws, an alliance with England appeared an opportunity and, more importantly, a necessity. One Cherokee chief, Scalileskin Retagusta, who journeyed to England in the delegation of 1730, expressed this poignant viewpoint clearly when he told English courtiers in London: "We came hither naked and poor as the Worm out of the earth, but you have everything and we that have nothing must love you and can never break the Chain of Friendship that is between us."[29] But younger Indians chafed under that same chain and other more visible ones, as the uprisings of subsequent generations of native Americans would continue to attest. There may have been some substance, as well as deep longing, behind the testimony of an Indian slave in Charles Town in May 1733, the year of Oglethorpe's arrival, "that an Indian Woman had told him that all the Indians of the Continent design'd to rise and make War, against the English."[30]

If the story of the Yamacraw burial mound can serve as a reminder of the chronological depth of the Georgia frontier, another Oglethorpe vignette illustrates that frontier's enormous geographic breadth. After a sojourn in England to shore up support for the colony and gather new recruits, the founder returned to Georgia early in 1736 with a party of Salzburgers who would relocate the colony's struggling German town of Ebenezer at a new riverside location. The group reached Savannah on February 19, "where Mr. Oglethorpe was received by the entire citizenry, constables and tythingmen, all under arms, with salutes from all heavy cannons and with every imaginable sign of joy. . . . The Indian King, Tomochichi, welcomed him and immediately sent two runners to bring news of his arrival to the Upper and Lower Creeks."[31]

Oglethorpe worked hard that year. On the one hand, he had to restrain his most dedicated local Indian allies from attacking the Spaniards; on the other hand, he needed to consolidate the support of distant nations in case war should break out. On July 13, 1736, when a Chickasaw delegation visited the governor in Savannah, an incident occurred that seems emblematic. These Indians had come all the way from northern Mississippi, in part, they said, because they had heard rumors that Oglethorpe, unlike officials in South Carolina, was the son of a red woman. They soon saw that in fact he had "as white a Body as any in Charles Town," but the General still managed to sway them by announcing that he was "an Indian in my heart" (rather the way President Kennedy reassured West German allies in Berlin in the 1960s by proclaiming "Ich bin ein Berliner"). To test his support, the Chickasaws repeated French charges that British powder and shot were inferior, prompting Oglethorpe to give them the munitions they desired—along with advice about how to fight the French, based on his experiences in Europe.[32]

The small but meaningful anecdote that dramatizes my second point —the geographic scope of the southern frontier—comes from that conference. As Phinizy Spalding relates the incident in his book, *Oglethorpe in America*, during the course of discussion the Indian leaders graphically illustrated to Oglethorpe their sense that both the Chickasaws and the English were in danger of being encircled and overwhelmed by a third party, the French. According to Spalding, "By drawing ever larger circles in the sand to represent the three forces the Indians pointed out not only their own weakness and vulnerability but the English weakness as well. The large French circle encompassed the Anglo-Indian marks with ease. Unless something was done, they said, the French would 'kill us like Hogs or Fowls.' "[33]

At first this Chickasaw sand sketch sounds as crude as it was ephemeral. But in fact it was probably a more graphic and inclusive picture of the southern frontier than historians have been able to manage in the two and a half centuries since that time. The geographical and cultural biases mentioned earlier have made it inordinately hard for generations of scholars to grasp what the Chickasaw chiefs understood firsthand. Yet it is possible to mention some of what they knew in the summer of 1736 and then to re-create in more detail the set of circles they traced out carefully for Oglethorpe.

To the west, first of all, we can assume that they were well aware of the increasing Spanish presence in East Texas. Spaniards had been traversing the Southwest for two hundred years since the days of Coronado, and in the half century since the great Pueblo Revolt of 1680 in New Mexico the Chickasaws had become participants in a lively trans-

Mississippi traffic in horses. (As Plains Indians learned to steal horses from Spanish colonizers and breed them for hunting and warfare, their eastern neighbors found that horses were becoming increasingly valuable for travel and trade among Indians and Europeans in the Southeast. The Chickasaws were well located to serve as powerful middlemen in this west-to-east trade.) After the French established the Louisiana colony in 1699, Spanish efforts to secure their claim to East Texas had increased. In 1718 the Spaniards had established the mission of San Antonio de Valero, which would later become the Alamo, and by the 1730s large cattle ranches were coming into existence on the western edge of the geographical South.[34]

To their south and north, the Chickasaws were intensely aware of increasing French influence in the Mississippi Valley. Louisiana now included 2,400 Europeans and nearly 4,000 Africans, and as the colony expanded it encroached on Indian lands. Between 1729 and 1732 the French had all but obliterated the once-powerful Natchez tribe, and survivors had taken refuge with their Chickasaw neighbors. When Bienville returned to New Orleans from France in February 1733 (the same month Oglethorpe first reached Savannah), he initiated plans to punish the Chickasaws for harboring Natchez refugees and English traders from Charles Town. In the spring of 1736 Bienville sought to crush the Chickasaws by converging on their fortified villages with separate contingents from the north and south. But the force of 114 Frenchmen and 325 Indians that descended the Mississippi from Fort de Chartres in Illinois country arrived too soon. Chickasaw warriors ambushed them successfully and captured dispatches outlining the intended campaign. Two months later Bienville arrived from the south with 700 Choctaw allies, 140 enslaved blacks led by free Negroes, and more than 600 French and Swiss soldiers. But this force too was ambushed and suffered a humiliating and expensive defeat.[35]

To the east, the Chickasaws were attentive to the shifting settlements and expanding horizons of the English along the Atlantic Coast. They knew that Red Sock (Mingo Onmastaba), a leader of their Choctaw enemies, though generally loyal to the French and suspicious that blankets from English traders were the cause of a recent outbreak of smallpox, had journeyed to Carolina and Georgia in 1734. They knew officials there were fearful of the possibility that the western nations —the Chickasaws and Choctaws, the Creeks and Cherokees—might

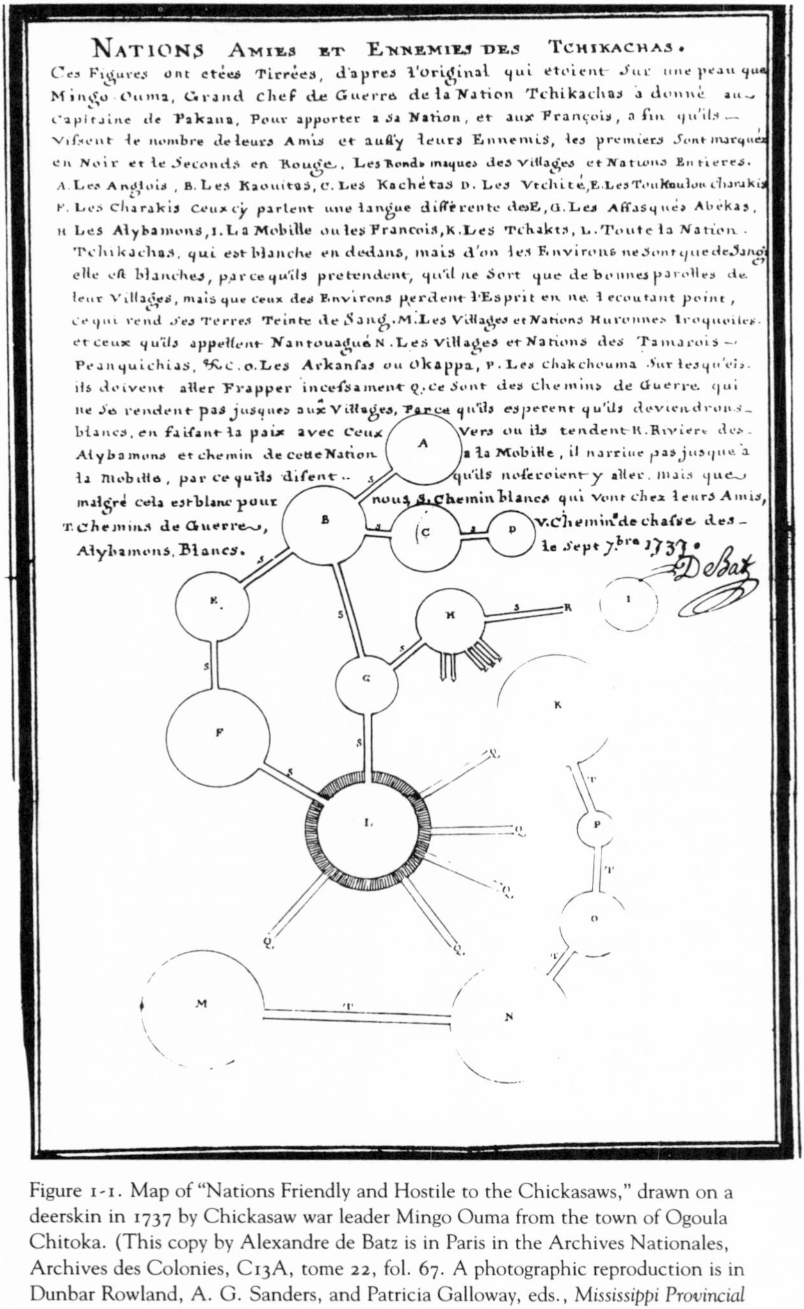

NATIONS AMIES ET ENNEMIES DES TCHIKACHAS.
Ces Figures ont etées Tirrées, d'après l'original qui etoient sur une peau que
Mingo Ouma, Grand Chef de Guerre de la Nation Tchikachas a donné au
Capitaine de Pakana, Pour apporter a sa Nation, et aux François, a fin qu'ils
vissent le nombre de leurs Amis et aussy leurs Ennemis, les premiers sont marqués
en Noir et les Seconds en Rouge. Les Ronds marqués des villages et Nations Entieres.
A. Les Anglois , B. Les Kaouitas, C. Les Kachétas D. Les Vtchité, E. Les Toukoulou charakis
F. Les Charakis Ceux cy parlent une langue differente de E, G. Les Affasqués Abékas,
H Les Alybamons, I. La Mobille ou les Francois, K. Les Tchakts, L. Toute la Nation .
Tchikachas, qui est blanche en dedans, mais d'on les Environs ne sont que de Sang
elle est blanches, par ce qu'ils pretendent, qu'il ne sort que de bonnes parolles de
leur villages, mais que ceux des Environs perdent l'Esprit en ne l'ecoutant point ,
ce qui rend ses Terres Teinte de Sang. M. Les Villages et Nations Huronnes Iroquoiles.
et ceux qu'ils appellent Nantouaguoé N. Les Villages et Nations des Tamarois —
Peanquichias, &c. o. Les Arkansas ou Okappa, p. Les chakchouma Sur les qu'eis.
ils doivent aller Frapper incessament Q. ce sont des chemins de Guerre. qui
ne se rendent pas jusques aux Villages, Parce qu'ils esperent qu'ils deviendrons
blancs, en faisant la paix avec Ceux Vers ou ils tendent R. Riviere des
Alybamons et chemin de cette Nation a la Mobille, il n'arrive pas jusqué a
la Mobille, par ce qu'ils disent.. qu'ils noferoient y aller, mais que
maigré cela est blanc pour nous S. Chemin blancs qui vont chez leurs Amis,
T. Chemins de Guerre, V. Chemin de chasse des
Alybamons. Blancs. le sept 7bre 1737.

De Batz

Figure 1-1. Map of "Nations Friendly and Hostile to the Chickasaws," drawn on a
deerskin in 1737 by Chickasaw war leader Mingo Ouma from the town of Ogoula
Chitoka. (This copy by Alexandre de Batz is in Paris in the Archives Nationales,
Archives des Colonies, C13A, tome 22, fol. 67. A photographic reproduction is in
Dunbar Rowland, A. G. Sanders, and Patricia Galloway, eds., Mississippi Provincial
Archives, French Dominion, vols. 4–5 [Baton Rouge, 1984], 4, facing p. 142.)

someday bury their own differences enough to "rise and make War, against the English," with possible support from the French and Spanish. And they knew that the Georgia newcomers, more than the established traders in Charles Town, seemed particularly solicitous with respect to fostering Chickasaw independence and cultivating their trade. The small Georgia colony, in fact, had provided direct support when the larger Indian tribe had turned back French raiding parties several months earlier.[36]

Now we return to the circles in the sand—the display used by Chickasaw diplomats in presenting the complex geopolitics of the southern interior to Oglethorpe, who had not ventured beyond the Atlantic seaboard. Their picture must have looked a great deal like the secret document shown in Figure 1-1.[37] Indeed, they had undoubtedly seen and discussed—or perhaps even helped to draw out on an animal hide —such a schematic map, illustrating the delicate balance of political forces in the South. According to its inscription, the map was copied from "a skin that Mingo Ouma, Great War Chief of the Chickasaw Nation, gave to the Captain of Panaka to take to his Nation [the Alabamas] and the French, in order that they might see the number of their friends and also their enemies." A copy of this diagram and its explicit key eventually found its way into the Archives Nationales in Paris, just as deerskin maps procured by the English during the same period ended up in the British Museum in London.

Though it has been copied and transferred across the Atlantic, the deerskin's central message is still readily discernible. At the center are the beleaguered towns of the Chickasaws, represented by a heavily fortified circle (**L**). It represents, according to the inscription, "The whole Chickasaw Nation, which is white within, but the space surrounding it is of nothing but blood. It is white because they claim that only good words come from their villages, but those of the surrounding country lose their minds by not listening to them at all, and this stains their lands with blood." The letter **S** marks the "White paths that lead to their friends," trails of peace that join the Chickasaws to their allies. **T** designates "War paths," and **Q** shows "warpaths which do not go as far as the villages, because they hope that they will become white when they make peace with those toward whom they lead."

The Chickasaw mapmakers place east at the head of the deerskin —whether to acknowledge the rising sun or the rising power of their

English allies, whose Carolina and Georgia settlements on the Atlantic Coast appear at the top as letter **A**. Not far inland are the two main centers of the Lower Creeks (relocated during the past generation from older sites near the headwaters of the Ocmulgee): Coweta (**B**), on the eastern bank of the Chattahoochee River near its falls, and Kasihta (**C**), located at that time on the opposite bank of the river some miles downstream. Further south on the same side of the river were smaller Creek settlements, symbolized here by the town of the Yuchis (**D**).

A trail from Coweta Town on the Chattahoochee reaches northward on the map to Tugaloo (**E**), the village where traders entered the mountain domain of the Cherokees. From the Lower Cherokee towns a path extends down the map toward the west to the Upper, or Overhill, Cherokee settlements (**F**)—where, according to the key, they "speak a different language from E"—and on to the home of the Chickasaws. Another more direct route from Coweta to the Chickasaw towns passes westward through the extensive lands of the Upper Creeks. For the Tallapoosas and Coosas (or Abikhas), their northernmost center, and the largest western "factory" for Carolina traders, is at Great Okfuskee (**G**) on the Okfuskee or Tallapoosa River. Further south along the river, where it becomes the Alabama at the French post of Fort Toulouse (near modern-day Montgomery), are additional Upper Creeks known as Alabamas (**H**). Carolina traders told Oglethorpe it took nearly four weeks for a pack train from Charles Town to reach these Alabama (or Alibamon) villages.[38]

On the Gulf Coast side of the map, the rival French are represented by an isolated circle (**I**), smaller than that for the English. And stretching from there around the bottom of the deerskin in an ominous crescent, like the jaws of a fish, are the allies and agents of the French, linked together by trails and waterways. At the top of these open jaws are the powerful Choctaws in east-central Mississippi (**K**), and below them to the west are smaller tribes, such as the Chakchiuma (**P**), one-time allies of the Chickasaws and Creeks near the Yazoo River.[39] Further west, where the Arkansas meets the Mississippi, is the somewhat larger Quapaw nation, centered at Kappa (**O**). Beyond them up the Mississippi are the combined forces of the Illinois country under the domination of French traders and missionaries, located around Tamaroa (**N**) below the confluence with the Missouri near present-day East Saint Louis. And far to the north, less well known but squeezed to fit within the deerskin, are the more remote French allies, the Hurons and Iroquois (**M**), remnants of the Hurons having long since been absorbed among their former enemies, the Iroquois.[40]

Viewed from the perspective of Mingo Ouma and the Chickasaws, the full span and complexity of the frontier in the 1730s can perhaps be glimpsed in something like its entirety. Societies that had coped with the brief expedition of De Soto two centuries before were now accommodating their cultures and their diplomacy to the established and intrusive presence of competing European empires along the fringes of the South. And it is this complex interaction, stretching over so many generations, that currently poses one of the most exciting challenges for historians of the colonial South.

My two brief toasts can hardly do justice to the broad dimensions of Georgia's early frontier. But they may provide a needed reminder of the varied context in which we must reexamine the life and times of James Oglethorpe. Granted, the abstract region known as the southern colonial frontier still seems vague and cumbersome, for as yet it remains inadequately explored and mapped. But its age, stretching back across two centuries from the 1730s, is epitomized by the Yamacraw burial mound on the eastern edge of Savannah, where Oglethorpe once walked. And its geographic scope, reaching westward from the low country across a third of the continent, is suggested by the elaborate circles that a Chickasaw ambassador once drew in the sand at Oglethorpe's feet.

Oglethorpe and the Earliest Maps of Georgia

Louis De Vorsey, Jr.

Maps *sent back to England by men like South Carolina's Thomas Nairne helped shape British policies toward the region that would be Georgia, and what they contained was frequently incorporated into later maps and used as evidence to support schemes for colonization and exploitation. In his essay, Louis De Vorsey, Jr., demonstrates how maps helped to influence the initial settling of the colony and how Oglethorpe and the Georgia Trustees were able to present the region as ripe for settlement.*

But according to De Vorsey, Oglethorpe went even further. As an ardent expansionist of British interests on the southern frontier, he knew that winning a battle of maps could be even more important than winning an engagement on the field of combat. Therefore, in his effort to expand his colony's boundaries, Oglethorpe may have actually altered maps (or at least supplied less than accurate information) so that his own ambitions for Georgia might be realized. This possibility is weighed by De Vorsey, whose treatment seems to enhance the founder's reputation as an effective—although not always quite forthright—imperialist.—Editors

As Verner W. Crane and, more recently, Kenneth Coleman have pointed out, the general location of the "peculiar" colony of Georgia was, in a manner of speaking, preordained.[1] The founding of Charles Town in 1670 marked the beginning of an intermittent but relentless contest for what came to be known as the "Debatable Land," that expanse lying between Carolina and Saint Augustine, the Spanish town established more than a century before.[2]

Coleman marks the precharter history of Georgia as beginning in 1708, when Thomas Nairne, South Carolina's first regular Indian agent, sent his famous memorial and map to Crown authorities in London. Crane termed that memorial "one of the most remarkable documents in the history of Anglo-American frontier imperialism." In it Nairne argued that only South Carolina, through aggressive Indian alliances and trading arrangements coupled with support from the mother country, could check accelerating French expansion in the southern interior. Nairne's map was based in large measure on his travels and exploits in the Southeast and was sent with his memorial "to the end your noble Lordship may at one View perceive what part of the Continent we are now possest off, and what not, and procure the Articles of peace, to be formed in such manner that the English American Empire may not be unreasonably Crampt up."[3] The original of Nairne's map is no longer extant, but a published version appeared in 1711 as an inset on Edward Crisp's large map of South Carolina (Figure 2-1).[4]

Although the main thrust of Nairne's memorial dealt with French encirclement, his map contained several elements that bear directly on the region ultimately designated as Georgia. The "Savanna R" (Savannah River) and "Allattamaha R" (Altamaha River) are prominently depicted with the Savannah being shown as the southern limit of the South Carolina area Nairne distinguished as "English Settlement." Also prominent are dotted lines indicating "The North Bounds of Carolina," stretching along the 36°30′ parallel from the Atlantic to the map's margin far to the west of the Mississippi River, and "the South Bounds of Carolina" following the 29° parallel from the Atlantic Ocean to the Gulf of Mexico, a full degree south of "S Augustin," the Spanish city located south of a correctly depicted "S Juans R" (Saint Johns River). These lines mark the generous limits specified in the 1663 Carolina charter, which Charles II bestowed on the eight Lords Proprietors.[5] As can be imagined, the southern limit infuriated the Spanish, who argued that their early system of missions and presidios had made the whole of that region an integral part of La Florida. Nairne's map is the first to show correctly the major outlines of the region between Port Royal, South Carolina, and Saint Augustine, Florida.[6]

In 1715–16 a far-reaching Indian uprising known as the Yamasee War shook the Carolina trading network across the Southeast. In Crane's view the results of the Yamasee War were so significant as to rank it "with the more famous Indian conspiracies of colonial times."[7] It struck

Figure 2-1. Thomas Nairne's map of the American Southeast, which served as the source of the Oglethorpe-Martyn first Georgia map. (Courtesy of William P. Cumming)

with unexpected fierceness at the dispersed Carolina farming frontier in Saint Helena's and Saint Bartholomew's parishes and the widespread trading posts serving distant backcountry Indian tribes. Probably included in the initial massacre were the traders operating among the Ochese Creek (named Okesee by Nairne) on the Ocmulgee River near the site of Macon, Georgia.[8] Carolina leaders were doubtless correct in identifying the Creeks and Yamasees as the major instigators of the uprising. Characteristically, however, the Indians soon lost the war's initiative and began to feel the punishment of attacks by the Carolinians reinforced by a large contingent from Virginia. The Creeks abandoned their fertile Ocmulgee flood plain farmlands to flee west to safer ground in the valleys of the Coosa–Tallapoosa and Chattahoochee river systems. As Charles Hudson recently pointed out, "at this juncture in history, the most favorable circumstance a southern Indian could hope for was to live deep in the interior of the South and to have around him the greatest possible number of European interests—Spanish, British, and French—contesting for supremacy."[9] As Oglethorpe was to discover, the Creeks had achieved this desirable circumstance through their westward withdrawal from the Ocmulgee watershed.

Most importantly, the Yamasee War and its aftermath led to a widely held realization that South Carolina could not be considered truly safe until the region beyond the Savannah River was secured. The withdrawal of the Creeks to the west of the Chattahoochee and the

Yamasees to Florida elevated Spanish Florida from a negligible rival to a formidable contender in the struggle for control of the "Debatable Land." Fortunately for the Carolinians, authorities in London were not slow in realizing that the Spanish threat in that quarter was an imperial problem and not simply a local one with which the inept Carolina Proprietors were unable to cope. As Crane observed, "the threatened ruin of South Carolina for the first time definitely focussed the attention of the colonial authorities upon the southern frontier."[10]

It was at this time that the most colorful of the pre-Georgia schemes for the settlement of the "Debatable Land" was projected by a Scottish baronet, Sir Robert Montgomery. Montgomery and his associates presented their proposal to the Carolina Proprietors in June 1717 and received the deeds of lease and release for "all that Tract of Land, which lies between the Rivers Altamaha, and Savanna," in early July of the same year. During the summer, Montgomery published an exuberant promotional tract describing his "future Eden": the flamboyant Margravate of Azilia he planned to establish in the area south of the Savannah.[11]

Drawing on the recent Yamasee War debacle, Montgomery correctly focused attention on the fatal vulnerability of the American colonists that resulted from, as he wrote, "a want of due Precaution in their Forms of settling, or rather, to their settling without any form at all." He continued:

> The Planters grasp'd at an undue Extent of Land, exceeding their Capacity to manage or defend: This scatter'd them to Distances unsafe and solitary, so that, living in a Wilderness, incapable of mutual aid, the necessary Artizans found no Encouragement to dwell among them; Their Woods remain'd unclear'd; their Fens undrained; The air by that Means prov'd unhealthy, and the Roads impassable; For want of Towns, and Places of Defence, they suddenly became a Prey to all Invaders; even the unformidable Indians took advantage of the Oversight; and Carolina, is, at present, groaning under a most bloody Persecution, from a wild, and despicable Kind of Enemy, who had not dar'd to think of the Attempt, but from an Observation daily made, how open and unguarded they might take the English.[12]

Published with his "Discourse" was Montgomery's blueprint for an ordered and militarily secure settlement pattern. This was the elaborate and well-known engraving titled "A Plan representing the Form of

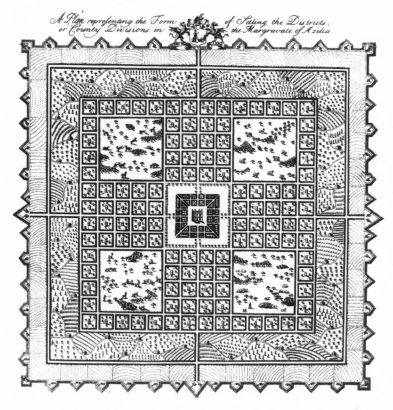

Figure 2-2. Sir Robert Montgomery's plan for laying out the district or county divisions in the Margravate of Azilia. (Courtesy of Hargrett Rare Book and Manuscript Library, University of Georgia Libraries)

Setling the Districts, or County Divisions in the Margravate of Azilia" (Figure 2-2). Azilia was not to be defended by "building here and there a Fort, the fatal Practice of America." To the contrary, Montgomery's plan was to make the "whole Plantation one continued Fortress" by enclosing habitations and farmlands by "Military Lines, impregnable against the Savages." [13]

In his "Discourse," Montgomery explained that the ordered settlement plan would require "a level, dry, and fruitful Tract of Land, in some fine Plain or Valley, containing a just Square of twenty Miles Each Way, or two hundred and fifty Six Thousand Acres."[14] Exactly where within the debatable land between the Savannah and Altamaha this well-endowed tract would be located was not mentioned, nor was any general map of the region included with the discourse.

While many have been tempted to dismiss the Margravate of Azilia as a mere chimera or interesting footnote to the early history of Georgia's settlement, Coleman correctly stressed the impact the scheme exerted in the decade following its failure to materialize. "The importance of Azilia," he wrote, "lies not in its failure nor in Sir Robert's rhetoric, but rather in the suggestions put forth which were later incorporated into the settlement of Georgia."[15] There is no need to restate here Coleman's review of Azilia characteristics that found their way into the Georgia designed by Oglethorpe and his fellow Trustees. What is instructive is to note the degree to which Azilia was incorporated into the maps appearing the decade preceding Georgia's founding.[16]

One of the most important and widely circulated of these was Herman Moll's "A New Map of the North Parts of America Claimed by France" (Figure 2-3). This important map was first published in London in 1720 and showed both Montgomery's "Margravate of Azilia" and "Golden Islands" prominently in the area of his grant. Montgomery had published his second promotional tract, *A Description of the Golden Islands*, in the same year Moll's map appeared.[17] He pointed out that the Golden Islands, "St. Symon," "Sapella or Sapola," "Santa Catarina, " and "Ogeche, now called Montgomerie" were a part of the Margravate of Azilia containing sixty thousand acres of "rich Plain clear'd Ground, ready prepared for the Plow."[18]

In addition to naming the area of Azilia, Moll used a dotted line to show the margravate's territorial limits. Significantly these dotted lines clearly included the bounding Savannah and Altamaha rivers, placing the whole of these important watercourses within Azilia.[19] This depiction accords well with the language of the "deed" describing the Azilia grant. In that document Montgomery and his heirs were to receive "all that Tract of Land, which lies between the Rivers Allatamaha and Savanna, together with the Islands, Ports, Harbours, Bays, and Rivers on that Part of the Coast, which lies between the Mouths of the said two Rivers to the Seaward . . . With Liberty over and above to make Settlements on the South Side of Allatamaha River." By specifying the

Figure 2-3. Detail from Herman Moll's "A New Map of the North Parts of America," 1720, showing the boundaries around the Margravate of Azilia. (Courtesy of Hargrett Rare Book and Manuscript Library, University of Georgia Libraries)

"Mouths" of the boundary rivers, it could be argued that the entirety of the rivers themselves were made contiguous with Azilia. This argument is based on the definition of river mouth as including at least two banks with an intervening stream emptying through them.[20] If such was the case, it would follow that the boundary between Azilia and South Carolina followed the line of ordinary high water on the South Carolina side of the river in the same way that the Maryland-Virginia boundary was located on the Virginia bank of the Potomac by the terms of Lord Baltimore's grant.[21]

Montgomery failed to fulfill his obligation to settle a considerable number of colonists on his grant in the required three years, and the Azilia scheme lapsed. Impatient Carolinians viewed the failure of Azilia as one more proof of the inability of the Lords Proprietors to forward the interests of the colony. The fact that the Board of Trade had approved the Azilia scheme was clear proof, however, that imperial decision makers were committed to the idea of settlement in the debatable land south of the Savannah River in 1720.

This was the year when South Carolina agents John Barnwell and Joseph Boone transmitted a detailed report on the need for a system of fortified outposts to protect the colony's frontiers and Indian trade. Most urgently required, they argued, was a fortification at the mouth of the Altamaha River. Such an outpost, it was felt, could become the center for settlement in the debated land. Barnwell's and Boone's arguments and proposals fell on sympathetic ears and within a week the Carolina plan was endorsed.[22] Barnwell returned to South Carolina and personally supervised the construction of the Altamaha fort, which was completed in 1721.[23] The Spanish were quick to denounce this incursion on territory that they had claimed for centuries. Unpretentious as the log blockhouse on the Altamaha may have been, it began, in Crane's words, "the actual English occupation of the old Spanish province of Guale, the future colony of Georgia."[24]

Fort King George, as the Altamaha outpost was grandly named, was never a popular duty station. It was severely damaged by fire, reluctantly rebuilt, and finally abandoned in the autumn of 1727. This in no way, however, signaled a diminution of British commitment to the Altamaha frontier. A series of Carolina raids and forays against unfriendly Indians, including the Yamasees living within one-half mile of Saint Augustine, created, during 1728–32, a very favorable situation for another English advance into the debatable land. Also contributing to the improved climate for expansion was the ending of proprietary rule in South Carolina.

In April 1730, the newly appointed royal governor of South Carolina, Robert Johnson, submitted his frontier township scheme to an enthusiastically approving Board of Trade. In an effort to provide a solution for the colony's many problems, Johnson's plan drew heavily on the earlier frontier fortification and settlement proposals of Thomas Nairne and John Barnwell. Basic to Johnson's scheme was the establishment of ten frontier townships to be settled by Protestant refugees from Europe. Significantly, he recommended that three of the new townships be located on the Savannah River with the remainder on the Santee, Pon Pon, Wateree, Black, Peedee, and Waccamaw rivers.

Johnson's plan was approved and the governor was ordered, with all convenient speed, to set out not ten but eleven new townships with two of them on the Savannah and another two on the Altamaha River.[25] Johnson's originally proposed townships were to be located at about sixty miles from Charles Town whereas the Altamaha was more than twice that distance. This fact encouraged Crane to conclude that the Altamaha townships reflected the Board of Trade's belated acceptance of the full southern frontier commitment advocated by Barnwell ten years before.[26] As Coleman pointed out, this was the first time that the British government specifically mandated settlement that far south.[27] The way was thus cleared for the establishment of Georgia, the last successful enterprise of English colonization within the limits of what would become the United States.

As both Crane and Coleman have made amply clear, the Georgia enterprise of Oglethorpe and his associates was the result of the "long-maturing policy of the colonial administration to occupy and protect the exposed southern American frontier." It was that policy, Crane averred, that "determined the precise *locale* of the colony of Georgia."[28]

In the summer of 1730, Oglethorpe and John Lord Viscount Percival (later the first earl of Egmont) began an energetic campaign to per-suade the king's advisers to issue a charter that would allow them and fellow philanthropic trustees to secure "a grant of lands on the south-west of Carolina for settling poor persons of London."[29] After long and tedious wrangling with George II's bureaucrats, the charter was com-posed, signed by the king, and, on June 9, 1732, witnessed and issued officially. To administer the new colony, a body known as "the Trustees for Establishing the Colony of Georgia in America" was created. The colony was to embrace

> all those lands Countries and Territories Situate lying and being in that part of South Carolina in America which lies from the most Northern Stream of a River there commonly called the Savannah all along the Sea Coast to the Southward unto the most Southern Stream of a certain other great water or River called the Altamaha and Westward from the heads of the said Rivers respectively in Direct Lines to the South Seas and all that space Circuit and Precinct of land lying within the said boundaries . . . wee do by these Presents make Erect and Create one independent and seperate Province by the name of Georgia.[30]

Although no official map was prepared to illustrate the de jure terri-torial limits described by the charter, a map was subsequently published

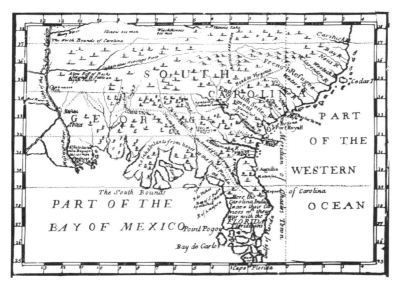

Figure 2-4. The original version of the Oglethorpe-Martyn first Georgia map that was printed with *Some Account of the Designs of the Trustees for Establishing the Colony of Georgia in America* (1732). (Courtesy of Hargrett Rare Book and Manuscript Library, University of Georgia Libraries)

by the Trustees that can assist in understanding that lengthy document. This is the untitled map (Figure 2-4) that was included with the tract titled, *Some Account of the Designs of the Trustees for Establishing the Colony of Georgia in America*. The tract was written in the summer of 1732 by Benjamin Martyn, and the Trustees in early August directed that it be printed; they also named Martyn secretary to the Trust.[31] Most authorities also credit Martyn, with the collaboration of James Oglethorpe, as drafting the map shown in Figure 2-4, basing it closely on the 1711 Nairne map discussed above.[32]

The untitled map included with *Some Account* is usually considered to be the first map to show and name the colony of Georgia. It shows the boundaries of Georgia as two finely dotted lines that follow the banks of the Savannah and Altamaha rivers from their mouths to headsprings. From the point marked by the head of each river, dotted lines are extended due west as straight parallel lines to the western margin of the map, which is drawn well beyond the Mississippi River. Thus the first

Figure 2-5. The erased and altered version of the Oglethorpe-Martyn first map of
Georgia. This version with the name Georgia compressed into the area east of the
"Chattahuchie R" was included in *Reasons for Establishing the Colony of Georgia* . . .
and Samuel Smith's *A Sermon Preached Before the Trustees for Establishing the Colony of
Georgia*, both printed by the Trustees in 1733. (Courtesy of Hargrett Rare Book and
Manuscript Library, University of Georgia Libraries)

map of Georgia repeats the important northern and southern boundary
configuration noted on the 1720 Moll map showing the abortive Margravate of Azilia (Figure 2-3). In both cases, the bounding rivers are
graphically included within the territory described in the charters. Recall that the Georgia charter specified the "most Northern Stream" and
"most Southern Stream" of the Savannah and Altamaha respectively
as the province's lateral limits. This fact was to have considerable significance in subsequent disputes involving Georgia's territorial limits.[33]

At least two versions of the first Georgia map were published under
the Trustees' auspices. They are readily recognizable, with the first version (Figure 2-4) containing much more in the way of information
that was displayed on the original Nairne map from which it was derived. The second and probably most influential version (Figure 2-5)
owed less to Nairne and compressed the name "Georgia" into the area

east of the "Chattahuchi R," whereas on the first version the colony's name covered the whole of the territory between the Mississippi and the Atlantic. This second version with the compressed name Georgia was included in two editions of *Reasons for Establishing the Colony of Georgia . . . With some Account of the Country and the Design of the Trustees* and in Samuel Smith's *A Sermon Preached Before the Trustees for Establishing the Colony of Georgia*, all of which were published by the Trustees in 1733. *Reasons*, which was written by Benjamin Martyn, was sent to each member of Parliament to support a petition by the Georgia Trustees for a large government subsidy for the new colony.[34]

Before leaving the second version of the first map of Georgia (Figure 2-5) and accompanying descriptions, a few additional points should be noted. For one thing, "St Augustin" is incorrectly shown far south of its actual site and appears to be located outside of "The South Bounds of Carolina." Note too, the caption "the line of the present French Possession" that appears along the west bank of the distant Mississippi River. On the Nairne map (Figure 2-1) this line was shown beginning on the Gulf Coast and then curving to the west to follow the Mississippi for a distance before turning sharply eastward to run behind South and North Carolina. A very large area astride the lower Mississippi is prominently captioned "French Settlement."

Thus the most widely distributed second version of the first map to show and publicize the Trustees' colony was judiciously altered to present Georgia in a more favorable light. The hostile French, whose strategy of encirclement was bemoaned by a legion of Carolinians, had, with a few strokes, been removed from harm's way to the trans-Mississippi west. So too the menacing Spaniards at Saint Augustine had been transported southward almost to Cape Canaveral. Oglethorpe and his associates had accomplished, with the engraver's stylus, what countless Carolina border raiders and regular troops had failed to pro-duce—frontier pacification in the debatable land. It was, of course, a clever bit of cartographic legerdemain calculated to convince members of Parliament to back the Georgia scheme with large government sub-sidies. Along the way it may have persuaded many an indigent London artisan or other prospective settler into a decision to cast his family's lot with the new colony abuilding in far-off Carolina.[35]

By the time this geopolitically bowdlerized map reached its primary audience of Lords and Commoners in the British Parliament, Oglethorpe had already arrived on the Savannah River bluff known as Yama-craw. The inspired manner in which he personally organized and led the original Georgia colonists through the arduous months following the founding of Savannah is amply chronicled and will not be repeated here. Rather, the remainder of this chapter will focus on Oglethorpe's efforts to have more accurate and detailed maps of Georgia, Britain's newest colonial adventure, produced and published.

After spending a bit more than a year in Georgia establishing Savannah and a number of outlying settlements on the northern margins of the debatable land, Oglethorpe returned to London. As Phinizy Spalding has pointed out, he lost no time in taking "some pains to withdraw his earlier comments that might lead prospective colonists to think that Georgia was the biblical land of milk and honey."[36] In fairness to Oglethorpe it should be noted that some of the misrepresentation had come from inaccurate information that he and the Trustees had at hand before settlement began. In a letter written from Savannah only a month after his arrival, Oglethorpe noted, "this province is much larger than we thought it, being 120 miles from this river to the Altamaha."[37] In *Reasons*, this coastal distance had been given as "between sixty and seventy Miles."[38]

In May 1734, Oglethorpe, accompanied by Tomochichi and a number of other friendly local Indians, sailed for England. It had been a year of incredible achievement. In the words of Hector Beaufain, written January 23, 1734, "the settling of Georgia is what Mr. Oglethorpe has so entirely at heart that every thought and action of his is directed to that favourite object." Beaufain continued: "when affairs are ordered in town . . . he visits the out-settlements, lays out new ones, examines the nature of the soil, appoints proper places for forts, mills and other public works, searches into inlets and rivers hitherto unknown, by means of which the inland navigation may be improved and even the great rivers made to communicate with one another."[39] Beaufain also accompanied Oglethorpe in his scout boat on an exploration of the Savannah River above the South Carolina settlement known as Purrysburg. His observations, based on that excursion, provide rare insight and ample testimony as to the energy and thoroughness of Oglethorpe as colony builder and explorer. Beaufain wrote:

> We might have reached Purrysburg in less than half a day, but Mr. Ogle-thorpe would visit some families which he has settled upon Abercorn

River. The River is large and joins the Savannah at about six miles below Purrysburg. We found the people very busy. They were extremely pleased with the honour Mr. Oglethorpe did them. We passed the night in the boat and next evening proceeded to Purrysburg. . . . Next day we continued our way up river. We made a progress of five days, lying at night either in the boat or in the woods. We had for two nights a very hard frost. This way of traveling I was an entire stranger to. I believe it would disagree with most people. We saw upwards of Purrysburg no human creature excepting an Indian warrior who was coming down with his family in a canoe. He was mightily pleased to meet with Mr. Oglethorpe, who has found means to keep a good correspondence with the Indians of these parts. The current of the river is very strong above Purrysburg. We went not only along the Savannah but turned into several fine creeks, or lagoons they are called so here though some of them are rivers. We landed on all places likely for settlements. I had much ado to follow Mr. Oglethorpe, for he walks the wood like an Indian.[40]

Although Beaufain made no direct mention of any sketches or surveys, it seems certain that Oglethorpe was actively preparing maps of his discoveries and settlements. In a letter to the Trustees written six months after his arrival in Georgia, he mentioned that he would soon send a map to illustrate his verbal reports and descriptions of the terrain he was so busily exploring and settling.[41] No record exists of this map's having been forwarded any time prior to the spring of 1734, so it would appear that Oglethorpe carried it with him on his return to London. This conclusion seems warranted in view of the fact that Oglethorpe provided a "Map of the Coast of Georgia" to the British War Office, probably shortly after his return.[42] In the register entry detailing the acquisition of this map, it is indicated to be an "Orig." (original) by "Mr. Oglethorpe." Unfortunately the map itself does not appear to have survived.

During the months following his return to London in 1734, Oglethorpe was also providing maps of Georgia to contacts on the Continent where German Protestants were being encouraged to emigrate to Georgia. As early as September 5, 1734, Henry Newman mentioned sending "A Mapp of Georgia which Mr. Oglethorpe desires me to convey to you in the best manner," in a letter to Philipp Georg Friedrich von Reck in Ratisbonne.[43] In the following month von Reck wrote to request that Newman "Procure for me from Mr. Oglethorpe a Plan of Georgia."[44] He continued by mentioning that "There is a little general Chart of the Coasts of Georgia Carolina and Cape Florida engraved at London. I should be glad [if] you would send me two Copies together with the Plan above mentioned from Mr. Oglethorpe which shall be presented to the King." Which German prince was to be so informed by von Reck is not revealed.

Somewhat belatedly Oglethorpe officially presented the fruits of his cartographic labors to the Georgia Trustees. That body's journal entry for February 5, 1735, noted: "Received of Mr. Oglethorpe as his Benefaction a Draught of Part of Carolina, Georgia and Florida, and another of the County of Savannah."[45] These maps were probably utilized by Oglethorpe as he read his "Short account of the present condition of the Colony" to his fellow Trustees.[46]

Like the maps that Oglethorpe delivered to the War Office and correspondents in Germany, the drafts he presented to the Trustees are no longer extant. The fact that the Trustees ordered "that the two Draughts . . . be put in Frames with a Glass over them and hung up in the Office" strongly suggests that they were finished products and not mere manuscript sketches.[47] Although modern usage of the term "draught" emphasizes its meaning in the sense of being a preliminary or preparatory sketch, ample eighteenth-century evidence exists to show that the term often indicated finished engraved and printed maps.[48] The hypothesis offered here is that Oglethorpe presented the Trustees with finished engraved copies of two maps for which he supplied essential firsthand geographical intelligence gained during his first sojourn in Georgia.

The first of these maps, described as "a Draught of Part of Carolina, Georgia and Florida," was very probably number 10 of Henry Popple's enormous twenty-sheet map titled "A Map of the British Empire in America with the French and Spanish Settlements adjacent thereto." This map, when the twenty sheets are joined, forms the largest printed map of America produced during the colonial period, measuring about ten feet square. Popple himself had no particular reputation as a geographer or cartographer prior to the first appearance of his map in 1733. An inscription near the southeastern corner (sheet 20) of the assembled map makes it clear that Popple compiled his map from sources already available in official files rather than from newly undertaken surveys.

Mr. Popple undertook the Map with the Approbation of the Right Honourable the Lords Commissioners of Trade and Plantations; and great

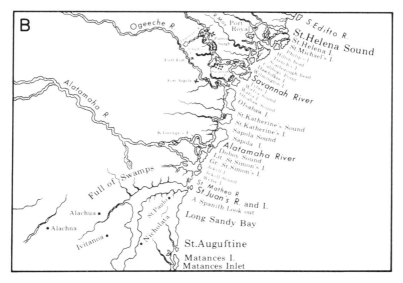

Figure 2-6. A tracing of the "B" or intermediate state of Henry Popple's depiction of the Georgia coast based on information supplied by Oglethorpe when he returned to London in 1734. Notice the branch of the "Alatamaha R." terminating at the gloss "Full of Swamps."

> Care has been taken by comparing all the Maps, Charts, and Observations that could be found, especially the Authentick Records & Actual Surveys transmitted to their Lordships by the Governors of the British Plantations, and Others, to correct the many Errors committed in former Maps.[49]

Popple's 1727 manuscript and very rare early stages of the 1733 engraved printed map show a highly generalized coastline in the area of South Carolina and Georgia.[50] Later states of the map were pulled from a corrected sheet 10 copperplate engraving and show a more detailed Georgia map. It is argued here that the source for the improved Popple map of Georgia found on sheet 10 was none other than the colony's founder and architect, James Edward Oglethorpe.

Exactly when and how Henry Popple obtained access to Oglethorpe's cartographic intelligence has not been discovered. In all probability Oglethorpe sought out the map compiler shortly after his return to London in 1734. Although barred by the colony's charter from officially

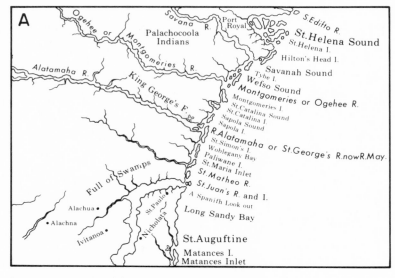

Figure 2-7. A tracing of the "A" or original state of Henry Popple's depiction of the Georgia coast.

holding any office in Georgia, he performed all the normal functions of governor and was thus expected to make any sketches, surveys, or geographical intelligence available to the Board of Trade and to the War Office.[51] In view of the statement printed on Popple's map quoted above and Oglethorpe's interest in broadcasting an updated view of Georgia, rapid transmission of his new knowledge was in no way surprising.

What is somewhat surprising is to find that many of the extant Popple maps, including the copy from the Cambridge University Library, reprinted in 1972, were taken from an incompletely altered copperplate (Figure 2-6). Most of the Popple maps show the configuration that is arbitrarily identified as the "B" or intermediate state of the alteration process that Popple undertook in his effort to bring the Carolina-Georgia map plate into agreement with Oglethorpe's reports. The reason for this assignment can best be understood by examining the area just to the north of the "St. Juan's River" where the inscription "Full of Swamps" occupies a prominent position on the earliest and presumably pre-Oglethorpe map (Figure 2-7).

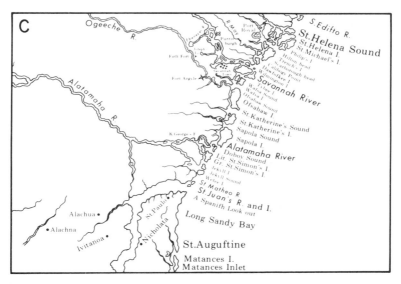

Figure 2-8. A tracing of the "C" or final state of Henry Popple's depiction of the Georgia Coast. Notice that the branch of the "Alatamaha R." is now connected to the Saint Johns River (St. Juan's).

It can be observed that Popple revised the entire area lying between the Altamaha and Saint Johns rivers. In the widely circulated "B" state (Figure 2-6) of the revisions, the Popple map exhibits an arm of the Altamaha that runs to the south to terminate abruptly at the "Full of Swamps" inscription. On the hypothesized final or "C" state (Figure 2-8), which had been pasted over the "A" state detail on maps owned by the American Philosophical Society and Colonial Williamsburg Foundation, the inscription has been removed and the arm of the Altamaha extended to the Saint Johns River.

Other puzzling changes occur on the Popple map that space will not allow to be explored here. Perhaps a tentative conclusion should be that Oglethorpe was laying the groundwork for a more southerly Altamaha river system than existed in nature. Recall that the southern bounds of Georgia had been fixed at the "most Southern Stream of a certain great water or River called the Altamaha." In an imperial power play against Spain, Oglethorpe might have reasoned, Britain and Georgia could only gain if such a hydrography was widely accepted. In fairness to Oglethorpe, such a hypothesis is certainly far from proven at this point. It might easily be that this portion of his geographical knowledge was based on Indian sources. The Lower Creeks were claiming *all* of the region from the Savannah to Saint Augustine, and Oglethorpe may have been reflecting their geographical interpretation of this incredibly difficult coastal terrain. He may have been, with good cause, more concerned with keeping the Lower Creeks closely allied with Britain than he was with the cartographic accuracy of this still remote and contested buffer zone.

If, as hypothesized above, Oglethorpe's two cartographic benefactions to the Georgia Trust were engraved map prints, there can be little or no doubt that the second was a copy of "A Map of the County of Savannah."[52] Cumming and other experts have interpreted the initials "T.F.L. fec" appearing on the map to mean that the copperplate, from which the map was printed, issued from the Augsburg shop of Matthias Seutter. After Seutter's death his son-in-law, Tobias Conrad Lotter, became a part-owner of the firm and eventually continued the business alone under his own name.[53] The fact that the middle initial is given as "F" rather than "C" should require that the attribution of the engraving to the well-known Tobias Conrad Lotter be a tentative one.

The County of Savannah map is found variously located in the monumental collection commonly known as the "Salzburger Tracts" that was edited by Samuel Urlsperger and issued in Hallé during the 1730s and 1740s.[54] The correspondence between Henry Newman and Philipp von Reck, mentioned above, makes it clear that Oglethorpe was providing maps to German contacts in the months following his first return from Georgia. Included in that correspondence network was Samuel Urlsperger, a key figure in efforts to aid displaced German Protestants for repatriation in Georgia.

Although no evidence has been found that unequivocally proves that Oglethorpe provided the sketch or survey that guided the eye and hand of "T.F.L." when he engraved the copperplate for "A Map of the County of Savannah," circumstantial evidence exists to support that conclusion. Some of that evidence suggests that "T.F.L." might have been located in England. It is found in a letter from Henry Newman to Samuel Urlsperger dated June 20, 1735, more than four months after Oglethorpe had delivered his cartographic "benefaction" to the

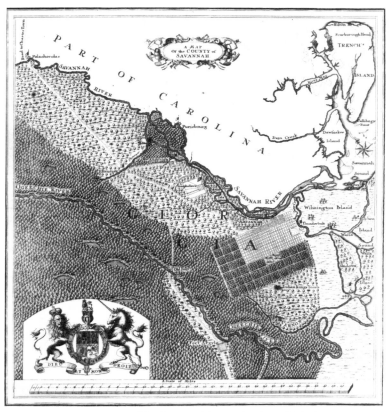

Figure 2-9. Copy of "A Map of the County of Savannah," first published in Germany by Samuel Urlsperger in 1735. (Courtesy of the Hargrett Rare Book and Manuscript Library, University of Georgia Libraries)

Georgia Trustees. In that letter Newman mentions that Urlsperger will be receiving "Instructions about placing the Meridians and Parallels to the Map of Georgia or rather that a Copy as engraved here will be sent to you."[55]

The fact that "A Map of the County of Savannah," which was published in Urlsperger's 1735 tract, lacks any lines or marks of latitude or longitude would lend support to the suggestion that the map, or plate from which it was pulled, originated in London. (See Figure 2-9.) So too does the fact that language appearing on the map is English. In his next series publication, dated 1736, Urlsperger included an explanatory "Advertissment" concerning the map. Among other things, including a latitude of 32° north, Urlsperger provided a list of German-language equivalents for several of the English terms that appear on the County of Savannah map.

Wherever it was engraved, "A Map of the County of Savannah" is a remarkable cartographic document. It shows the geography of the farms, settlements, towns, roads, forts, and outposts that Oglethorpe had ordered established during his first active year of colony building. In this respect it forms an excellent cartographic record of that year and the accomplishments of Georgia's energetic founder. It was for exactly this reason that Georgia's preeminent early historian, Charles C. Jones, wisely included a reprint of it in his seminal *The History of Georgia*, published in 1883.

More recently, the internationally recognized historian of American urban design, John W. Reps, characterized the 1735 County of Savannah map as showing "the general regional pattern of land settlement as it then existed" in Georgia.[56] That regional plan was subsequently modified and refined by the ingenious Oglethorpe, but its broad outlines first shown on the County of Savannah map are still discernible on the landscape and continue to help shape the dynamic growth of modern Savannah.

Reasonable as it may be to assume that James Edward Oglethorpe's military career provided him many opportunities to prepare and use maps, nothing in the historical record treats this aspect of his manifold accomplishments. In the case of his endeavors in promoting and executing the establishment of the Trusteeship Colony of Georgia, however, the record is replete with evidence that he was an accomplished surveyor and compiler of what were, for their day, extraordinarily complete and accurate maps. Perhaps even more important was Oglethorpe's demonstrated ability to structure maps that could be expected to forward the ambitions and goals of the Georgia scheme he and his fellow Trustees launched.

This analysis of several of the earliest maps of Georgia has revealed the active hand of the colony's chief promoter and founder, James Oglethorpe. In the case of the first Georgia map, his zeal to promote the innovative colonization scheme led him to adapt and alter one of the best available map sources in order to compose a cartographic image that was both acceptable to potential critics and attractive to supporters and prospective colonists.

After a bit over a year spent in laying out Georgia's first settlements and gaining a wealth of firsthand knowledge, he returned to London and set about to broadcast more realistic images of Britain's newest colonial possession. In part Oglethorpe accomplished this task by providing maps to the War Office and the quasiofficial map compiler Henry Popple. Popple's "A Map of the British Empire in America with the French and Spanish Settlements adjacent thereto," first published in 1733, was the largest printed map of America to appear in the eighteenth century and was not superseded until the appearance of John Mitchell's "A Map of the British and French Dominions in North America" in 1755. Even in Popple's great map, however, evidence suggests that Oglethorpe may have distorted nature to promote the idea that Georgia's southern boundary river, the Altamaha, connected with the Saint Johns River. Had such a hydrography been accepted it could have given weight to British claims to an area already claimed by Spain. Without doubt, the "Map of the County of Savannah" best serves as clear testimony to the high quality of Oglethorpe's cartographic skill. Published in Germany and frequently incorrectly dated, this map has not been as closely associated with Georgia's founder as it deserves to be. As mentioned above, it is an amazingly accurate and complete cartographic inventory of the condition of the colony when Oglethorpe made his first trip back to London.

While questions concerning the details and implications of Oglethorpe's role in the preparation and use of the earliest Georgia maps remain to be answered, enough has been revealed in this analysis to demonstrate the need to search beneath the maps' surfaces and discover the underlying motives and ambitions they reflect and exemplify. The early maps of Georgia have lain too long neglected in the search for a better understanding of Oglethorpe's singular role in the conception and founding of the Trustees' noble experiment.

Parson and Squire
James Oglethorpe and the Role of the Anglican Church in Georgia, 1733–1736

Harvey H. Jackson

In this study, Harvey H. Jackson assays the difficult task of determining exactly where James Edward Oglethorpe thought the man of the cloth belonged in an American frontier society. Oglethorpe was a traditionalist in spiritual matters and felt that religion played a seminal role in the lives of Englishmen in Old and New World alike. But he made it obvious in Georgia that although ministers were important, the function they played was definitely secondary to the secular leader. The province's ministers basked in the warm sunlight of the founder's approbation in the early stages of their careers in Georgia, but when they slipped over the bounds into Oglethorpe's executive and administrative competency the parson-squire relationship he had known in England went into effect on the banks of the Savannah and the Altamaha.

This exposition by Jackson delineates what Oglethorpe's notion of the parson-squire relationship was, while at the same time exploring specific areas in which the leader looked for support from his ministers. The ramifications for the Church of England of this unequal coupling between minister and lay leader are carefully orchestrated by Jackson, and the imprint fixed on the new colony is discreetly suggested.—Editors

The Church of England embraced the Georgia Plan as if it were its own. Anglican ministers praised it from their pulpits, and churches throughout the country took up collections to further the design. Only Parliament gave the colony more financial support than the various agencies, parishes, congregations, and individuals that made up the Anglican establishment. But in spite of these efforts the Church of England never became the force in Georgia that many wanted and expected it to be. Some scholars have blamed this failure on the handful of "fractious, overzealous, youthful and inexperienced, discouraged, narrow, immoral" clergymen sent to the colony. Yet many of these ministers became successful, indeed famous, after leaving the province, which suggests that clerical talent was not the critical factor. Other accounts point to a lack of priests, rather than ability, and cite John Wesley's complaint of having to serve "a parish of above 200 miles in length [that] laughs at the labours of one man." But when Wesley raised his lament at least three others were fulfilling clerical responsibilities in the province, which made Georgia's small Anglican congregation as proportionally well churched as early Carolinians.[1]

If the preceding were not major problems, was there something inherent in Trustee religious policy that worked against the Church of England? The Georgia charter did not officially establish the Anglican church but rather promised that "there shall be a liberty of conscience allowed in the worship of God . . . and that all such persons, except papists, shall have a free exercise of religion." This policy was intended to attract persecuted Protestants from Europe, the sort of colonists who made Pennsylvania prosper, and once they arrived keep them "contented with the quiet and peaceable enjoyment of the same, not giving offence or scandal to the government."[2] Concerned that religious intolerance would breed civil disorder, the Trustees excluded those they considered dangerous, protected those who were allowed to enter from the excesses of each other, charged all to keep the peace, and made the colony a haven for more than England's worthy poor. But official toleration did not mean that all religious groups were equal. Supported financially by the Society for the Propagation of the Gospel in Foreign Parts (SPG), the missionary arm of the Church of England, and with five of the church's clergymen sitting as Trustees, Anglicanism seemed assured a favored place in the province. Encouragement to foreign Protestants notwithstanding, the Board apparently believed in the beginning that the colony would be populated largely by Englishmen, and Englishmen needed an English church to comfort their sick and distressed, bury their dead, exhort them to live better lives, and impress upon all *The Whole Duty of Man*—incidentally the title of the orthodox tract that, next to the Bible and the Book of Common Prayer, was most often sent to the colony. The church was also expected to preach obedience to ordained authority and instill in the people a respect for the rules and regulations that kept humankind's baser instincts in check —rules and regulations with which Georgia would be amply supplied.[3]

Thus although official policy might appear to limit Anglican influence in the colony, in reality the Church of England was expected to play a central role in the lives of Georgians. Toleration was a reasonable approach to religion in a century that "was not so much an age of reason as of reasonableness,"[4] and it was reasonable that the Trustees would not knowingly put ministers of England's established church at a disadvantage, particularly when contributions from that church were being sought. But if policy was not a serious obstacle then application of that policy becomes suspect, especially when one considers that it was in the application phase that those much-criticized clergymen became directly involved. To assess this aspect, to examine what the Anglican church in early Georgia was actually allowed, expected, and able to do, one must look to the man most responsible for carrying out in America the design decided upon in London—James Edward Oglethorpe.

Not surprisingly, Oglethorpe agreed with the principles of religious toleration set down in the charter. Raised in a family tainted by past Catholic sympathies, he early learned the prudence of doctrinal ambivalence and ambiguity, both in his own actions and in his attitude toward the actions of others. Apart from a dislike of things popish, which was more nationalistic than ecclesiastical, he was a man without religious prejudices. This makes it difficult to determine just what he did believe. One biographer, Amos Aschbach Ettinger, cautiously observed that "what little is known of his personal faith is found in the labours for his fellow men, his reverent attitude toward the clergy, his recurrent expressions of devout trust in, and a deep gratitude to, the Almighty, and the testimony of those about him," but even this general list presents problems. His "labours for his fellow men" might well have been motivated by his sense of social obligation, while his dealings with the Anglican clergy in Georgia were more often perfunctory than reverent. Although he did refer occasionally in his letters to things occurring through "the manifest interposition of God" or to how

"God was pleased to provide," such statements were common to correspondence of the period and may be ascribed as much to literary style
as to religious convictions. And finally, the "testimony of those about
him" is contradictory at best. Johann Martin Boltzius, the Lutheran
pastor at Ebenezer, believed Oglethorpe had "a great Esteem for God's
holy Word and Sacraments, . . . and wishe[d] to see the Name of Christ
glorified everywhere," but John Wesley chided him for seldom attend-
ing divine services and for his apparent indifference to things spiritual.
Careful as he was, Ettinger may have overstated the case.[5]

Compounding the confusion is the fact that even when religious
motives were present Oglethorpe's actions usually reflected secular concerns. His desire to bring "poor *Germans*" to Georgia was, he admitted,
"for the Glory of God, and for the Wealth and Trade of *Great Britain*,"
while his concern for converting the Indians was more diplomatic and
defensive than evangelical. With Catholic Spain holding Florida, the
advantage of making the natives "Converts and good Subjects" was
obvious. Yet if this were to be done others would have to do it. As
Oglethorpe indicated in a 1734 letter to the Reverend Samuel Wesley,
if an aspiring missionary was "eager to take up the Cross and follow his
Crucified Master" in Georgia, he (Oglethorpe) "should be far from dis-
couraging him to undertake this Task."[6] However, the Trustee was not
willing to join the priest in his work. James Oglethorpe would hardly
hinder a clergyman from doing his duty, and at times might even aid
him if that was needed, but matters spiritual were the ministers' concern, not his. And as events unfolded it became apparent he preferred
it that way.

In this regard James Edward Oglethorpe was scarcely different from
other English country gentlemen of good estate and ancient lineage.
Like his counterparts in landed society, Squire Oglethorpe "accepted
that a right-minded man loved God, believed in His mercy, and prac-
tised kindness and charity towards his fellow-creatures." He held "a firm
belief in the moral and social values of religion" and, though he might
appear lax in his own personal faith, he "generally supported the parson's spiritual authority and lent him material assistance."[7] Such was
the natural order of things in the world of the "Country *Sunday*," described only half in jest by Joseph Addison in the *Spectator* as "the best
Method that could have been thought of for the polishing and civilizing
of Mankind." "It is," Addison observed, "certain the Country-People

would soon degenerate into a kind of Savages and barbarians, were there not such frequent Returns of a stated Time, in which the whole Village meet together with their best Faces, and in their cleanliest Habits, to converse with one another upon indifferent Subjects, hear their Duties explained to them and join together in Adoration of the supreme Being." It was a system Oglethorpe saw function so well in the Church of Saint Peter and Saint Paul in Godalming, Surrey, and he apparently believed it would work as well in Georgia.[8]

Because these expectations were assumed rather than defined, it became James Oglethorpe's task to clarify the role of the parson even as he established his own status as leader of the community of Georgia colonists. This process began as the ship *Anne* weighed anchor, and in the weeks that followed he appointed officials, passed out favors, settled disputes, dispensed justice, stood as godfather to a child born on board, and even gave a member of the crew "a good kick on ye arse" when he harassed some of the settlers. Confirming the authority conferred on him as a Trustee, Oglethorpe so completely established himself as patriarch, patron, and protector that the people called him "father" and marked his birthday with food and festivities equaled only by Christmas. Actually the celebration for Oglethorpe may have been more enthusiastic, for though both meals were essentially the same the secular holiday was marked by "Cudgill playing . . . for a pair of Shoes" instead of "Prayers wth. a Sermon."[9]

Spiritual matters, however, were not neglected, and on this first voyage Oglethorpe set an example by frequenting divine services where the Reverend Doctor Henry Herbert, who had volunteered to "assist in settling the Colony . . . by performing all Religious and Ecclesiastical Offices," could be depended upon to deliver "an Exhortation suitable to the present undertaking," just as a country parson might have preached to the squire who controlled his living. Together Herbert and Oglethorpe, parson and squire, visited the sick, buried the dead, calmed the fearful, and cooperated to such a degree that before landing the minister felt confident enough in their relationship to intercede on behalf of a passenger who incurred Oglethorpe's wrath by feeding a sheep's head to the dogs. The man was pardoned, a public act that at once enhanced the parson's prestige, even as it impressed upon the colonists the goodness *and* the authority of their squire.[10]

By the time they arrived in Georgia lines of obligation and respon-

sibility between and among parson, squire, and people seemed well
drawn and understood, so Oglethorpe confidently gave each family an
"iron pott, frying pan, and three wooden bowls, a Bible, Common
Prayer Book, and [The] Whole Duty of Man," and turned religion over
to Herbert. From that point the church played a decidedly secondary
role in what was taking place. The Indians who greeted them indicated
a "desire to be instructed in the Christian religion" (probably because
that was what they knew the English wanted to hear), but the parson was not involved in the deliberations. Furthermore, on Sunday,
March 4, Oglethorpe ordered that after divine services the men should
go under arms into the woods where he set up a target to be shot at for
a prize. This practice was continued "for many Sundays afterwards," because it was the only day that "could be possible spared from labour, and
with some success." No record survives to indicate if Herbert protested
this violation of the Sabbath, but a few weeks after Oglethorpe's order
it was reported that the minister, like so many in his congregation, had
taken ill. Convinced his health would improve only if he returned to
England, Mr. Herbert left the colony in April. He died on the voyage
home.[11]

The Reverend Samuel Quincy, Herbert's successor, arrived in August
to find the colony rife with rumors of Catholic spies and the colonists suffering from a sickness their leader blamed on drinking rum.
Newcomers quickly joined the drinkers and in their intemperance grew
"very mutinous and impatient of labour and discipline." In fact, while
Oglethorpe was visiting Charles Town one of the more daring "had in
a barefaced manner insulted all order and threatened the chief people."
The whole duty of man needed to be preached and Samuel Quincy was
expected to preach it.[12]

There was much in Quincy's appointment to indicate that the Trustees did not give the matter the attention it deserved. One might argue
that the minister's background, which included "education at the College in New England, . . . studies at the Dissenters academies" in
London, time spent at Cambridge, plus experience as an "Independent
preacher" and later as a Presbyterian parson before he finally conformed
to the Church of England and was ordained, certainly recommended
him for service in a colony dedicated to religious toleration; but there is
little to suggest this was considered as an advantage. With a character
described as "unexceptional," he hardly seemed well suited for such a

demanding post, but the SPG was willing to pay him and Georgia was in need, so he was sent. Even so, he arrived so ill-prepared that Oglethorpe was "forced to lend [him] provisions out of the Store, otherwise [he would] have suffered for want." It was not a particularly auspicious beginning.[13]

Quincy was further handicapped by the fact that he did not experience the close shipboard association with Oglethorpe that Herbert had enjoyed, so the shared understandings on which to base a relationship were missing. To make matters worse he found Oglethorpe so "taken up when in town with the political and civil part of the administration, the business of grants, the settling and providing new inhabitants, [and] keeping a good order among the people," that he had little time to advise and direct his parson. Instead the Reverend Mr. Quincy was treated to a tableau of images and activities, with Oglethorpe the central figure, that were created and carried out to establish and reinforce both social and political bonds—bonds Quincy and his church were expected to sanctify. One such event occurred in early 1734 when six couples from Purrysburg, South Carolina, came down to Savannah to be married. From the outset it was apparent this was more than a religious ceremony. Oglethorpe, aware that the river joined as well as divided the two colonies, and anxious to use that fact to Georgia's advantage,

> received them in the most obliging manner and with much generosity. He ordered presently a fine hog to be killed for the entertainment of the company. Beer, wine, rum [interestingly enough], and punch were very plentiful. They were all very merry and danced the whole night long. The next day [the couples] went to Mr. Oglethorpe to take their leave and thank him for all his kindnesses, and as their boats were passing the river they were saluted from the fort by a volley of the great guns.[14]

From their landing to their leaving it was an occasion marked by a consciousness of the roles that all involved were required to play, roles not unlike those acted out in rural England by the gentry and by the people whom they protected and who served them. And the church did what was expected of it. Nevertheless, the impressions left by this social drama may have confused Quincy, for one observer noted that "some of these wives will hardly stay the nine months out to create a progeny," adding with tongue firmly in cheek that "whether [this was] by reason of the fruitfulness of the air or some trial of skill beforehand [he could] not determine." But it was not for the minister to pass judgment. He was simply to give his blessing to what took place, if it was in the interest of his squire.[15]

By early 1734 Georgia's population was over six hundred, and nearly half of the people lived in outlying garrison settlements. This meant that Oglethorpe, increasingly concerned with defense, spent less time in Savannah. While he was absent Quincy appeared to conduct himself to the satisfaction of most, and soon reports reached England that commended him "for his care and good example." Despite Trustee instructions, no church had been built, but a "spot of land" had been reserved where one was to be erected "as soon as possible." Meanwhile "a place [was] . . . set apart for public worship on Sundays, [and] where the children [were] educated all the rest of the week." It was not the best arrangement, but no one seemed to complain, least of all the minister. Then in late March, Oglethorpe sailed for home. A few weeks later Samuel Quincy, troubled by one of the sicknesses that plagued the southern coast, departed for New England, leaving the Reverend Lewis Jones, "the missionary from Port Royal," to serve in his stead.[16]

Thus began the pattern of absenteeism that has been considered the primary cause of Quincy's downfall. Although he attempted to provide for his flock while he was away, reports reached London that he left "a Wheelright to read Publick prayers, comfort the Sick and bury the dead [which] was a behaviour the Trustees could not excuse."[17] Equally upsetting was the fact that Quincy did not send the Board a report of his activities for over a year, a neglect which his excuse—that he lacked precise instructions in that regard—did not rectify. But had he written the Trust, as he did the SPG, his candid assessment of Anglicanism in the colony would hardly have commended him to the proprietors. "The Public Worship of God is very much neglected," he admitted, "& Vice and Immorality are Very open and flagrant amongst us." "Excessive Drinking . . . Reign[ed] as much amongst the Women as the Men," social gatherings turned into brawls, sexual misconduct was prevalent and in some cases public, and to make matters worse the people showed little inclination to reform. Quincy may have summed up the situation best when, upon being asked if "Romish Missionaries" were active in the colony, he replied that although there were Catholics there, none were "Proselyting others." But if they tried to convert colonists, Parson Quincy concluded, they would be disappointed, for "Religion seems to be the least minded of anything in the place."[18]

But Quincy's ministry was not without some successes. He was able to promote a "society" of seven or eight young men who met to study the scriptures, and on the whole the people "judge[d] him to be a good natured, friendly, peaceful, sober[,] just man and . . . they [had] no complaint against him either relating to his private life or to the execution of his office as Clergyman except his absence from them."[19] Quincy's error was not that he failed to make Georgia a religious colony, but rather that he failed to support those who, in Oglethorpe's absence, were responsible for making it an orderly one.

Soon after his squire sailed for England, Parson Quincy got involved in politics, which might have been forgiven had he not chosen the wrong side. By early 1735 he had become a critic of Chief Magistrate Thomas Causton, whom he described as "a most insolent and tyrannical fellow." A calico printer before immigrating, Causton was accused of using his position as Keeper of the Trustees' Store to force colonists to bend to his will. That Causton did this as a matter of policy is debatable, but Quincy was soon identified with those who believed he did; and because many who opposed Causton also advocated changes in land tenure and called for the introduction of slave labor, the Trustees concluded that the Reverend Samuel Quincy was "in League with the Malecontents." Meanwhile the minister, convinced that Georgia, which was once "intended to be the asylum of the distressed, unless things [were] greatly altered, [was] likely to be itself a mere scene of distress," asked to be relieved of his duties—a request the Trustees gladly granted.[20]

Even before Quincy resigned, efforts were underway to secure a more acceptable minister for the colony. Oglethorpe, in England but preparing to return to Georgia, took particular interest in the proceedings, and although it may be overstating the case to say, as Ettinger did, that he "stepped in and found the men he wanted," his involvement was significant. Acting on the advice of friends and contacts at Oxford, he and his fellow Trustees selected John Wesley to serve as minister in Savannah. Wesley's brother Charles, who was ordained before leaving, was to be Oglethorpe's secretary, and the Wesleys' friends, Benjamin Ingham and Charles Delamotte, were to go along to assist them. They seemed ideal candidates—intelligent, from good families, familiar (in varying degrees) with the life of the parish parson, committed to their calling, and eager to go "over to help the cause of religion as a particular providence and mark of God's favour to [the Trustees'] design."[21] What most who sat on the Board did not know, or did not appreciate, was that John and, to a lesser degree, his companions had designs of their own. On the day he was appointed, John Wesley confided to Trustee Dr. John Burton that his "chief motive, to which all the rest are subordinate, is the hope of saving my own soul" and that he "hope[d] to learn the true sense of the gospel of Christ by preaching it to the heathen." It was not exactly what James Oglethorpe had in mind for his parson, but if the minister could satisfy himself while satisfying the needs of the colony, that would be well enough.[22]

Thus began what Ettinger characterized as the religious phase of Georgia's development, although E. Merton Coulter observed that the two-vessel flotilla that carried Oglethorpe and more than two hundred colonists across the Atlantic looked very much "like a military expedition." Actually it was both, for with the Anglican ministers were Salzburgers and Moravians, religious refugees from Europe, as well as other colonists who, according to John Wesley, "knew little more of Christianity than the name." Most of this latter group (Highland Scots, Lowland Scots, and English) were bound for Saint Simons Island, where Oglethorpe would build Fort Frederica to guard Georgia's southern flank; but when the voyage began they seemed to the clergymen ideal candidates for conversion, subjects upon whom they could test their ideas and abilities. With this end in mind the ministers "had Prayers twice a Day . . . expounded the Scriptures, catechised the Children, and administer'd the Sacrament on *Sundays*," all of which they carried out with an attention to form and order that gave them the epithet "Methodists" and with such energy that their small flock increased even as their zeal alienated others on board.[23] Meanwhile "Mr. *Oglethorpe* shew'd no Discontenance to any for being of different Persuasions in Religion," a policy the Anglicans, impressed with the dissenters' faith and devotion, generally approved. However, John Wesley was concerned by his leader's failure to attend divine services regularly and by his reluctance to discuss matters of doctrine. The parson persisted, and at one point Oglethorpe did appear "quite open" to a religious experience, but no commitment was made and things soon returned to normal.[24]

As on the previous voyage, Oglethorpe exhibited "a patern of fatherly Care and tender compassion," which the clergymen considered evidence of religious devotion, although others on board saw his activities in a more secular light. Frequently he "cal'd together the Heads of families . . . and gave them several excellent and usefull instructions relating to their living in Georgia," and (as Ingham noted, with perhaps more emphasis than it deserved) "exhort[ed] them likewise to love God and one another."[25] This pleased Wesley, and despite his other concerns he reported to Dr. Burton that

> we can't be sufficiently thankful to God for Mr. Oglethorpe's presence with us. There are few if any societies in England more carefully regulated than this. The very sailors have for some time behaved in a modest, regular manner. The knowing that they are constantly under the eye of one who has both power and will to punish every offender keeps even those who, it is to be feared, have no higher principle, from openly offending against God or their neighbour; so that we have an appearance at least of Christianity from one end of the ship to the other.[26]

Seldom had a squire carrying out his responsibilities for the promotion and protection of religion and order been described more succinctly.

If what Oglethorpe expected from his parson in return was not made evident on the voyage, an incident occurred soon after they arrived that may have been an attempt on his part to bring their relationship more clearly into focus. About a week after dropping anchor, a party of Indians came down to the ships. Because it was obvious that such meetings were of some significance to the colony, the ministers, seeking to add visually to the ceremony, "put on [their] gowns and Cassocks . . . and then went into the great Cabin to receive them." The conference continued into the next day, and before the Indians departed the Wesleys and their friends "put on [their] Surplices, at Mr. Oglethorpe's desire, and went to take leave of them." The addition of this garment may have no significance beyond revealing how Oglethorpe believed he could impress the natives with formal Anglican attire; however, his insistence that the ministers wear the surplice, a white outer ecclesiastical vestment, raises an intriguing possibility. During the preceding century the surplice, called by some Puritans "a rag of the whore of Babylon," had come to symbolize not only enduring Catholic practices associated with the High Church party (practices with which, at the time, the Wesleys and their friends agreed) but also the subordination of clergy to the state. Such an order from James Oglethorpe, if indeed it was an order, could have been calculated to alert the priests to the fact that he was the authority over them as well as over the colony. If that was the case, it was a message they would have done well to heed.[27]

If the new arrivals needed further guidance as to what Oglethorpe expected from clergymen, they had only to look to the frequently praised communities of Ebenezer, where "religious, industrious and cheerful" Salzburgers, guided by their ministers, gave "a good Example to the Inhabitants" of the province, and Darien, where Highland Scots performed equally well under the influence of the Reverend John MacLeod, "a very good Man, who is very careful of instructing the People in religious Matters, and will intermeddle in no other Affairs." In contrast the citizens of Savannah conducted themselves much as they had under Quincy, and the discontent that developed earlier continued unabated. If ever a people needed the restraining influence of religion these did, so Oglethorpe concluded that John Wesley should concentrate on their needs and their regulation. Wesley's plans to carry the gospel to the Indians would have to wait.[28]

After settling the ministers in town, Oglethorpe took an expedition, which included Benjamin Ingham, and went south to build Fort Frederica. There problems between parson and squire began. Oglethorpe arrived on February 19, and three days later, on a Sabbath morning, the main party, with the minister, landed. As they disembarked Ingham observed that "Several of the people were firing guns" and quickly "ask'd Mr. Oglethorpe if Sunday was a proper day for Shooting." It was an awkward question, for when Savannah was settled Oglethorpe had set aside Sunday afternoon for target practice, an activity that seemed all the more important at the Saint Simons garrison. But rather than not support the church in its initial effort to regulate society, the commander relented and Ingham happily observed that "We immediately put a Stop to it." After breakfast parson and squire "joyn'd in the Litany, and then [Oglethorpe] returned to Savannah, having already put the people into a method of proceeding."[29]

Ingham soon found that the "method of proceeding" Oglethorpe "put the people into" did not guarantee that they would accept the parson's authority when the squire was away—especially if that authority was exercised in what colonists considered an arbitrary and unreasonable manner. The minister's own account makes clear what took place:

> My chief Business was daily to visit the People, to take care of those that
> were sick and to Supply them with the best things we had: for a few days
> at the first I had every Body's good word; but when they found that I
> watch'd narrowly over them and reprov'd them sharply for their faults,
> immediately the Scene changed; instead of blessing came cussing, and
> my Love and Kindness was repay'd with Hatred and ill will.[30]

Rather than reconsider what he was doing, Parson Ingham ignored one
settler's suggestion that "new laws in America" allowed more personal
freedom, and he announced instead that the "Lord's day . . . ought to be
Spent in his Service, that they ought not to go ashouting or walking up
& down in the woods and that [he] would take notice of all those who
did." This threat gave rise to the rumor that Ingham "had made a black
List and that [he] intended to ruin" those who opposed him. Relations
between priest and people went rapidly from bad to worse, and when
Oglethorpe returned with new colonists he found the community in an
uproar.[31]

Among those arriving with this second wave of settlers was Charles
Wesley, come to serve as the leader's secretary. Considering Ingham's
sunken state, it is hardly surprising that "the people seemed overjoyed"
to see Wesley and that he quickly assumed many of the duties normally
performed by his fallen colleague. But what might have been the beginning of a more successful parson-squire relationship quickly dissolved
when two women in the village confessed to Charles that they had
engaged in "misconduct with Oglethorpe" and the minister believed
them. The women soon told others, apparently using Wesley's knowledge of the affair to give their story credibility, and by the time the tale
reached Oglethorpe his parson was implicated in the telling.[32]

Preoccupied with military matters, and feeling "the thing [was] in
itself a trifle and hardly deserve[d] a serious answer," Oglethorpe apparently decided that an occasional "harsh word" and "rougher" response
would warn Wesley of his displeasure. In fact, as he observed with unusual candor in a later reference to the rumors: " 'Tis not such things
as these which hurt my character. They would pass for gallantries and
rather recommend me to the world." But Wesley, not realizing he stood
accused as well, did not understand and "knew not how to account for
[Oglethorpe's] increasing coldness."[33]

Although this issue contributed to Oglethorpe's growing lack of confidence in the clergyman's judgment, it was not what finally turned squire against parson. What ultimately drove the wedge between them was a report that Wesley was "stirring up the people to desert the colony"—a charge based on the fact that those "desiring leave to go were such as constantly came to prayers" and the resulting assumption that the priest was "the spring of [it] all." Outraged, Oglethorpe called his secretary before him to answer the charge of "mutiny and sedition," a charge no simple denial could satisfy. This scene was followed the next day by an even more revealing exchange between the two. Attacking what he felt was the root of the matter, Oglethorpe asked Wesley to explain why there was "no love, no meekness, no true religion among the people? but instead of that, mere formal prayers." The colonists, he insisted, "were full of dread and confusion" and Charles Wesley was to blame. The parson had committed the ultimate offense: he had disrupted the community.[34]

With that, James Edward Oglethorpe "entirely excommunicated" Wesley from what Oglethorpe called "my little church within." "Determined to make an example" of the offender, Oglethorpe began a deliberate campaign to discredit the minister and force colonists to choose between parson and squire—which was really no choice for most. In less than a month Wesley was "in effect debarred of most of the conveniences, if not necessaries, of life," people "turned out of the way to avoid" him, and his congregation was reduced to "two Presbyterians and a Papist." "I could not be more trampled upon," he confided in his journal, "was I a fallen minister of State."[35]

Distraught, Wesley persuaded Ingham to return to Savannah and seek his brother's help in resolving the conflict. In contrast to what had befallen Charles, John's efforts had been marked by success at almost every turn, and his report that in the town "all is smooth and fair and promising[;] Many seemed to be awakened[; and] All are full of respect and commendation" must have made conditions at Frederica seem all the more dismal. Oglethorpe apparently approved of Ingham's mission and when John arrived he "received him with abundant kindness." However, Charles's explanation of what had occurred, and later conversations with the women, left the older Wesley confused, concerned, and not entirely convinced of Oglethorpe's innocence. Nevertheless, when he left the island about a week later some progress toward reconciling parson and squire had been made.[36]

Having "found so little either of the form or power of religion at Frederica," John Wesley was "sincerely glad [to be] removed from it." Yet he
did not consider conditions there to be entirely the fault of Charles and
Ingham. In a thinly veiled reference to the poor example of piety being
set by the man to whom the people looked for leadership, the Savannah
minister wrote Oglethorpe of how he was sure "that no one, without
a virtual renouncing of the faith, can abstain from the public as well
as the private worship of God." It is uncertain when this admonition
reached Frederica, or how it was received, for at about that same time
Oglethorpe was putting all his energy into preparations for an expedition against the Spanish, who were rumored active along the southern
frontier, which left little time for a personal reformation. Interestingly,
these preparations did contribute to the improving relations between
the colony's leader and his secretary-parson. Hardly the sort of man one
would think superstitious, Oglethorpe nevertheless became convinced
that he was "now going to death" and that before he departed to meet
the Spanish he had best set right his affairs. Therefore he sought out
Charles Wesley, and when the interview was over the minister was convinced that James Oglethorpe's "old love and confidence" in him were
restored.[37]

When the expedition and its leader returned safely, Charles sought
to use this "deliverance" as the foundation for a conversion experience,
but Oglethorpe resisted. Instead he turned his attention to the delicate task of restoring his parson's shattered image without alienating
the anti-Wesley element still prominent in the settlement. The conse-
quence of this effort was a compromise that left each side with a sense
of satisfaction but without a clear advantage over the other. Charles
could take pride in the fact that "the people had observed [he] was
taken into favour again, which [he] found by their provoking civilities,"
although that feeling was diminished somewhat by the knowledge that
the husband of one of the women involved in the scandal had been appointed "head bailiff." In the end the real victor was James Oglethorpe,
for through his efforts order was restored, the parson was put back in
his proper place, and it was apparent to all that the squire was still in
charge.[38]

On May 11, 1736, Oglethorpe left for Savannah and a few days later
his secretary followed, to be there when Indian traders came to town to
take out licenses. Religion on the island was left largely in the hands of

the Reverend Edward Dyson, chaplain of the Independent Company of Foot that had just arrived from South Carolina. A man whose "moral character did not recommend him" and whose reputation was such that Charles Wesley had once "run away into the woods" to "escape his visit," Dyson was criticized by the pious for his inattention to priestly duties and for his less than exemplary personal conduct; but Frederica was rapidly becoming the most military of Georgia's garrison towns and Dyson was a soldier's parson. Those he served complained very little and, apart from the few times he sent John Wesley to the island, Oglethorpe seemed inclined to leave well enough alone.[39]

In spite of assurances that all was forgiven, Charles Wesley remained uncomfortable in his relationship with Oglethorpe. This discomfort, along with his increasing dissatisfaction with the office that nearly three months earlier he had vowed he "would not spend six more days in . . . for all of Georgia," brought him to a decision, and a few weeks after arriving in Savannah he announced his intention to resign and return to England. He continued to serve until all obligations were fulfilled and on July 26, 1736, having "entirely washed [his] hands of the traders," Charles recorded in his journal: "The words which concluded the lesson, and my stay in Georgia, were 'Arise, let us go hence.' Accordingly at twelve I took my final leave of Savannah. When the boat put off I was surprised that I felt no more joy in leaving such a scene of sorrows."[40]

James Oglethorpe accepted Wesley's decision with mixed emotions and at their last meeting asked his former secretary not to inform the Trustees of his resignation until his own return in the fall. The reason for the request, he candidly admitted, was because there were "many hungry fellows ready to catch at the office; and in my absence I cannot put in one of my own choosing." In an attempt perhaps to appeal to any Anglican chauvinism Wesley might harbor, Oglethorpe added that without his help the best he could hope for was "an honest Presbyterian, as many of the Trustees are such," but doctrine and denomination were not his main concern. James Oglethorpe wanted a man upon whom he could depend, and he did not want to leave so important a decision to others—even his fellow Trustees.[41]

Meanwhile John Wesley's work continued to draw praise. Although some colonists were uncomfortable with his zeal for form and regularity, few could fault the results of his efforts. Even Oglethorpe noted with satisfaction that "the change [in the people was] . . . very visible, with respect to the increase of Industry, Love and Christian Charity among them." But this success also worked against Wesley and his friends, for the community appeared so dependent upon them that when they asked permission to go and preach the gospel to the Indians—the primary motive for their coming—Oglethorpe refused, arguing that "on their removal . . . we shall be left entirely destitute, and the People by a relapse, if possible, worse than before."[42] There were heathen enough, English ones, in and around Savannah, and it was the parson's first duty to preach to them. If he could not save his soul while serving his squire, there was little use for him in James Oglethorpe's Georgia.

Wesley's disappointment at this decision was no doubt eased by Oglethorpe's increased reliance on him and by the prestige that reliance brought. Even before Charles resigned, John began to assume some secretarial duties, and when his brother departed that office fell unofficially to him. This placed the minister in the position to offer both political and religious advice. Less experienced in the former, his counsel was not always the best—as when Oglethorpe, acting on the priest's suggestion, announced that if anyone had "been abused or oppressed by any man" he should "deliver in his complaints in writing" to him and he would "do every particular man justice." It was the sort of thing a country squire who was also justice of the peace might have done in England and, indeed, Squire Oglethorpe might have done the same on his first visit. But by 1736 local civil authority was taking hold in Savannah and the magistrates saw this action as one that might "discourage government" if continued. They protested and Oglethorpe, reconsidering, withdrew.[43]

Although this particular advice proved inappropriate, the fact that it was given, and taken, points to the cooperation that characterized the relationship between Wesley and Oglethorpe/parson and squire through the summer and into the fall of 1736. Appearing less dogmatic in matters of faith, careful to follow Oglethorpe's lead in supporting Trustee policies and the efforts of those officials chosen to promote them, Wesley was heralded as a force for order and stability in the colony. Meanwhile the minister concluded that he had "long been under a great mistake in thinking no circumstances could make it the duty of a Christian priest to do anything else but preach the gospel" and began to take more interest in "what less directly conduces to the glory of God and peace and goodwill among men." Although this change hardly made him as worldly as the stereotypical English parish priest, it represented a softening of previous positions and made him more comfortable dealing with the day-to-day activities of those under his charge. John Wesley was beginning to act like the parson James Oglethorpe had envisioned.[44]

Squire Oglethorpe did not remain in Georgia to see how well or how poorly Parson Wesley ultimately played his role. In late November 1736, he sailed for England, leaving government in the hands of magistrates whom the minister initially praised as being "not only regular in their own Conduct but desirous and watchful to suppress . . . whatever [was] openly Ill in the conduct of others." Wesley was still disappointed that he had "less Prospect of preaching to the *Indians,* than [he] had the first Day [he] set Foot in America," but he appeared to accept his leader's priorities and soon reports reached England of how civil and religious authorities were cooperating "both to repress open vice and immorality, and promote the glory of God by establishing peace and mutual goodwill among men." Then when it appeared that the parson-squire arrangement Oglethorpe had sought was becoming reality, in his absence John Wesley, like Quincy before him, became associated with malcontents "who were closely link'd in opposing the Magistrates in the Execution of Justice." Thus "the Town was divided, and very few remained neutre, but exposed one Party or the other." This political indiscretion, augmented by his well-known personal quarrel with Chief Magistrate Thomas Causton, his niece Sophy, and her husband, discredited the parson in the eyes of those Georgians to whom the Trustees listened. With his reputation suffering both at home and abroad, Wesley concluded that his only recourse was to return to England, and in December 1737 he took his leave of Georgia.[45]

Wesley's departure acknowledged what most Georgians no doubt knew already—that despite some deceptive successes, the parson-squire arrangement could not survive without James Oglethorpe. He alone had the prestige and the power to assume the principal role, but he was unable (or at least unwilling) to delegate his patriarchal authority to those who governed in his stead. This failure reveals as much about the evolution of Georgia's sociopolitical system as it does about the singular significance of James Edward Oglethorpe. One might have expected the vacuum left when Oglethorpe departed to have worked to the advantage of the Anglican church and its ministers, for his absence seemed to place them in a position to play a part in colonial affairs at least equal to that of magistrates, inasmuch as civil officers were generally the ministers' social, and certainly their intellectual, inferiors. But these officials were not ready to share their new authority and the status it conveyed. Oglethorpe and Wesley learned this when the squire, on the advice of his parson, attempted to administer justice outside the recently established civil order. How quickly and firmly, albeit politely, the magistrates challenged this intrusion into what they now considered *their* affairs made it clear they were prepared to defend their prerogatives against all assaults—even those by James Oglethorpe. Thus the ministers found themselves subject to the authority of men like calico printer Causton, which made them more receptive to malcontent agitation against Trustee policy and those who enforced it.[46]

But even when Oglethorpe was present, the Anglican ministers received less support than they wanted or expected. Religion was high on his list of priorities only when it served the needs of Georgia, and it shrank in importance when the colony was calm and the people orderly. This attitude was apparent not only from the way Oglethorpe personally dealt with the clergy, and from his less than admirable attendance at worship, but also from the material assistance he provided. Despite specific instructions and sufficient contributions, no Anglican church was built in Georgia during these initial years. Early in 1735 Quincy acknowledged the disadvantage at which this placed him when he complained of how dissenters were "talk[ing] much of Building a meeting house and getting a Minister," and he expressed his belief that "if we had a Church it would lend very much to keep the English Dissenters especially in our Communion." But by this time Oglethorpe had apparently concluded that peaceful, productive Presbyterians, even if "rigid that way," might serve Georgia as well as Anglicans, so when the Wesleys arrived a year later they found the congregation still meeting in the large "hut" where court was also held. When Oglethorpe ordered a new courthouse constructed instead of a church, even if it was to be used "for Divine Services till a Church could be built," he simply indicated once again the relative significance these institutions held for him. Also revealing was that the "Parsonage House" was erected on the edge of town, outside the "Pallisadoes" line (Figure 3-1), which put the ministers close enough to serve but not so close as to be in the way.

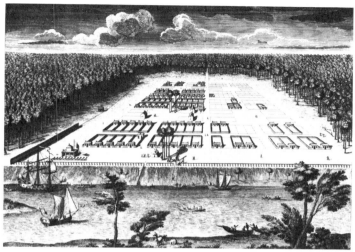

Figure 3-1. Peter Gordon's "A View of Savannah." Note the "Parsonage House" off to the left, by itself, outside the unfinished "Pallisadoes." (Courtesy of Hargrett Rare Book and Manuscript Library, University of Georgia Libraries)

The message thus conveyed to colonists could hardly have helped the clergy's cause.[47]

Yet this should not be taken to suggest that James Oglethorpe knowingly pursued a policy calculated to injure Anglican interests, but rather that his perception of the circumstances he confronted in Georgia caused him continually to rank religion lower and lower on his scale of concerns. Soon after he arrived in the colony, defensive matters began to take precedence and the role of the squire, which to Oglethorpe was essentially civil and social, became secondary to that of commander. The decision to make Frederica his headquarters in 1736 acknowledged this new direction, and when he returned to Georgia in the fall of 1738, at the head of the Forty-second Regiment of Foot, it was obvious that the *squire* was now the *general*. This shift in priorities did not alter Oglethorpe's opinion of what the clergy should accomplish. It only meant they were supposed to succeed with less help than they anticipated. This new burden dashed evangelical hopes as more emphasis was placed on preserving the community than on saving souls —which Charles Wesley discovered at Frederica and John later learned when Oglethorpe refused to let him go to the Indians because it would "leave *Savannah* without a Minister." Frustrated in their expectations and confused over what was expected of them, it is hardly surprising that the priests accomplished so little.[48]

But parson and squire were not alone accountable for what did and did not take place. On the whole, the Georgia Trustees approved of Oglethorpe's priorities and were as quick as he to condemn priestly shortcomings. They made no serious attempt to clarify clerical duties or to analyze and explain colonial conditions to those going over, which resulted in Quincy's failure to send required reports and the Wesley party's setting out with hopes and plans that proved unrealistic. Even fundamental material needs were overlooked, as graphically illustrated when Oglethorpe was "forced to lend [Quincy] provisions" when he arrived or "otherwise [he would] have suffered for want." More important still, despite Anglican influence on the Board, the Trustees never cooperated with the SPG to the extent one might have expected. Although John Wesley's complaint of having to minister to "a parish of above 200 miles in length" may have been a bit dramatic, more personnel might have improved the situation. Instead the Georgia Trustees, fearing they might lose control of the clergy, even tried to renege on their agreement to grant ministers a glebe, to which the SPG responded by temporarily cutting off what funds it did provide. Complacent when all was well and oblivious to most problems the clergy faced, the Trustees became concerned only when their priests conducted themselves in a way that threatened the grand design. Like Oglethorpe, they wanted Georgia to be a godly colony so long as they were sure God was a Georgian.[49]

There remains yet another factor that contributed to the inability of the Church of England to play a prominent role in the life of the colony—the colonists. Most of the settlers who arrived with Oglethorpe in 1733 were English, but soon Georgia began to receive Germans and Austrians, Highland and Lowland Scots, Jews, and a sprinkling of French, Irish, and Swiss, many brought specifically to defend the frontiers. Thus by 1736 the colony's composition and, in many ways, its purpose were quite different from what had been initially envisioned, and a population less English and more military handicapped the Anglican church. John Wesley was probably correct when he claimed that most of the passengers on his voyage "knew little more of Christianity than the name," if by Christianity he meant the Anglican communion. The human cargo in those vessels—Englishmen and Scots, most bound for Frederica and other garrison towns, plus a handful of Protestant refugees—was a microcosm of what the colony was becoming. With the exception of the Germans and Austrians, and perhaps the Jews, most Georgians put religion low on their list of priorities. Oglethorpe's attitude toward the church reinforced this relegation and Anglican clergymen found themselves ministering to an increasingly unenthusiastic flock.[50]

This condition was compounded by the rise of the "malcontents" —those Savannah-based dissidents who sought prosperity and power through alterations in the Trustees' restrictions on land, labor, and government. Coming from the most English area in the colony, many of them were, or at least should have been, Anglicans. If the Church of England were to succeed in shaping the lives of the colonists, surely Savannah was the place, but even there it was less than successful. Although Quincy sided with the protestors on some issues, and even Wesley was suspected to be sympathetic to their cause, statements by the latter *"That he never desir'd to see Georgia a Rich, but a Religious Colony"* convinced many that he and the Church he served were instruments of the Trustees, seeking "to enslave our *Minds,* as a necessary Preparative for enslaving our *Bodies.*" Agreeing with Ingham's unidentified antagonist who claimed that "new laws in America" supplanted the paternal patterns of security, dependence, and deference that gave religion authority in England, Georgia malcontents (who included more than those who signed proslavery petitions) rejected the restraints inherent in eighteenth-century Anglicanism, even as they rejected the rules, regulations, and relationships that were the basis for the Georgia Plan. In the end these malcontents, and those less vocal who shared their views, may have been the real reason why the Anglican church south of the Savannah was never what it was south of London, just as ultimately they were why Georgia was never what James Oglethorpe and the Trustees wanted it to be.[51]

James Edward Oglethorpe, Race, and Slavery
A Reassessment

Betty Wood

O*f all the elements of the so-called Georgia Plan, none has generated more interest than the prohibition of slavery. Why this was done and what part James Oglethorpe played in formulating the policy is the subject of Betty Wood's essay. What comes clear in Wood's analysis is that, as is the case with so much of the Georgia Plan, Oglethorpe took a leading role in defining, implementing, and ultimately defending Trustee policy.*

By carefully examining the circumstances that led Oglethorpe and the Trustees to exclude slavery, the author is able to place the slave prohibition in its proper context. With that done, Wood sheds light on why the Trustees were so opposed to any change in the antislavery policy. But Wood suggests that Oglethorpe went further than just a defense of the Georgia Plan and in so doing took a stand on the natural rights of Africans and the consequences of the trans-Atlantic slave trade that would not be repeated for decades.—Editors

James Edward Oglethorpe has been universally acclaimed by successive generations of scholars and has been usually depicted if not in saintly then certainly in heroic terms.[1] However, the generally flattering picture of, as Austin Dobson dubbed him, this "Paladin of Philanthropy" is at odds with the opinion held by several of the participants in the Georgia project and, more specifically, by those settlers who by the mid-1730s were demanding fundamental alterations in the Trustees' scheme. The man to whom they had once referred as "father" was now being denounced in the most blistering language as unsympathetic and indifferent to the needs of the colonists; as a tyrant; as one whose reputation was so closely linked with the Georgia Plan that, regardless of the cost to those being called upon to implement that plan, he refused to consider, let alone to admit, that he and his colleagues might be mistaken in their land and labor policies.[2]

Oglethorpe also had critics in London. Within months of the first settlement of Georgia some of the other Trustees were already complaining about his failure to keep them fully informed about events in the colony, a concern that in 1737 led them to appoint William Stephens as their resident secretary.[3] Moreover, the extent to which Oglethorpe took matters, and especially financial matters, into his own hands caused growing alarm and consternation on the Georgia Board of Trustees.[4]

Oglethorpe had opponents, but on both sides of the Atlantic there were those who, whether out of fear or admiration, were prepared to stand by him. Albeit for rather different reasons, he could rely upon the continuing loyalty of most Salzburger and Highland Scots settlers and, in London, on the staunch if not always uncritical support of the earl of Egmont.[5]

Oglethorpe's association with the Georgia project, like earlier and later phases of his public career, proved highly controversial. However, his friends and enemies alike concurred on one important point: that, depending upon their standpoint, he personified either the deep, selfless concern or the intransigence of the Trustees and was primarily responsible for denying the settlers that which many of them deemed to be "The one thing needful" for the success, if not the very survival, of Georgia. That "one thing" was black slave labor.[6]

The prohibition of chattel slavery was the cornerstone of the Georgia Plan, and it was this dramatic departure from what, by the 1730s, was the norm everywhere else in British North America that made the early settlement of Georgia unique in the annals of colonial American history. Given prevailing British and colonial attitudes toward race, slavery, and the African slave trade, no compelling reason existed for contemporaries to have supposed that any new American colony founded after 1700 would embark on such a course. Neither was there any reason to suspect that James Oglethorpe would be a prime mover of such a scheme.

Such early eighteenth-century English discussions as there were about slavery and the slave trade did not call into question either the morality of enslaving the African or of continued British and colonial involvement in the slave trade. By the same token, few doubted the economic value to the home country of the slave-based plantation economies of the Caribbean and southern mainland colonies. If anything, the reverse was true.[7]

Indeed, it was during the 1720s that the Anglican church and the English legal establishment finally arrived at two decisions that, for the foreseeable future, confirmed the status of "slave" on Africans in British America and held that slavery might exist in England itself. In 1727 the bishop of London, whose ecclesiastical authority encompassed the Anglican communities of North America, resolved the long-standing question of the relationship between Christianity and chattel slavery to the satisfaction of Anglican slave owners when he declared that conversion to Christianity made no difference whatsoever to an individual's secular status. Christians, and not least Christian masters, were called upon to attend to the spiritual welfare of their bondsmen but were placed under no obligation to manumit those of their slaves who professed themselves to be Christians.[8]

Two years later came a legal decision that overturned that of Lord Chief Justice Holt in the case of *Smith v. Gould* (1706). This earlier case had attempted to clarify the question of whether slavery could exist in England. Holt's judgment had been unambiguous: "By the common law no man can hold property in another." In 1729, largely to determine the legal status of those blacks who might be sent or brought by their colonial owners to England, the attorney general, Philip Yorke, and the solicitor general, Charles Talbot, took the contrary view and held that such blacks would "not become free." Moreover, they gave significant judicial backing to the bishop of London's opinion by declaring that "baptism doth not bestow freedom."[9]

In 1776 Oglethorpe explained to Granville Sharp that the Trustees had refused to condone chattel slavery in Georgia because they believed it to be "against the Gospel, as well as the fundamental law of England."[10] There is no evidence, however, that Oglethorpe or any other Trustee dissented from the bishop of London's interpretation of the relationship between Christianity and bondage.[11] Neither is there any suggestion that they favored Holt's decision over that advanced by Talbot and Yorke.

Unfortunately, Oglethorpe's views on slavery and race during the 1720s are not on record. However, it is clear that down to the end of 1732 he gave his tacit support to the continuation of the African slave trade. In December 1730, some ten months after he had first met with Egmont to broach the possibility of founding a new American colony, Oglethorpe was elected to the Court of Assistants of the Royal African Company. In January 1732, having purchased the requisite £1,000 worth of stock, he became a deputy governor of the company. Why he decided to sell his stock at the end of that year must remain a matter for speculation.[12] If he had any qualms about the propriety of enslaving the African, or felt any personal guilt about his close association with the Royal African Company, such feelings did not find expression in an outright condemnation of this appalling branch of British and colonial commerce.

Oglethorpe's and the other Trustees' opposition to slavery was strictly confined to the single case of Georgia. At no stage did they demand or even hint that the institution ought to be brought to an end everywhere, or indeed elsewhere, in British America. Of course, it could be argued that Oglethorpe and his colleagues had sound political reasons to limit their concern to Georgia. Influential, and for Georgia absolutely vital, British and colonial support would almost certainly have been alienated had they launched into a wholesale verbal assault on chattel slavery. In fact, the Act of 1735, which outlawed slavery in Georgia, served to reassure colonial slave owners and merchants involved in the slave trade that the Trustees harbored no such intentions. Indeed, by promising to return to bondage any black fugitives apprehended in Georgia they were not only acknowledging but also helping to ensure the continuation of chattel slavery in the other mainland colonies and, more especially perhaps, in neighboring South Carolina.[13]

The main impulse behind the momentous decision to proscribe black slavery in Georgia came not from a climate of opinion in the England of the 1720s which held that slavery was contrary to either the scriptures or the common law. Oglethorpe would have been much closer to the truth had he explained to Sharp that the Trustees' policy stemmed from two other considerations. First, it was the logical extension of their concern with white virtue, white manners, and white morals. Second, once it had been decided to locate this new colony in the southern borderlands, there seemed to the Trustees to be compelling military and economic reasons for dispensing with black slaves.

If the plight of the African slave was not a burning issue in England in the 1720s, the state of contemporary English society most certainly was. In the aftermath of the South Sea Bubble, a range of social, economic, and moral ills were identified by and attracted the deep concern of several prominent churchmen and parliamentarians. As is well known, the Georgia project was rooted in this wide-ranging and intense examination of English society.[14]

The original, but by no means novel, idea of trying to resolve at least some of England's problems by founding an American colony was Oglethorpe's. Although we cannot be entirely certain of his precise contribution to the social theory that underpinned the Georgia Plan, it is in *A New and Accurate Account of the Provinces of South-Carolina and Georgia*, published in 1733 and generally attributed to Oglethorpe, that we find one of the clearest expositions of what he and the other Trustees regarded as their primary purpose: the creation of a particular set of social values and relationships in Georgia. *A New and Accurate Account* also reveals quite clearly Oglethorpe's close familiarity with earlier proposals to colonize the borderlands and, moreover, the extent to which he and his associates accepted at face value accounts that depicted that region's physical environment in the most extravagant terms.[15]

Although Oglethorpe and the other Trustees were greatly swayed by previous schemes to settle the borderlands, none of their predecessors had made absolutely explicit the possible nature of the relationship between chattel slavery and the manners and morals of white society. Insofar as such earlier proponents of colonization as Sir Robert Montgomery helped to define the Trustees' thinking about slavery, then it was primarily in persuading them of the need to establish a compact settlement pattern for defensive reasons (a point readily appreciated by Oglethorpe the military man) and reassuring them that black slaves would not be required for the cultivation of the Mediterranean-type crops that would soon make Georgia such a valuable addition to the Old Colonial System.[16]

The Trustees' social purpose was twofold. One purpose was to remove from Britain those people who, reputedly because of their lack of virtue, were not contributing to the general welfare. Poverty and un-employment, which in the Trustees' opinion largely reflected the moral deficiencies of those concerned rather than any defects in the national economy per se, might lead such people into various "bad courses" likely to threaten the well-being of other, more upstanding members of society. The poor, the unemployed, and the unemployable, these "mis-erable wretches" and "drones," as the Trustees referred to them, would be relocated in the southern borderlands where, through the medium of work, they would become useful and virtuous citizens.[17]

The nature of the social and moral threat posed by chattel slavery to the productive, and thereby virtuous, society envisaged by Oglethorpe and his associates had been touched on during the 1720s by George Berkeley, a close friend of Egmont.[18]

Neither Berkeley nor Egmont, or for that matter Oglethorpe, dis-puted the economic value of the plantation colonies to Britain. But they were concerned by the rampant materialism of these slave soci-eties. The "luxury" and "idleness" of the Caribbean and southern main-land colonies, or at least of the elites that dominated them, constituted the very antithesis of the values the Trustees hoped to cultivate in Geor-gia. Work, not "idleness," was to be the hallmark of Georgia society. The ownership of land would comprise the all-important incentive to work and, thereby, self-improvement and moral regeneration. Wealth would not necessarily be distributed equitably in Georgia, but there was a very real sense in which, not least through the equal distribution of land among the charity settlers, the Trustees intended to create an initial equality of opportunity and access to the means of production. Thereafter, the precise manner in which wealth came to be distributed would depend upon the initiative and attitude, the aptitude for work—in essence the virtue—displayed by the individual.[19]

Before 1732 these themes were discussed and the Georgia Plan for-mulated in the abstract. The military, economic, and above all the social and moral reasons for wishing to dispense with slavery were all in place by mid-1732, but as yet the Trustees did not feel it necessary to legislate against that institution. Indeed, they were even prepared to employ black workers borrowed and hired from South Carolina to help with the construction of Savannah, and in 1734 they also allowed the Salzburgers to use slaves at Ebenezer.[20]

Two things persuaded James Oglethorpe, the only Trustee ever to set foot in Georgia, of the need for the Trustees to make explicit their intention never to allow slavery in the colony on a permanent basis: his visit to South Carolina in the summer of 1733, and what he found upon his return to Savannah.

What outraged Oglethorpe so much during the course of his trip to South Carolina, his first lengthy encounter with that colony's slave society, was not so much the plight of Carolina's blacks as it was the attitude of certain planters toward the new colony of Georgia. The South Carolinians had made every profession of good will toward the Georgia project and had supplied invaluable material assistance, including black workers, during the initial stages of settlement. But it soon became apparent to Oglethorpe that some Carolinians had rather different, and decidedly more devious, intentions: they hoped to be able to expand their rice interests, and thereby black slavery, across the Savannah River. As if this were not bad enough, some of them had the audacity to try to bribe Oglethorpe into securing a reversal of the Trustees' land and labor policies.[21] Oglethorpe's scornful response to these overtures was entirely predictable but, at an early date, he had been alerted to what was likely to prove a potent and potentially irresistible threat to the integrity of the Georgia experiment.

Oglethorpe's worst fears, which had been heightened by his experience in Carolina, were realized upon his return to Savannah. Prior to his departure, the first settlers, no doubt encouraged if not intimidated by his energetic presence, had worked hard and enthusiastically at the many tasks involved in founding Savannah. What Oglethorpe found upon his return "shocked" and appalled him; the settlers had "Grown very mutinous and Impatient of Labour and Discipline."[22] Within a matter of weeks, two of the values that formed the very essence of the Trustees' social design seemed to have evaporated. But why? To Oglethorpe, the answer seemed obvious: the presence of black slaves. Here was proof, if any were needed, of the moral infirmity of the early settlers and, moreover, of the way in which chattel slavery threatened to undermine the Georgia project. Oglethorpe immediately returned the slaves to their Carolina owners and tried to impress upon the other Trustees the need for firm and decisive action to make crystal clear their long-term intentions regarding slavery.

In 1735, largely at Oglethorpe's insistence, the Trustees obtained what, in theory at any rate, was the ultimate legal and political backing for their prohibitory policy: an act of Parliament. Significantly, however, this legislation emphasized not so much the unfortunate consequences of chattel slavery for white manners and morals as it did the military and economic reasons for excluding that institution from Georgia's vulnerable frontier society. The Trustees, and Oglethorpe especially, were keenly aware that Spain would not hesitate to manipulate any black slaves brought to Georgia as part of its war effort and, moreover, that such slaves would need little external encouragement to strive for their freedom.[23]

The reasons why the Trustees emphasized the military dangers implicit in the introduction of slaves, and stressed that the commodities to be produced in Georgia simply did not necessitate their use, reflected an important and often underestimated degree of political pragmatism on the part of the Georgia Board. The House of Commons, committed as it was to the African slave trade and convinced of the economic value of the plantation colonies, had to be persuaded that it was in the national interest to finance a colony that excluded slavery. Georgia's role as a military buffer and its anticipated economic importance to the home country constituted rather more persuasive arguments than a case that rested on the probable consequences of chattel slavery for the social, moral, and political virtue of the colony's white inhabitants.

James Oglethorpe was dismayed and angered, but surely not entirely surprised, by the fact that the Act of 1735 did not quell the growing demand for slaves in Georgia or completely eradicate the South Carolinian interest in the colony's potentially rich rice lands. After 1735 the malcontents' increasingly strident proslavery argument rested exclusively on the comparative profitability of slavery. Like the Trustees, but by 1739 with the notable exception of Oglethorpe, they paid little heed to black rights, to the legitimacy or otherwise of enslaving the African.[24]

The turning point in the slavery debate came in 1739 when Thomas Stephens, who had gone to Georgia in 1737 to act as his father William's assistant, threw in his lot with the malcontents.[25] According to Stephens, who felt deeply aggrieved at the high-handed manner in which Oglethorpe had treated him, the Trustees in London were being consistently and deliberately misinformed about conditions in Georgia. In Stephens's view (and his opinion was endorsed by Patrick Tailfer and the other authors of *A True and Historical Narrative of the Colony of Georgia*), Oglethorpe was the main culprit. Georgia, claimed Stephens and Tailfer, was not in the flourishing condition depicted by Oglethorpe but, on the contrary, was on the point of collapse.[26]

But why should Oglethorpe have so misrepresented the situation in Georgia? Stephens's answer, which he presented in person as well as on paper to Egmont, the other Trustees, and ultimately the House of Commons, was that Oglethorpe's reputation was so closely bound up with the Georgia project that he stubbornly refused to concede that he might be wrong, that the Georgia Plan was proving to be an abject failure. Egmont, in spite of certain reservations about Oglethorpe's behavior, steadfastly refused to accept Stephens's analysis of his colleague's motives.[27]

Thomas Stephens and the other malcontents were correct in their assessment of the comparative profitability of black slavery.[28] Moreover, they were not mistaken about the determination of the man they identified as being the main stumbling block to the realization of their economic aspirations for Georgia. However, time was to show that they seriously underestimated the determination of the South Carolinians to expand their slave-based rice economy. They also overestimated their own ability to diminish the physical and psychological cost of chattel slavery to Georgia's white inhabitants through the introduction of such devices as a strict numerical ratio between blacks and whites.[29]

James Oglethorpe's reputation was indeed closely linked to the Georgia project, but then so were those of the other Trustees. Yet in the public eye it was Oglethorpe, far more than any other individual, including Egmont, who personified the endeavor to colonize the southern borderlands. However, the stiff resistance offered to the malcontents by Oglethorpe in Georgia, and organized by Egmont in London, went far beyond personal pride and vanity. These men were deeply and genuinely committed to the social design elaborated in the Georgia Plan and firmly believed that under their paternalistic stewardship Georgia would soon develop into one of Britain's most highly prized American possessions.

Between 1735 and 1743 Oglethorpe played a triple role in what by the former date had already become the defense, as opposed to the promotion, of the Georgia project. First, his mere presence in the colony acted as a fairly effective deterrent to most of those who toyed with the idea of evading the ban on slavery. Second, Oglethorpe encouraged those settlers who, for whatever reason, supported or could be persuaded to support the continuing exclusion of slavery to make their views known to the Georgia Board. Finally, together with the other Trustees, but notably with Egmont, he consistently warned the malcontents of the difficulty, if not the sheer impossibility, of introducing into Georgia a modified version of South Carolina's slave society.[30]

By 1739 a propaganda war raged in Georgia and, more significantly, in London. The malcontents bombarded the Trustees and Members of Parliament with a range of literature in which they set out in often forthright language their analysis of the causes of and most appropriate remedies for the many ills that beset Georgia. They argued that Oglethorpe would go to any lengths to protect his reputation and accused him of misleading the Georgia Board and thereby Parliament and the British people; they also accused him of bribery, coercion, and corruption.[31] Their ploy was, quite simply, to discredit Oglethorpe and all those who sided with him.

The Trustees' labor policy received significant support from two groups in Georgia: the Salzburgers at Ebenezer and the Highland Scots at Darien. Early in 1739, in response to the proslavery petition sent from Savannah in December 1738, both settlements dispatched counter-representations to the Trustees.[32] The malcontents argued that the Salzburger petition demonstrated the degree of spiritual and temporal tyranny exercised by Pastor Johann Martin Boltzius over his congregation; they depicted the Darien petition as a prime example of the depths to which Oglethorpe would sink in order to get his way, in order to safeguard his reputation.

What had persuaded the Highland Scots to "Act Inconsistent with their own or Posterity's Interest" by declaring their unequivocal opposition to chattel slavery? To the malcontents the answer was clear enough: Oglethorpe had bribed them with "the promise of a few cattle."[33] In fact, as Harvey Jackson has argued, the Darien petition represented not so much a sordid bribe as a compromise between Oglethorpe and John Mackintosh Mohr that offered the hard-pressed Scots much needed economic assistance in exchange for an unambiguous declaration of their support for the ban on slavery. But had the Scots been coerced by Mohr and Oglethorpe? Although at least one of the petitioners claimed that this was the case, there is no conclusive evidence on this point.

But as Jackson has commented, "If coercion was involved, it was as much the coercion of circumstances and events as coercion by Mohr" and Oglethorpe.[34]

The Darien petition of 1739 reiterated what by that date were the thoroughly familiar military and economic reasons that had prompted the Trustees to outlaw slavery. But the unknown author of this document opposed chattel slavery for reasons that, as one recent historian has noted, "would reverberate through the anti-slavery movement and culminate in Lincoln's Second Inaugural Address."[35] The sinfulness of slaveholding was emphasized as were the natural rights of the African, including the right to freedom. As with all sins, sooner or later God would punish the sin of slaveholding, possibly through the device of a "bloody" rebellion. Here was an entirely new dimension to the debate as to whether or not slavery should be permitted in Georgia. But who was responsible for penning these words? The possibility cannot be ruled out that even if he did not personally draft the Darien petition, Oglethorpe concurred with the sentiments it expressed.

Although his main concern was with the implications of chattel slavery for Georgia's white society, by January 1739 Oglethorpe had gone further than any other Trustee in emphasizing the natural rights of the African and, of no little significance, the consequences of the slave trade for African society. By implication, he rejected the notion favored by George Whitefield, among others, that Africans benefited if not materially then certainly spiritually by their enforced removal from the heathen "darkness" of Africa to the Christian societies of the New World, and that this "benefit" in itself provided sufficient justification for their enslavement.[36]

Shortly after the Darien petition had been dispatched, Oglethorpe, who urged his fellow Trustees to stand firm against the malcontents, drew attention to the fact that the introduction of slavery into Georgia would "occasion the misery of thousands in Africa . . . and bring into perpetual Slavery the poor people who now live free there."[37] Oglethorpe, who unlike the other Trustees was familiar with the contours of South Carolina's slave society, had firsthand evidence of some of the "misery" caused by the enslavement of the African. Moreover, in 1733 he had been instrumental in securing the release from slavery of Job Jalla, an episode that may well have helped to persuade him of the fundamental injustice as well as the human "misery" inherent in chattel slavery.[38]

Although we cannot positively identify the author of the Darien petition, and Oglethorpe never claimed responsibility for it nor had it directly attributed to him, it seems clear that he approved of this scathing indictment of slavery. Yet despite his comments, the natural rights of the African and a concern for African society never featured in the antislavery case argued publicly by either Oglethorpe or the Trustees as a whole. Perhaps even the often outspoken Oglethorpe sensed that, given contemporary British and colonial racial attitudes, such a line of argument would have proved counterproductive. But the fact remains that the author of the Darien petition, and Oglethorpe in a letter to his fellow Trustees, had anticipated arguments that were to blossom during and after the era of the American Revolution.

The year 1742 marked the beginning of the end of the Georgia Plan. In that year the House of Commons for the first time voted down the Trustees' annual money petition; a demoralized Egmont resigned from the Common Council of the Trustees; and Oglethorpe defeated the Spanish at the Battle of Bloody Marsh.[39] Ironically, the military triumph that virtually guaranteed Georgia's survival demolished what over the years had proved to be one of the Trustees' most potent arguments for excluding slavery. With the removal of the Spanish threat, and given the hostility they were encountering from a House of Commons being primed by Thomas Stephens, the Trustees' position seemed hopeless. Oglethorpe's final departure from Georgia in 1743 meant that the Trustees were denied the services of the man who, although no longer able to claim the affection, loyalty, and respect of all the settlers, still acted as a fairly effective brake on the illicit employment of slaves. After 1742, and not least because of the connivance of the South Carolinians, black slavery came to exist in practice, if not yet in law, in Georgia.[40]

Between 1742 and 1749 the Trustees, led by James Vernon, fought a spirited and stubborn rearguard action to maintain their ban on slavery and thereby to preserve what they could of their original plan for Georgia. But neither Oglethorpe nor Egmont took a prominent part in the deliberations that preceded the Trustees' final admission of defeat in 1750 and the introduction of black slavery in 1751. Perhaps because of his marriage, the '45 Rebellion, and his court-martial, Oglethorpe found that he had neither the time nor the political credibility to get deeply involved in these discussions.[41] It is also possible that, given his uncompromising commitment to the original Georgia Plan, he had no wish to lend his support and such prestige as he enjoyed to what in effect was the final dismantling of the Georgia experiment.

Oglethorpe's views on the decision to permit slavery in Georgia, and the subsequent development of slavery and race relations in that colony, are not on record. Down to 1776, and in his remarks to Granville Sharp, he maintained a public silence on the Georgia project. But looking back over the years he must have felt a sense of bitter disappointment, if not betrayal. He and his associates had offered the early settlers of Georgia an alternative path of social and economic development, but it was one the people had deliberately, and with full cognizance of the likely outcome, rejected. Yet there was a very real sense in which Oglethorpe would have been perfectly justified in taking some pride in what he and the other Trustees had fought so long and hard to achieve in Georgia.

Oglethorpe, with the faithful backing of Egmont, had been relentless, even ruthless, in his determination to ensure that Georgia's settlers were never exposed to the physical, psychological, and perhaps above all else the moral dangers posed by chattel slavery. But there is evidence that by 1739 his concern for the well-being of Georgia's white society was tempered with a genuine and farsighted concern for something else: the natural right of the African to freedom and the consequences for African society of the trans-Atlantic slave trade.

As Phinizy Spalding has commented, James Oglethorpe was not, and did not claim to be, "a political or moral philosopher."[42] It would not be doing an injustice to the Oxford-educated Oglethorpe to describe him as a man of action, a doer rather than a thinker. Oglethorpe never developed his views on slavery into a coherent or systematic critique of that institution. However, he did anticipate most of the concerns that underpinned the later antislavery movement. By the end of the 1730s he was advancing, albeit in a tentative and somewhat fragmentary fashion in his private correspondence, views on race, slavery, and the African slave trade that were so far in advance of contemporary British and colonial opinion as to be politically unattainable. British policy makers cared even less about Africa and the African than they did about the virtue, or lack of it, of Georgia's white inhabitants. The latter saw in neighboring South Carolina a slave society, an agricultural capitalism, that although not without its flaws and risks was there to be copied rather than avoided. For the majority of settlers, and not just those who had paid their own way to the colony of Georgia, the prospect of profit outweighed all other considerations.

Given the political and economic priorities and the aspirations and racial attitudes that characterized the Anglo-American world of the 1730s and 1740s, Oglethorpe and his associates stood little chance of realizing their original ambitions for Georgia. In a purely political sense they failed. Yet Oglethorpe had succeeded in grasping the nature and long-term significance of the fundamental issues posed by chattel slavery. This fact alone, and not least his genuine concern and compassion for Africa and Africans, must surely secure for him an important niche in the history of British antislavery thought.

Oglethorpe, William Stephens, and the Origin of Georgia Politics

Phinizy Spalding

One of the fascinating—but perplexing—aspects of the Georgia Plan is the almost total absence of provisions for a system of government that could settle local political differences. It was as if the Trustees believed that a well-regulated colony would have no such divisions, and therefore nothing more than a few local officials were necessary. But political divisions emerged quite early, and in time they came to threaten the Georgia Plan itself.

In this essay Phinizy Spalding uncovers the origins of the anti-Trustee party, the "malcontents," and discusses how James Oglethorpe was himself the catalyst for this political factionalism. Also evaluated is the career of the Trustees' secretary, William Stephens, who initially seemed capable of playing the role of impartial arbiter but who was ultimately forced to take sides in the controversy. Stephens's decision to support the Trustees further divided the colony and thus a bitter factionalism became a distinct feature of Georgia politics even before the decade of the 1730s ended.—Editors

Even before James Oglethorpe and the first settlers left Great Britain on the Anne, opposition to the Trustees' various regulations surfaced. The tail-male tenure, restricting inheritance of land to a male heir, was singled out for criticism, and serious questions were raised as to the desirability of limiting most land grants to fifty acres. When the Georgians arrived in the New World, they began to have misgivings on other points where, it seemed, new directives might be issued. The evolving notions that both strong drink and black slavery be barred from the colony seemed unwise, and other less important ideas also caused them to be apprehensive.[1]

Dissatisfaction with the Trustees' ideas soon appeared on the banks of the Savannah, and Thomas Causton, designated storekeeper and bailiff for Georgia, wrote his wife on March 12, 1733, and reported that "tho' we want for nothing we have some Grumbletonians here also."[2] Scarcely a month later Samuel Eveleigh, a prominent and perceptive Carolina merchant, told the Trustees that prohibiting slavery would be "a great prejudice" to Georgia and might completely "Overset your Noble design." In Georgia's debilitating climate, Eveleigh claimed, it was even harmful for whites "to hoe and tend theyr corn," much less do heavier work.[3] In South Carolina, the attitude toward Georgia, initially friendly to the point of obsequiousness, turned to ridicule and scorn after barely more than a year. The new experiment, with its quirks and odd fancies, was derided; Georgians wanted everything provided them, and with no attendant responsibilities. In October 1734, the *South Carolina Gazette* waxed sarcastic about the new colony:

> . . . furnish us still with whatever we've need,
> Provide us with bread with beef and with pork
> For we've never the least Inclination to work. . . .
>
> The King it is true has provided us Lands
> But what signifies that unless he'd find hands
> To make use of the same: as for us tho' we're poor
> You'll never persuade us to work we are sure. . . .
>
> We cannot abide this drinking all Water
> So beg, to your Bounty you'd add some small beer
> As you know you did freely enough the last year.
>
> Consider our case now, and pray sirs be civil
> Or else we shall wish you all kick'd to the D____l.[4]

The Carolina rhymester touched upon the three subjects that were to provide the most difficulty in Georgia in the coming years: land, labor, and the obnoxious rum prohibition.

But Oglethorpe was determined that the Trustees' dictates be observed to the letter. He was also convinced that two of these curious features of the colony should be sanctioned as acts by the Georgia executive in England—which was done in the case of the Rum and Negro acts in 1735.[5] Having these pieces of legislation on the statute book and enforcing them, though, were two different things, as Oglethorpe soon discovered.

During his first stay in America, Oglethorpe, acting the role of founding father, tended generously to the wants of his colonists. He was paternal, understanding, constructive, patient, and widely admired by the settlers. Still the Trustees in England, although deeply impressed by the unselfish motives that drove him across the Atlantic, were concerned about what they detected in him to be a tendency to take over complete control of the plantation. Even more alarming to the Trust, which desperately desired accurate information about Georgia, was his failure to correspond as frequently as the Board wished. Oglethorpe pleaded overwork and lack of time, and certainly, when one considers the staggering number of small items with which he dealt, his plea was justified. On the whole, he was successful in transmitting to the colonists his own enthusiasm for what Georgia might be. Although modest murmurings came from several quarters during his first stay in Georgia, there appears to have been a general consensus among the majority of the settlers to give their driven leader the benefit of any doubts that they may have had. The project, then, just might work.

Oglethorpe was absent from America for almost two years (March 1734 to February 1736), during which period the colony bided its time. The dominant figure in Georgia was the storekeeper Thomas Causton —a haughty and arrogant man, although one with strong virtues too. Causton handled the store, from which provisions were allotted to the colonists, as though it were his personal fief; his reports to London were both infrequent and unsatisfactory. Elizabeth Bland wrote in 1735 that she had been sorely mistreated by Causton and, as a result, despised the colony he headed: "But did king Georg Use his people as they are Used here he woud Soon loose his Crown. Such lying Such Scandle & false Swearing as I never heard in my life, in Short its a very hell upon Earth"; the colony was a "terable place" ruled by "ville wretches." But she held out hope that if Oglethorpe could hear the grievances of the people he would rectify the situation.[6] Other settlers seemed to echo her wish that the situation would improve when Oglethorpe arrived.

Oglethorpe had any number of opportunities to calm events in Georgia upon his return in 1736. He was, however, caught up in the escalating international situation with Spain and, on the domestic front, by the problems associated with settling Frederica and quieting concerns associated with the Wesley brothers. Therefore, he had little time to devote to the petitions and remonstrances of his settlers during this short eight-month stay in Georgia. Causton, whose accounts were badly awry, was not properly instructed to make the necessary economies to put the colony aright financially. At this point the Trustees began to believe that Oglethorpe was pursuing a defined policy of keeping them ill informed, and they began to draw back from their former unquestioning admiration of the founder. His bills of credit—large sums drawn directly on the Trustees to cover expenses in Georgia—confounded the gentlemen of that body and seemed to threaten the good name not just of the colony but of the individual Trustees as well. It was clearly time for reforms to be instituted that would bring full and reliable information into the Georgia Office and that would put Oglethorpe in his proper place in relation to the other Trustees. Accordingly he was summarily recalled to England and arrived January 2, 1737.[7]

Also in January 1737 the Georgia Board, with Oglethorpe in attendance, received an application from William Stephens, from the Isle of Wight, former member of Parliament, to fill the newly created post of secretary. "This was highly pleasing to us," the earl of Egmont wrote, "he being a Man of cool temper and excellent Sense, and great industry and punctualness, and by him we were sure of having constant information of the State of the Colony concerning which hitherto we had been kept too much in the dark."[8] Stephens, born in 1671, son of Sir William Stephens, had been educated at Winchester, King's College, Cambridge, and the Middle Temple. In 1697, he married Mary, the daughter of Sir Richard Newdigate of Warwickshire. Five years later Stephens stood for Parliament from Newport, Isle of Wight, and was elected. Under Queen Anne, Stephens was a staunch Tory, was reelected from his conservative constituency in 1715, and although he lost his Newport backing in the parliamentary elections of 1722, he offered for Newtown, also on the Isle of Wight, and was once again returned. While in Parliament he held various posts, the most important being commissioner for the victualling—a position that required him to entertain often and lavishly. The result was that he was financially ruined and his parliamentary career came to an end in 1727.[9]

He secured a job with the York Buildings Company, which dealt in lumber and speculation in lands in Scotland,[10] but when that business reorganized and sold its assets, Stephens, pursued from the Highlands to London by swarms of creditors, was out of a job.[11]

In 1736 Stephens took on a commission for an old friend and York Buildings Company associate, Colonel Samuel Horsey, to go to South Carolina to inspect a land grant Horsey had been given on the Carolina side of the Savannah River. Stephens, at the age of sixty-five, arrived in Georgia in April 1736. For over a month he waited in Savannah with increasing impatience as Oglethorpe tended to affairs in the southern part of the province. When, at the end of May, Oglethorpe did finally arrive, their exchanges appear to have been testy. The men obviously knew one another during overlapping terms in Parliament, but neither has left a record that he was pleased to see the other on the banks of the Savannah. Oglethorpe advised Stephens of what to look for when going upriver to scout lands for Horsey, but Stephens had the distinct impression that Oglethorpe—who had land interests in Carolina as well —was bent on reserving the best properties for himself.[12]

After six exhausting weeks inspecting possible sites for Horsey's barony, Oglethorpe and Stephens met once again before the latter returned to England. Stephens's feeling that Oglethorpe was too critical of the Carolinians, simply because they disagreed with Georgia policy, was underscored. Whenever the men discussed Carolina's reluctance to follow Georgia's lead, Oglethorpe waxed hot. The "many Slippery tricks" that the Charles Town leaders had pulled on Georgia concerning land were recounted by Oglethorpe, but Stephens did not put much credence in the denunciation because relations between the two colonies were so bad that neither could think well of the other. During one four-to-five-hour diatribe, Oglethorpe spoke darkly of revenge on the Carolinians. In "great warmth," Oglethorpe said he "would make some of them repent dearly." To the politic Stephens such talk seemed overheated. He wrote simply: "Much more pass'd in Conversation, tending the same way, not fit to be committed to Paper."[13]

Stephens, after performing his necessary duties in Charles Town for Horsey, took ship for England. The initial contact in America between Stephens and Oglethorpe, later to be lukewarm allies against the burgeoning opposition faction in Georgia, had not been auspicious. Oglethorpe viewed Stephens as a potential competitor whose loyalty to

Georgia was by no means proven; Stephens apparently saw Oglethorpe as a spoiled hothead sorely lacking in a softening objectivity.

The American journal that Stephens wrote for Horsey outlining these and other events was done so thoroughly and efficiently, and his observations seemed so fresh and pertinent, that his name was mentioned favorably to Egmont, who more than likely suggested that Stephens apply to the Georgia Trustees for the secretarial position.

In April 1737 Stephens was proposed as secretary—a proposition readily agreed to by the Georgia Board. He was to serve a six-year term and to take his third son, Thomas, with him should he fail to complete the assigned number of years. In return Stephens received a 500-acre land grant, free passage to the New World, servants to help him clear his lands, £50 in hand and £50 more upon demand. A committee was designated to draw up his instructions, which were sealed on April 27 with "a paper Sign'd of more private instructions to him."[14] Three months later Stephens was reported to be leaving any day for Georgia.[15]

With the creation of the office of secretary, the Trustees established the first legitimate executive position, albeit a weak one, for their colony. Stephens's orders and instructions reflect the wide range of matters about which the Trust wanted to be informed but about which it at that time knew precious little. He was empowered to get regular reports from all the Trust's officers in Georgia and to see that these reports were sent to England; he was to send word to England as to the "progress or decay" of the province; he was to look into the reasons Georgians had for failing to cultivate the land given them; he was to list those who were industrious and those who were not; he was to report on the church attendance of the settlers and the officers of the Trust; and he was to advise the Trustees' officials on the spot on questions of morality and vice. In general, Stephens was told to inform London of the behavior of the inhabitants of the colony, report on their adherence to Georgia's laws, inform the Board of any events of particular interest, keep a careful record of all correspondence sent or received, and suggest policies to the Trustees for the good of the colony. Privately, he was expected to send confidential information to the Georgia leaders in London reporting on the reliability of their officers in the province, keep a close watch over the distribution of the colony's stores, and chronicle the grievances the colonists had with their officers.[16] On close inspection it can be seen that the various instructions were primarily

private or investigative in nature and lacked a true grant of governmental power. As James Ross McCain has commented, the office of
secretary in Georgia "was to aid the executive power in England rather
than to strengthen it in Georgia."[17] It is clear that the Trustees, having
failed earlier to establish the sort of machinery in Georgia that would
keep them abreast of events, were trying to correct this error by creating the office Stephens was named to fill. His appointment was to
make up for the oversight that had permitted the Trustees to go at times
for months without hearing anything wholly reliable from their colony.
Although the position lacked executive strength, at least it was a start.

Late in July 1737 Egmont reported that Stephens would be leaving
"next week" on the ship *Mary Anne*,[18] but for some reason he did not
get underway until after August 10. Causton, the Georgia storekeeper
whose activities were under a cloud, was instructed to give the new
official all due encouragement in the performance of his duties. After
an uneventful voyage, Stephens arrived in Charles Town on October 20, discharged numerous semiofficial duties there, and landed on
Savannah's Yamacraw Bluff on November 1.[19]

By the time of Stephens's arrival in Georgia, Oglethorpe had been
absent from the colony for roughly one year. During that period dissatisfaction with the Trustees' ideas had grown and numerous letters and
informal representations had been composed and sent to London. John
Brownfield, mercantile factor for an English firm and register of the
colony, frankly wrote to the Board in February that many lands given
out "lie in cypress swamp and are continually covered with water." It
was either too expensive or was impossible to drain such lands. Other
grants fell upon barren ground, thus forcing some of the Georgians
to abandon their farms and move to Savannah to support themselves.
Many of the most industrious people lost crops owing to the lack of
roads, wild cattle, or because "deer and insects consumed much of their
produce."[20] To Brownfield the most legitimate complaint of the colonists was that if the laws of Georgia were, as the Trust claimed, not
incompatible with English law, "why don't the Trustees send a book of
statutes with their by-laws annexed that every person may be satisfied
of the constitution of the province he lives in?"[21] Furthermore, Brownfield, in the same May letter from Savannah, refuted point-by-point a
glowing report about Georgia that appeared in a London newspaper.
The colony in truth, he said, instead of burgeoning, had never been so

depressed. It was short of basics; provisions were low or exhausted in some instances; the colonists had no credit because they did not have absolute title to their lands. Without clear title they lacked the power to put up their property as collateral against loans. "I wish that hunger may not bring distempers amongst us, more fatal than the sword of an enemy," he concluded.[22]

The situation was not so desperate as Brownfield said, but it was not easy, and the colonists saw that their complaints were being ignored. In fact, the Trustees felt that even to respond to letters critical of their policies was to condescend too much in the colonists' direction. Still, the Trustees were anxious to correct glaring problems in Georgia, but they were unsure how. One of the functions Stephens was to perform was to help them with these painful and difficult decisions.

Stephens was received with civility in Savannah by Causton, who showed him to the modest little house he was to occupy. That evening the two of them, joined by Thomas Christie, recorder of the colony, and Hugh Anderson, keeper of the Trustees' garden, resorted to one of Savannah's many public houses for conversation and entertainment. Robert Williams, a promising merchant on Yamacraw Bluff, joined them and "began to lay open his Mind pretty Freely" on the difficulties under which Georgia's population lay. The restricted tenure of land and the "Want of Negroes" were singled out as major grievances. Williams denounced "vehemently" the Georgia Board's policies and said he and others would leave the colony were changes not made. Stephens tried to calm him and promised Williams that he would transmit his suggestions to the Board.[23] All of this on his first night in town must have seemed to Stephens a portent of things to come—and it was.

Stephens spent over a month familiarizing himself with the various characters that populated the bluff, many of whom he had met when on the Horsey mission in 1736. He dined with Causton and his family at the Caustons' well-run plantation at Ockstead; he breakfasted with John Wesley and assured him of his objectivity in the various controversies that swirled about the young Anglican minister; he talked extensively with Williams again—as well as with the dissatisfied Patrick Mackay and John Brownfield; William Horton spoke on the question of his feud with Causton; John Fallowfield, with whom Stephens had stayed when he was in Georgia earlier, also spoke against Causton; and Henry Parker, second bailiff, came for dinner with Stephens and impressed the secretary favorably.[24] By December 8—about six weeks after his arrival—he and Causton were consulting on how to break up "this stubborn Knot of ill-designing People."[25] Even so, Stephens thought of his position as being more an arbiter between groups than as Trustee partisan, and he tried diligently to retain credibility with the various factions in Georgia. In the midst of the celebration for Oglethorpe's birthday on December 21, his trusted son Thomas arrived, an irony that probably did not go unnoticed by readers of Stephens's *Journal* some years later when Thomas headed the opposition to the Trustees'—and, coincidentally, to his father's—policies in Georgia.[26]

Secretary Stephens found that Causton was widely disliked in Savannah. A group of Lowland Scots, some of whom had come into town from their plantations when they found it too difficult to make ends meet on their land grants, seemed to control the social and political activities in Georgia's first settlement. They met in a sort of club, like "a Coffee-House," once or twice weekly to talk over their complaints and problems and to seek solutions. Stephens began to attend these meetings as well so he could feel out "the Disposition of the People" and report to the Trustees on what he had learned.[27] The dissidents seemed to welcome him; the members freely spoke their minds to him, and he answered their questions—or tried to—with decorum and dignity. He was incorporated easily into the normal life of the town. The club seemed to be less vehement by early spring, although in April Stephens noted that he wished they could be less aggressive in advocating slavery.[28] Still Stephens could report early in 1738 that most people were content and that spring planting was well advanced with a good crop anticipated.

Meanwhile in England, the Trustees were laying the groundwork for controversy. The Common Council of the Trust, determining upon drastic reform to bring about economies in government and responding—partially at least—to many complaints from Georgia, severely cut expenses, forbade Oglethorpe to draw on them for military outlays, dramatically reduced funds allocated for Indian presents, dismissed Causton as storekeeper, and ordered the Trustees' store closed.[29] But for the time being, and before word could cross the Atlantic, spring in Georgia seemed sweet, or at least mostly so. Stephens could write in May: "perfect Tranquility every where, People following their own Business."[30]

As good as his word to both the Board and the dissenters, Stephens attempted to present one of the colonists' most serious grievances to the Trust in its true light. He suggested to Georgia's leaders that they permit female inheritance, thereby relieving the minds of the landowners on that score and moving gradually along the road toward full *fee-simple* ownership. Egmont agreed, and such was recommended to the Common Council of the Trustees. However, Oglethorpe, who was still in England when Stephens's recommendation was received, rallied his forces on the Board and defeated the motion. For his trouble Stephens, who had tried to live up to his instructions to hear all sides of a question, found that his position was being eroded from both ends. The Trustees, largely because of Oglethorpe's opposition to Stephens's stance, began to look warily at their secretary. And the unhappy colonists, feeling that Stephens had not expressed their desires with enough authority, began to lose faith in him as a go-between. The embattled secretary in Savannah was in a no-win situation.[31]

In the realm of American reality, the promise of Georgia's 1738 spring was destroyed by an extended drought and an extraordinary heat wave. The high hopes that so many had for bountiful crops were blasted when May passed into June without rain and as the sun beat down unmercifully. Stephens wrote that such heat had "not been known before, since the first Comers settled." When a good shower finally came on June 19, most of the colony's crops had long since been devastated. With provisions running short and no changes in the system foreseen the prospect for continued harmony on Yamacraw Bluff was not a fair one. Even so, and in spite of the failure of his land reform to be adopted by the Trust, Stephens managed to retain his image of "honour and integrity" with many of Georgia's citizens.[32]

In September 1738, though, Stephens found that even he was being attacked during a revival of factional tensions in Savannah. At about the same time it was rumored that Oglethorpe had arrived in Georgia—an event that probably stirred mixed emotions in the secretary. Finally on September 27, word reached him that the General had arrived at Saint Simons Island nine days earlier. "So long was this good News in finding its Way to us," Stephens reported laconically.[33] But he surely must have taken it as an intentional slight that Oglethorpe had made no effort to write him personally and that news of his arrival reached Savannah in an offhand, unofficial manner.

On October 10, Oglethorpe made his long-awaited appearance on Yamacraw Bluff. His new favorite, Thomas Jones, busied himself looking into the confused accounts of the Trustees' store. The inhabitants were delighted to greet their old leader, but then, on October 17, Oglethorpe made a harsh pronouncement. In Stephens's words, Oglethorpe "made a pathetick Speech"[34] to the town, commenting on how deeply in debt the Trust was as a result of Causton's fiscal indiscretions. Complete retrenchment was necessary; most of the contents of the store would have to be applied to the debts under which the Trust now labored. On the following day Causton was relieved of office, as was surveyor Noble Jones. Thomas Jones was designated as Causton's replacement and, clearly, as Oglethorpe's new confidant as well.

During this episode it would seem that Oglethorpe's and Stephens's relations were coolly correct. The former largely ignored Stephens, but he also depended heavily upon him to carry out the details of his work. The secretary hardly had time to sleep during Oglethorpe's two-week stay in Savannah. New constables, tythingmen, and bailiffs were named, a new byword—Austerity—was now to be the order of the day on Yamacraw Bluff. When he returned to Frederica on October 25, Oglethorpe left behind him "a gloomy Prospect . . . and many sorrowful Countenances." No one, Stephens wrote, had any notion that the colony had fallen on such hard times until its leader "laid the Whole open."[35] Stephens saw only grim work ahead for the entire colony.

Stephens must have realized that his charge—to "appease the Discontents"—would now be impossible to fulfill. Although the dismissal of Causton was applauded by some, the new economies and the failure of the Trustees to deal with the issues of slavery and land tenure convinced the opposition leaders that more radical action would be necessary if ever they were to make their points to London. And surely the Trustees, by ignoring the advice that Stephens had given them—advice for which they had asked—helped undermine the authority of their officials in Savannah. Specifically, by failing to back their appointed secretary the Trustees put Stephens into the awkward situation whereby he would have to join the disaffected element or close ranks with Oglethorpe and Thomas Jones, men for whom he had no personal affection and in whose political judgment he apparently had little faith. Causton, a person whom Stephens at least initially respected, had been humiliated by Oglethorpe. Had an indigenous, organized pro-Trustee faction emerged in Savannah by October 1738, Causton would have been the logical person to head it. But thanks to Oglethorpe's determination that the old storekeeper must go, Causton not only was out of power and out of a job but he was now persona non grata as well. With Causton discredited, Stephens became the reluctant leader of the dispirited, unorganized elements in Georgia that espoused the side of the Trust. It was a disagreeable, necessary choice for Stephens and meant losing his role as impartial arbiter. Faced with the alternative of alienating the malcontents or Oglethorpe, he naturally chose the former, but with no great gusto.

The malcontents in Savannah, many of whom had been unusually quiet during the summer and early fall of 1738, received new heart from Oglethorpe's abrasive October speech. An intemperate feud developed between Thomas Jones and Causton—a feud that taxed the patience of Stephens and threatened the stability of the settlement; he spent many hours listening to each side. And the more Stephens thought about the situation the more annoyed he became. It began to look to him as though Oglethorpe had come to Savannah, made his startling announcements, and had then left the beleaguered secretary to handle repercussions. The General had been besieged by pleas for aid from the poor inhabitants when he had been in town, Stephens pointed out, but had been too busy to settle such trifling problems; he simply left these problems for Stephens to handle. Stephens had no authority to issue provisions and the Trustees' store was closed until further notice. He was powerless to help the settlers, and the wails of the disaffected mounted. "The greatest Part of the Clamour," Stephens wrote with chagrin, "fell to my Share, which indeed gave me great Disquiet."[36]

Oglethorpe returned to Savannah unexpectedly on November 11, not to calm the growing tumult, but to upbraid Causton further. Thomas Jones had informed Oglethorpe that Causton had been casting aspersions on the founder's good name. Jones scolded Causton and warned him that Oglethorpe would not permit his honor to be impugned. After bluntly informing Causton of the trouble he might get into, Oglethorpe left town without attacking any of the substantive domestic issues that were facing Georgia at the time.[37] Stephens's silence in his *Journal* speaks more than words on Oglethorpe's failure to approach Savannah's factional disputes head-on; but on the General's behalf, it must be noted that his regiment, now situated at Frederica, consumed his waking hours. Only a slight on his honor could have lured Oglethorpe to Savannah at this particular frantic moment as he prepared for the coming war with Spain.

The sniping continued between Causton and Jones—Stephens felt that the former deserved "a temperate and candid Hearing" while getting his defense together, but Jones was not giving him this privilege —and reports began to filter into Savannah that the Darien settlement was threatening to leave Georgia en masse if the land tenure provisions were not changed. Stephens, of course, lacked authority to make any alterations, and he watched futilely as this rumor fueled the dissatisfaction in Savannah.

On December 5, 1738, Stephens first heard that the leaders of the developing anti-Trustee element had prepared a representation to be sent to London. If "Darien led up the Dance, they were not wanting others elsewhere, who were ready to fall in with them." On December 9, Williams and Patrick Tailfer "accosted me [Stephens] with an open, frank Air," saying that the representation was complete and that it would soon be signed by the citizens, shown to Oglethorpe, and sent to the Trustees. Stephens went to see the document at Williams's house and gave his opinion that it was an ambitious piece with its aim being "an absolute new Form of Establishment."[38] Stephens assumed that he was not expected to sign because of the nature of the statement and the fact that he was an employee of the Trust.

To Stephens's apparent surprise the representation became "the common Talk of the Town." Its cordial reception was equally astonishing to him. The "Concurrence it met with from almost every Body, shewed plainly the Contents of it were what they had at Heart, though they had hitherto refrained from making such open Complaint." The representation "ran like Wild-fire" through Savannah, many people even thinking, in their naiveté, that Oglethorpe himself would be won over by it.[39] Ultimately 121 people signed this document, dated December 9, 1738, making it impossible for the Trustees to ignore it.

The petition was couched in the most respectful terms, but under its deferential exterior is reflected a hard sense of the plight in which Georgia found itself and a crystal-clear prediction that should the Trust choose once more to ignore the requests of the settlers then the colony might well cease to exist. The signers pointed out that even the greatest diligence and expense had failed to enable the colonists "to raise sufficient produce to maintain their families." The practicalities of the situation in Georgia—expensive and unreliable white labor and the lack of clear title to the land—could in no way be negated further by Trustee dreams based on "any theoretical scheme or reasoning." With an agricultural potential currently ruled out because of London's wrong-headed ideas, it would appear that the only alternative for prosperity in the colony lay in the evolution of useful and profitable mercantile ties. But here too, because labor was so expensive in Georgia, timber could not be cut and processed "fit for a foreign market but at double the expense of other colonies." In Carolina, only a few miles from stagnant Savannah, businessmen utilizing black labor were constantly loading ships bound for foreign markets with timber products, which were then traded in exchange for goods to be brought into Charles Town. There was no way, the petition argued, that Georgia could compete in such an economic cycle given the present makeup of the province. (William Stephens, whose main function for the York Buildings Company only a few years before had been oversight of the Scottish timber interests of his firm, could only have agreed with this particular pessimistic assessment of Georgia's potential in the timber trade.)

The December representation admitted that silk and wine might one day be successfully produced in Georgia but reasoned that even these endeavors would be impossible without black labor. Carolina could produce anything Georgia could and, accordingly, "will always ruin our market unless we are in some measure on a footing with them." Because Georgia was so unproductive, the ships calling at Savannah and elsewhere charged excessive fees because they left port with empty holds, Georgia having no produce to export. A traditional trade pattern had not emerged by the end of 1738 because the settlers could not put up their lands as security inasmuch as they had no fee-simple title to them. The colony was caught in a vicious economic circle from which there seemed no escape. As a result, all currency was drained from the settlement and Georgia was in extremis.

In the past, the petitioners concluded, we "have entirely relied on and confided in your good intentions believing you would redress any grievances that should appear." Permit true title to lands in the colony and revoke the prohibition on blacks and see how such actions "will soon make this the most flourishing colony" in America, they urged. Such reforms would effectively perpetuate the fame of the Trustees as

Georgia's "first founders, patrons and guardians." But to deny the demands would bring about the colony's ruin, the petitioners warned, and cause the ruin of the Trustees' collective reputations as well, henceforth to be known as the originators of Georgia's "misfortunes and calamities."[40] This closely argued representation, brief and to the point, stated the crisis in which Georgia found itself. Should the colony continue on its strange, unchartered course under the guise of the Trustees, or be permitted to evolve the way other southern continental colonies had?

Oglethorpe denounced the entire representation and its authors, particularly Robert Williams, whose role in its writing he obviously thought seminal. He had used anger and intimidation to get the signatures, Oglethorpe said, and was particularly effective among those citizens of Savannah who were indebted to him. Oglethorpe called the assertion that white men could not work effectively in Georgia absolutely in error and added that he could refute such charges "by hundreds of Witnesses," including the Salzburgers, the Scots at Darien, and many in Frederica and even Savannah. It was only the idle, he said, who asked for black labor. Accede to this element, Oglethorpe warned, and "the Province is ruined"; Tailfer and Williams would buy up most of the lands in and around Savannah; and the settlers would flee to other provinces, their places being taken by Negroes.[41]

On the other hand, Stephens appears to have been generally in favor of what the petitioners asked, although denouncing those individuals he considered most responsible. Having presided over a deteriorating situation before, such as the one he headed during the York Buildings Company's ill-fated speculative enterprises in Scotland, Stephens was armed with firsthand knowledge that might have been valuable to the Trust. But by 1739 it was obvious that the Trustees did not really want to hear the plain language and sound advice their secretary had to offer. He hinted in his writings that some of the malcontents' demands were not unreasonable, but he obviously could not add his name to the list of signers without completely jeopardizing his credibility in the eyes of the Georgia Office. And he needed the salary desperately in order to support both himself and his beleaguered and separated family. So Stephens tempered his judgments on the situation with the stark realities he had to face.

The representation signaled the start of a general campaign on the part of the opposition to bring about the changes deemed most desirable. The December petition was followed soon after by Hugh Anderson's two able letters, one to Oglethorpe and the other to Egmont.[42] Then came more petitions and, finally, pamphlets in which the opposition's demands, along with the language, became more strident. Nothing in Georgia or, for that matter, in the Georgia Office was ever quite the same after December 1738.

Stephens, who had already been rendered uncomfortable because of the tie made in the representation between land tenure and slavery, feared that should he seem too receptive to the opposition's ideas he would lose the support not just of the Trustees but of Oglethorpe as well. Although the administrative style and the fiscal policies of the latter had, by 1739, been repudiated by the Trustees, Oglethorpe was still the person to be reckoned with in Georgia. And he bitterly resented the December 1738 petition, denounced its originators, and began to associate Savannah with disloyalty to him and to the Trust. As was so often the case with Oglethorpe, he took criticism leveled at the colony as a personal slight. He encouraged his allies in Frederica, Darien, and Ebenezer to start counterpetitions aimed at diluting any impact the December 1738 representation might have in London.[43] It is worth noting that he sought no outward support at this time from Savannah.

Not long after the first of the year, when the Trustees' store in Savannah ran out of meat and was desperately low on other provisions, it was rumored on Yamacraw Bluff that Oglethorpe intended to starve upstart Savannah into submitting to his will. Stephens could give little credence to such a bizarre story, but he must have thought that Oglethorpe only added fuel to the flames by not coming to Savannah to give the lie to such rumors. And when he finally did come, in March 1739, Oglethorpe went out of his way to pick a quarrel with Stephens's son Thomas.[44] This quarrel so offended Thomas that he continued the political flirtation that he had already begun with the opposition. The result led ultimately to his being chosen head of the anti-Trustee faction in Georgia and England—much to his father's chagrin and sorrow.

For the moment William Stephens appeared in a very delicate situation indeed. And when the Georgia Board, with some indignation and dispatch, rejected the 1738 petition out of hand,[45] Stephens's position in Savannah began to polarize even more. The inflexibility of the Georgia Trustees circumscribed the political area in which their secretary could effectively operate. Even before word reached Georgia of the

Trust's rejection, Stephens discovered that his attendance at the social functions of "the club" was no longer as welcome as it once was. His arrival at a meeting on February 9 promptly put an end to a debate between the members. The situation served as an omen to him that he was no longer being taken into the confidence of the evolving opposition group. Even earlier, in a frank letter to the Trust's accountant, Harman Verelst, Stephens bemoaned his inability to act decisively to prevent opposition from forming. He was, in fact, being treated derisively by the Trust's enemies because he was short not only on authority but also on some of the basic physical necessities of colonial life. Surely it had not been the design of the Trustees "to render me contemptible, & thereby defeat the Intent of my Service."[46]

But why, really, should he continue to be trusted and asked for advice? As the Williamses and the Joneses probably saw it, Stephens had no influence to convince the Trustees of their error, nor did he have the authority to act in any substantive way in America. As Savannah teetered on the brink of want and anarchy early in 1739, Stephens was powerless to institute policies needed to ease any part of the situation. Authority to act rested in Oglethorpe—or, at least, Oglethorpe assumed such power to himself. The nature of Stephens's instructions restricted him from the exertion of true executive initiative, so he found his influence declining rapidly. Unable to impact policy in London and lacking the grant to create it in Savannah, Stephens's plight seemed hopeless by June 1739.

Stephens, though, was never one for giving up without a struggle. The Trustees' abrupt rejection of the 1738 representation hardened evolving factional lines in Georgia by making inevitable the division of the province on political issues relating to pro- and anti-Trustee policies. Stephens was faced with a major decision that would affect not only his immediate career but the future history of the colony as well. Should he reflect his true feelings that the Trustees' opposition had much merit, or must he close ranks behind Oglethorpe and become a champion of the Trustee line?

Even before mid-1739, it was clear that the latter path would be the one taken. Although he had little in common with Oglethorpe and held Thomas Jones in low esteem, he had come to like even less the opposition, whom he dubbed variously "our Madcaps," "our wise Schemists," and the like. That they were overwhelmingly Scotsmen may have been an invisible factor in his dislike and ultimate decision, for Stephens had just lived through the most difficult period of his life in Scotland and had come away from the Highlands embittered. But his nature, personality, and normal preferences seemed as well to dictate that Stephens should side with the Trustees. His relationship to Egmont, his friendship with Samuel Horsey, and ties that drew him to other members of the Trust, such as James Vernon, naturally inclined Stephens to their views. Furthermore, Stephens could not risk losing his job, particularly with the cries of his creditors still fresh in his ears. Stephens's innate personal caution, his ingrained conservatism, and his religious preferences also dictated loyalty to the Trustees. His staunch Anglicanism must have been an important albeit unmeasured factor that tied him naturally to the friends of Oglethorpe, for few if any of the Georgia "Madcaps" followed Church of England procedures in Georgia.

Finally, the dominant figure of Oglethorpe must also have acted as a determinant in Stephens's mind. Oglethorpe, whose powerful personality encouraged controversy, was factionalism personified. Given the founder's status and prestige, it would have been exceedingly unwise for Stephens openly to challenge Oglethorpe in a colony he considered to be his own. The secretary, though, was never at ease with Oglethorpe, and ultimately the two fell out when Stephens was given executive control of the northern segment of Georgia in 1741. But they joined forces in 1739 in temporary, uneasy alliance to present a united front to the malcontents on the several issues that so sorely vexed Georgia. That these political alignments would last for years and bring about one of colonial America's most ardently waged pamphlet wars was not, of course, comprehended at that time.[47]

The 1737 decision by the Georgia Trustees to send a secretary to their colony had important ramifications. Although William Stephens was open-minded and impartial for a year or more—an impartiality the Trustees did not fully appreciate—he was finally forced to choose sides. The catalyst that caused the political factionalism in Georgia to peak was James Oglethorpe, who, by his brusque and at times even casual dismissal of the opposition's requests, worsened a situation he tried to calm. Stephens, his ambitions and judgments tempered by his sobering experiences in public life and by the heavy indebtedness that resulted from earlier mistakes, was more conciliatory and diplomatic than the younger, driven Oglethorpe. The secretary's counsel, though, did not hold sway with Oglethorpe or the Trust, and Georgia rushed pell-mell into genuine organized political factionalism less than six years after its establishment. The representation of December 9, 1738, was the first shot in a full-blooded political war that would have as its spoils the kind of colony Georgia would ultimately be. In the background of this representation and the reaction it spawned in Oglethorpe and Stephens can be found the origin of Georgia politics.

Oglethorpe's Contest for the Backcountry, 1733–1749

Edward J. Cashin

James Oglethorpe's Georgia was more frontier than colony, a *frontier that was contested for by three European powers and numerous In- dian tribes. As if French, Spanish, and Indian competition were not enough, Georgia's founder also had to face South Carolina rivals who were happy to have the new colony as a buffer but were not willing to surrender the trading advantages they had gained over the years since Charles Town was founded.*

In the following essay, Edward Cashin examines the various interests that competed with James Oglethorpe for economic and diplomatic control of the region, and he evaluates Oglethorpe's efforts to gain control of the backcoun- try for his colony. What emerges is a different view of James Oglethorpe, colony builder. From this new interpretation comes insight into how an aggressive policy, combined with good luck, made it possible for Oglethorpe to succeed in the face of overwhelming odds.—Editors

If, as Louis De Vorsey has demonstrated, James Edward Oglethorpe was preoccupied with reshaping the map of North America, he had good reason to be. The French claim to the southeastern region was graphically illustrated in a 1718 map (Figure 6-1) by Guillaume Delisle, the king's cartographer. The map has been called one of the most important mother maps of the North American continent.[1] It is the first to show Texas and the first to attempt to trace De Soto's route. The fact that it included the Savannah River within the borders of Louisiana must have caught Oglethorpe's attention. The Delisle map

Figure 6-1. Guillaume Delisle's "Carte de la Louisiane." This map dates from 1718.

represented the extent of the French territorial ambitions; Oglethorpe was determined to redraw the boundary lines.

Oglethorpe's protagonist in the backcountry was the experienced Jean Baptiste Lemoyne, Sieur de Bienville, founder of Mobile and New Orleans. It was one of history's ironies that within a month of Oglethorpe's landing at Yamacraw Bluff, Bienville returned to New Orleans to begin his fourth and final tour of duty as governor of Louisiana. It would appear that Bienville had all the advantages in the contest for the backcountry: over thirty years experience in Indian affairs, thirteen new companies of soldiers to bolster his garrison, Fort Toulouse in the very heart of the Creek country, and the allegiance of the largest tribe of southeastern Indians, the Choctaws. Bienville's immediate objective was to destroy the Natchez and their protectors, the Chickasaws. The Creeks and Cherokees would then be won over by one means or another.[2]

Nothing in Oglethorpe's previous experience had prepared him to act

as a backcountry strategist. With his fellow Trustees he had given much
consideration to the problems of the English poor, to the complexities
of silk manufacture, and to the way the first Georgians should behave.
But he knew little about Indians until he met Tomochichi and less
about the Indian trade until he counted twelve large boats coming down
the Savannah River during his first month in Georgia. The boats, laden
with deerskins, were on their way from New Windsor to Charles Town.
He quickly calculated the value of the trade and almost as quickly
realized its importance in the contest with France.[3] New Windsor,
formerly known as Savannah Town and protected by the guns and
garrison of Fort Moore, was situated at the place where the Creek and
Cherokee trails merged to cross the Savannah River into Carolina.
Charles Town merchants maintained storehouses there, and it was the
rendezvous for the English traders who carried goods into the Indian
country as far as the Mississippi River.[4] Among their clients were the
French-threatened Natchez and Chickasaws. Whether from love of the
English or fear of the French, a band of Chickasaws under Squirrel
King had settled near Fort Moore. Similarly, the Uchees had separated
themselves from the Creeks to occupy a tract on the lower Savannah
River. A superiority of trading commodities was the great advantage
the English had over their French rivals. Although their wares were
preferable to those of the French, the conduct of the English traders
left much to be desired. Fraudulent measurements and the abusive use
of rum had caused the Yamasees to take up the tomahawk against
the English in 1715. The complaints of Tomochichi and his Creek
friends convinced Oglethorpe that the same practices could drive the
Georgia Indians into the waiting arms of the French. By June 9, 1733,
Oglethorpe had grasped the heart of the matter. If the trade is "ill
managed it may draw on the war," he warned his colleagues of the
Georgia Trust, "but if it is well managed it will bring in £2000 Sterling
a year and secure the Indians in our Interest."[5]

Other than Tomochichi, Oglethorpe's tutor in matters relating to
trade was the prominent Charles Town merchant, Samuel Eveleigh.
Eveleigh maintained a store at Savannah Town and was anxious to
move his operations into Georgia. He had selected the site of his Georgia post, if Oglethorpe would agree. It was across the river from Fort
Moore and up the trail a few miles on an elevation called Kenyon's
Bluff. Eveleigh echoed the opinion in Charles Town regarding the vital

importance of a new fort in the Creek country. In fact, he offered to build one at no expense to Georgia in return for a three-to-five-year monopoly of the trade.[6]

The clamor on the part of Carolinians reached a crescendo in March 1734 when they heard that Governor Bienville had summoned the Choctaw chiefs to Mobile for a war talk. Unless a new English fort could be erected, war was "unavoidable," a Carolina correspondent informed Lord Egmont. The Carolina Assembly invited Oglethorpe to Charles Town to convince him of the importance of building a fort to counter the French influence.[7]

Thus, Oglethorpe was thoroughly briefed when he returned to England in 1734. He knew he needed a fort in Indian country and that he had to gain control of the Indian trade. Before he left, he named a recently arrived Scot, Patrick Mackay to investigate the condition of the Creek trade. Samuel Eveleigh, doing his all for Georgia, outfitted Mackay with horses and supplies.[8]

Oglethorpe received credit for an impressive diplomatic victory just after his departure. One of the spies he had employed to gather intelligence, a half-breed named Tommy Jones, brought a contingent of the dreaded Choctaws into Savannah to meet Oglethorpe. "Your Honour's name is Spread very much amongst them," Mary Musgrove reported to the absent Oglethorpe. He had done what Carolina had vainly tried to do: he had detached the Choctaws from the French interest at least for the moment.[9]

As Oglethorpe's reputation waxed in the Indian country, it waned in Charles Town. The reason was that Patrick Mackay had begun acting in an arbitrary and arrogant fashion. "I find a great many Saucey Villains in this Country," Mackay wrote to Thomas Causton in Savannah. Mackay tried to flog one and sent to Causton for handcuffs in order to arrest others. He made it clear that in the future the trade would be regulated by the Georgia authorities. That kind of talk, together with Mackay's resolute action, caused even greater concern in Charles Town.[10]

The Carolina officials had another cause for concern when the French commander at Mobile wrote an angry letter to the effect that Mackay had boasted that he would pull down Fort Toulouse. If necessary, French troops would arrest such troublemakers.[11] This threat prompted a new memorial by the South Carolina Assembly amplifying upon the latest danger. Natives of Canada were said to be moving "in shoals" to Louisiana. The French governor sent five hundred men out to live among the Indians for the purpose of winning them over. The Cherokee Indians were increasingly insolent, probably because of French intrigue. All of these reasons compelled Carolina to build a fort among the Cherokees, and the province was willing to raise money for an additional fort in Georgia. To that end the Carolina Assembly put a tax on deerskins and increased the cost of the trading licenses. Samuel Eveleigh was convinced that the new taxes would drive traders to do their business in Georgia and undercut the Carolinians by 20 to 25 percent.[12]

The Georgia magistrates did nothing to assuage the irate feelings of Carolina's Lieutenant Governor Thomas Broughton when they wrote that Patrick Mackay was simply following Oglethorpe's orders and that the traders who were forced to leave the Indian country probably deserved it. Broughton was indignant that "men of your rank and station would take that tone." He expressed the opinion that the king would never permit the province of Georgia to preempt the Indian trade. Meanwhile, he would withhold the money being raised for the Georgia fort, and as commander of all militia in Georgia and Carolina he would take steps to protect Carolina's interests.[13] The note of petulance was unmistakable.

If Broughton expected Oglethorpe to reprimand his surrogates, he was mistaken. In fact, the Georgia Trustees did the very thing most feared by Carolina: they attached the Indian trade. The Indian act, which became effective June 24, 1735, was entitled an "Act for maintaining the peace with the Indians in the Province of Georgia." Unlicensed traders were forbidden to visit, frequent, haunt, trade, traffic, or barter with any Indian within the province of Georgia. The commissioner, who was to be Oglethorpe, was empowered to keep bonds of all traders as guarantees of good conduct. Significantly, a provision of the act stated that the commissioner could apply for enforcement of the act to the commander of the garrison nearest the place where the Indians resided. This wording revealed that the Trustees had accepted the contention that a garrison should be posted in the Indian country. A separate piece of legislation banned the importation and use of rum and brandies in Georgia. A preamble explained that several Indian chiefs had complained about the abuse of rum.[14]

There is no way to tell exactly when the Trustees decided upon the location of their Indian garrison. The name Augusta was probably chosen to commemorate the royal wedding between Frederick, Prince of Wales, and Augusta of Saxe Gotha on April 26, 1736. The occasion provided the name of the other new frontier settlement of 1736, Frederica. Augusta would guard the French frontier, Frederica the Spanish. Oglethorpe was so taken up with the latter that he did not attend to the former until June. He may have been prodded into action by a delegation of Indians and traders who visited him in Savannah and offered to build a town at their own expense three hundred miles up the river for forty families. Kenyon's Bluff was three hundred miles upriver by Oglethorpe's reckoning, and it was likely that he had already been influenced by Samuel Eveleigh's favorable description of the site. The fact that Kenyon's Bluff was outside the area of settlement permitted by Oglethorpe's treaty with the Creeks in 1733 seemed never to have bothered either Oglethorpe or the Creeks.[15] The Indian act required a fort in the Indian country, but not necessarily a town. Yet, on June 14, 1736, Oglethorpe ordered Noble Jones to lay out a town of forty lots, similar to the basic plan of Savannah. Roger Lacy, whose enterprise in building a fort at his Thunderbolt plantation outside Savannah had attracted the notice of Oglethorpe, was given responsibility for building Fort Augusta. Lacy was also named agent to the Cherokees and had to spread the news that Carolina licenses were no longer valid. He was instructed to seize goods of unlicensed traders and smash all the rum kegs he could find. John Tanner, an eighteen-year-old neighbor of Oglethorpe from Surrey who had come over "for his amusement," was given the same task in the Creek country.[16] (We might note how supremely self-assured these Englishmen were. Like Oglethorpe himself they were amateurs in the forest and yet they dealt with native Americans and veteran traders with an attitude bordering on arrogance. At least they had the good sense to take along experienced woodsmen as deputies. Even with an escort, real danger existed. The Creeks remarked that "he from Georgia was a child" and donned their war paint. Roger Lacy was well aware that the Cherokees were ready to "knock him and the rest on the Head." In both instances the Carolina traders persuaded the Indians that this was a white man's argument.)[17]

In July 1736, while the two agents were spreading consternation among the Carolina traders in the Indian country, William Stephens took a trip up the Savannah River. The future Indian commissioner and secretary to the Trustees reported that the inhabitants of New Windsor were very much disturbed by Oglethorpe's effort to take over the Indian trade. Stephens did not blame them for being worried. He predicted that the traders and storekeepers at New Windsor would simply move across the river and settle along the Indian trail without waiting for Lacy to lay out the town properly. Stephens foresaw that the Savannah, which "glides smoothly on as the river Thames at Putney," would soon become famous for the volume of its commerce.[18]

Oglethorpe waited for his two agents to return to Savannah before he took ship for England in November 1736. Young Tanner went home with Oglethorpe and had more amusement when the sailors panicked in a storm off the coast of Wales and he and Oglethorpe had to help haul down the sails.[19]

Roger Lacy would have returned to Augusta, but Carolina was more than usually nervous about a combined French and Spanish attack that winter. In fact, Governor Bienville launched a two-pronged offensive against the Chickasaws in 1736—an offensive that ultimately failed because of poor coordination. Bad weather and a brave Chickasaw resistance were also instrumental in turning back the French. Bienville wrote that he could blast the Chickasaws out of their huts if he had artillery.[20]

The Fort Moore traders and the Savannah River Chickasaws were ready to march if called upon, but the expected attack from Florida never materialized. By May 1737 the danger had dissipated and Roger Lacy took some of his workers up to Augusta. According to Thomas Causton, several houses already stood there and a crop of corn had been planted. Because Squirrel King and his band were so cooperative, Lacy ordered the surveyor to run out a town for them on the Georgia side below Augusta. Although the town plan was never developed beyond the blueprint stage, the place was given the name New Savannah. The Chickasaws had no clear title to the land as they had to the tract opposite Augusta on the Carolina side. Later, they testified that New Savannah belonged to their friend Billy Gray, a veteran trader to the western Chickasaws. William Stephens explained that the Chickasaws moved across the river because they had been "disobliged" by the Carolinians and preferred a "friendly commerce" with Oglethorpe's people.[21]

While his laborers were building the fort, Roger Lacy went on a

second round of smashing and seizing in the Cherokee nation. He was
back in Savannah by December 1737 and reported that the fort was in
"great forwardness." In his absence he had left in charge another one
of Oglethorpe's young neighbors, Richard Kent, son of a member of
Parliament from Reading. Kent had expressed a certain diffidence in his
ability to manage a settlement where the whites were as unaccustomed
to restraint as the Indians.[22]

From the first year at least two types of merchants operated in
Augusta. One was the resident storekeepers like Kennedy O'Brien,
Samuel Brown, and John Rae who bought their supplies from Charles
Town. The other type included the traders and packhorsemen who
took goods on credit from the storekeepers and traveled out to the Indian country. Traders were assigned to specific Indian towns. They built
houses, took Indian wives, sired children of mixed blood, and established ties of kinship and trust. James Adair wrote a firsthand account
of Indians and the trade, and he dedicated his book to two Augusta-
based traders whom he especially admired, Lachlan McGillivray and
George Galphin. Adair described the condition of the trade at this time
as a happy one. Those involved were generally "men of worth" whose
interests were the same as the government's. Every Englishman from
the king to James Oglethorpe to the humblest packhorseman wanted
to win the Indians away from the French. According to Adair, "the
traders could not be reckoned unhappy; for they were kindly treated
and watchfully guarded by a society of friendly and sagacious people,
and possessed all the needful things to make a reasonable life easy."[23]
These men of the forests who formed close personal ties with the Indians were perhaps the most important auxiliaries Oglethorpe had in his
contest with the French.

Roger Lacy did all that was asked of him. He finished building the
fort and put ten of his own men in it as a garrison. In July 1738
he contracted the fever that was spread from Charles Town to New
Windsor to Augusta and even to the Cherokee country. He returned
to his plantation and died there on August 2, 1738.[24] A month later
Oglethorpe arrived in Georgia with his regiment and proceeded to
Frederica.

A contingent of Choctaws was disappointed not to find Oglethorpe
in Savannah. They were poorly entertained by the Trustees' storekeeper, who had barely enough provisions for his own people.[25] The

disgruntled Indians returned to their own country and joined the second great French offensive against the Chickasaws.

In June 1739 Oglethorpe received an urgent summons from the Creeks to come to a tribal gathering at Coweta Town. "Tomochichi and all the Indians advise me to go up," Oglethorpe reported.[26] Therefore he would go up, even though it meant carrying an expensive caravan of presents. A compelling reason for Oglethorpe's decision, in addition to Spanish intrigues among the Creeks, was the news that the French had begun their campaign in the west.

Governor Bienville countered the English construction of Fort Augusta by building a fort on the Tombigbee River in 1737. Additional troops and supplies, including the requested cannon and bombardiers, arrived from France. During the same July 1739 when Oglethorpe went to meet the Creeks, the English governor of New York alerted the governor of South Carolina to the fact that the Senecas with Canadian militia were on the march to join Bienville.[27] The backcountry was center stage.

Oglethorpe's conference with the Creeks went wonderfully well. He was as impressed by them as they were by him. He promised to punish misbehaving Carolina traders, and the Creeks ratified the original land cessions made by Tomochichi. No one questioned the legality of the Augusta settlement.[28] The Indians wanted the town there as much as did the English. Oglethorpe's departure was delayed by a violent attack of fever. On August 27, 1739, he was well enough to set out for Augusta and arrived there on September 5. Lieutenant Richard Kent received him with a seventeen-gun salute. Samuel Brown presented a delegation of Cherokees to Oglethorpe. They had suffered from fever and smallpox and were in need of food. Oglethorpe was able to supply them with 1,500 bushels of corn, a portion of the bountiful harvest of the crop planted by Lacy's men. Oglethorpe was pleased with the manner in which Richard Kent had kept the veteran traders within bounds. On the spot, he made Kent a captain as well as conservator of justice of the peace not only for Augusta but for all the "Indian Nations within the colony of Georgia."[29] The scope of his jurisdiction must have seemed staggering to the young man from Berkshire.

Oglethorpe singled out Kent for special praise in his report to the Trustees. He was a youth "of great worth and merit" who had a fine tract of land under cultivation. Even before he had seen Augusta, Oglethorpe called it the "Key of all the Indian Countrey" and of great service to the king. He was convinced that his policy under Kent's management had averted a possible war with the Indians. Later, Oglethorpe asked the Trustees to ratify his promotion of Kent and his promise to maintain a garrison there at Trust expense. Augusta, he wrote, was "the great resort for the Indian trade and there is a very pretty Town built with a number of white families without any expense to the Trust except the Garrison for their protection."[30]

While at Augusta, Oglethorpe received word that the long-expected war with Spain had begun. Thomas Eyre, a cadet in Oglethorpe's regiment who had accompanied the General on his backcountry tour, was made agent to the Cherokees. Eyre was another of those impetuous young Englishmen Oglethorpe relied upon to do his business in the backcountry. Eyre delivered commissions to veteran traders Samuel Brown and Thomas Holmes in Augusta. They were to bring down a company of Cherokees. William Gray was given a captain's commission and ordered to organize the Chickasaws and Uchees.[31]

The war flared first on the western front. The northern French force arrived at the rendezvous point in the Chickasaw country in August 1739. Lack of coordination plagued the French again. Bienville's force, encumbered with heavy artillery, began a ponderous march from New Orleans in September. The ever-fretful Carolinians were convinced that the French intended to invade their province by way of the Tennessee River. Oglethorpe welcomed the great confrontation; his brave pledge to the Trustees deserves to be remembered: "The French have attacked the Carolina Indians and the Spaniards have invaded us. I wish it may not be resolved between them to root the English out of America. We here are resolved to die hard and will not lose one inch of ground without fighting."[32]

Again the Chickasaws fought well and again the weather was their ally as the French artillery bogged down in the mud. The northern force managed to gain some success. The Chickasaws agreed to give up their French prisoners and promised not to harbor the Natchez. The remnants of the Natchez tribe fled to the Cherokees for protection. However, Bienville's expedition failed in its main objective to crush the Chickasaws. One of his officers blamed a divided command that produced contentions and bickering.[33]

Contentions and bickering played a part in Oglethorpe's limited success in his invasion of Florida in the same year, 1740. If blame there was, he was entirely willing to lay it at the feet of the Carolinians who retreated from Florida prematurely. Then, too, traders from that province had tried to prevent the Cherokees from going to Oglethorpe's assistance. His Indian allies, on the other hand, won his praise. "The Indians, particularly the Creeks, showed the utmost intrepidity and were of the greatest service," Oglethorpe told Egmont.[34] The Creeks were left to guard the frontier after the English left Florida.

Oglethorpe never returned to the backcountry. With his prestige dimmed by the failure of his second Florida expedition, he left Georgia in July 1743. By a quirk of history, his rival Bienville took ship for France on May 10 of the same year, his reputation also under a cloud.[35] The difference between them was that Oglethorpe had provided for eventual control of the backcountry by his Indian diplomacy and by policing the trade. Augusta continued to perform the great service for which he had hoped. Critics would argue that Augusta's prosperity was due to the widespread use of slave labor and no credit should go to the Trustees whose policy forbade slavery.[36] Though black people in Augusta undoubtedly contributed to its prosperity, its significance in the international struggle stemmed from the work of Oglethorpe's man, Richard Kent.

While Oglethorpe was fighting the Spaniards in Florida, Kent took his men into the Creek country and arrested some of the worst offenders of the Indian act. In 1741, Kent mediated a dispute between Cherokees and Creeks. His authority was bolstered when Oglethorpe increased the Augusta garrison from twelve to twenty rangers. This allowed him to station men at a post called Fort Oakfuskee in the Creek Nation. Kent took seriously the charge to police the Indian country and supplied Oglethorpe with a continual stream of intelligence reports by means of the patroons or captains of the seven riverboats that served Augusta.[37] One of Kent's most celebrated coups was his capture of a man who had caused some consternation in Charles Town. Christian Priber, a German who came to Georgia with the Trustees' permission, had settled among the Cherokees and had begun to convert them to a utopian scheme he called the Kingdom of Paradise. Carolinians were not sure which shocked them more, Priber's advocacy of free love or his advice to the Indians to free themselves from European influences. The Cherokees refused to surrender their friend to the Carolinians, but

Figure 6-2. "A Map of the British and French Dominions in North America," by John Mitchell, first printed in 1755.

Kent's Creek allies intercepted Priber on his way to Mobile and brought him to Kent, who delivered him to Oglethorpe in Frederica. There Priber amazed everyone with his erudition and there, it would seem, he died, for his story abruptly ends.[38]

In 1746, Captain Kent won the admiration of the hard-bitten traders by facing down one hundred sullen Creeks who had come to demand powder and shot. The Chickasaws told Kent that the Creeks had boasted that they would kill three or four Englishmen and then return to their nation. Kent told them boldly that the only powder and shot they would get was from the mouth of his cannon. He prudently sent a request for help to Frederica, and Major William Horton came up with a supply of presents and fifty rangers, ready for a fight or a feast. The Indians took the presents and went away.[39]

Kent's good record prompted the inhabitants of Augusta to request the Trustees to increase his authority in settling disputes.[40] The Trustees agreed. Kent carefully reviewed each application for a grant of land and, after rum began to be sold openly, each application for a "vict-ualling house." Meanwhile, a self-regulating process was taking place in the busy Indian trade. The traders, described as "jangling" among themselves earlier, gradually merged under the name Brown, Rae and Company. The company spokesmen boasted of the fact that they "were the best acquainted with Indian affairs of any." They took credit for keeping the Indians on good terms and for preventing the Choctaws from going back to the French.[41] There was a measure of truth in their boast.

With the Treaty of Aix La Chappelle in 1748, Oglethorpe's regiment was disbanded. Captain Kent decided to sell his property in Augusta and go home to England, but other former soldiers took grants of land in the town. A sure sign that a more civilized era was dawning was the fact that in 1749 the people of Augusta built a church and asked for a resident minister.[42]

James Oglethorpe might have congratulated himself as he welcomed Richard Kent back from America. In 1733 there were loud alarms over the incursions of the French and frantic cries for a fort in the Indian country. Oglethorpe had chosen to put his fort in the precise place where he could intercept the Carolina overland trade and thus gain a measure of its control. His own diplomacy and that of his agents, together with the organization of the trade, had ensured the loyalty of Georgia's Indians during the colony's first critical war and foreshadowed success in the next. Oglethorpe's victory is illustrated by the John Mitchell map of 1755 (Figure 6-2). On it, Louisiana was forced back to the Mississippi River as if in anticipation of the final outcome of the Great War for Empire.[43]

Oglethorpe must have been pleased to read in the very first history of Georgia, written by Benjamin Martyn in 1751, the passage that Augusta "is in a thriving Condition and is and will be a great Protection to both the Provinces of Carolina and Georgia against any Designs of the French."[44]

James Oglethorpe in Europe
Recent Findings in His Military Life

Rodney M. Baine and Mary E. Williams

Those interested in the life and times of James Edward Ogle-thorpe have often wondered what Georgia's founder did during the exciting period of the 1750s. Lacking hard evidence to prove that he engaged in any particularly stimulating pursuits, most historians and biographers have assumed that he contented himself in his late middle age with a quiet domestic life centered upon his landholdings and his wife, Elizabeth.

The truth is quite the contrary. Oglethorpe, it seems, got restless. Dissatisfied with current politics, out of favor at court, feeling something of an anachronism, he became once again stimulated by the urge for adventure. So the old soldier raised adequate funds to join one of his longtime friends, Field Marshal James Keith, on the Continent where together they fought the hated French. Rodney Baine and Mary Williams clarify these little-known exploits of Georgia's founder and put these acts of military derring-do in the proper context of Oglethorpe's long, useful, and varied life.—Editors

In view of the extremely public nature of most of James Oglethorpe's life, it is surprising to realize that two periods have been virtually unexplored: three years in his youth and four in his middle age.[1] Bits and pieces of information uncovered here and there are beginning to throw light on these mysterious periods in the life of Georgia's founder.

Oglethorpe's military experience before coming to America was far more extensive than his recent, scholarly biographers have shown. They have asserted only that Oglethorpe acted briefly as an aide-de-camp to Prince Eugene of Savoy during the siege and battle of Belgrade in 1717.[2] Earlier, less careful biographers agreed that he served with Prince Eugene as secretary and aide-de-camp from 1716 until 1718.[3] Now, thanks to a letter Oglethorpe wrote to his friend Field Marshal James Keith in 1755, and to notes James Boswell took years later toward a biography of the General, we know that Oglethorpe entered the imperial service on August 3, 1716, and took part in the 1716 campaign in which the imperial army defeated the Turks at Petrovaradin and Timisoara; he participated in the winter campaign of 1717 in the Wallachian Banat and finally in the imperial campaign of 1718–19 against the Spaniards in Sicily.[4]

The Oglethorpe family had a distinguished military tradition. Following in that tradition, James was enrolled in 1706, at the age of ten, in Queen Anne's First Regiment of Foot Guards, a largely ceremonial regiment. In 1713 he was commissioned as lieutenant, "to rank as Capt. of Foot" in that regiment, a commission he resigned on November 23, 1715.[5] Perhaps the young lieutenant thirsted for action; perhaps his mother was prudent enough to suggest that her son leave England before he could be compromised by her and her daughters' work on behalf of the Pretender. Perhaps he was simply like his father, tempering his admiration for the Pretender with reason. In any case, Oglethorpe left England for Paris.

At Paris, Oglethorpe enrolled at the Academy of Lompres, where he apparently received practical military experience. There he was joined by James Francis Edward Keith, a prominent young Scotsman from a distinguished Jacobite family. While Oglethorpe was at Lompres, war between the Turks and the Austrian Empire began to threaten, and zealous young men made plans to serve as volunteers under the imperial commander, Prince Eugene of Savoy. Armed with letters of introduction from the duke of Argyll, from his brother, Theophilus Oglethorpe, and from various other friends and relatives, Oglethorpe decided to join them. At Ulm on the Danube some time in June or July of 1716, doubtless by prearrangement, Oglethorpe joined Louis-François Crozat, son of Antoine Crozat, Marquis du Châtel, and then proprietor of the Mississippi Company; and they floated down the Danube to the scene of action.[6]

On August 3, 1716, they reached Petrovaradin and there joined the imperial army. Oglethorpe was accepted by Prince Eugene as a "Volontaire attache" and was, with Prince Emanuel of Portugal, assigned as aide-de-camp to the adjutant general for the Latin and Spanish languages.[7] Only two days later Oglethorpe saw action in his first battle. Although outnumbered by the Turks almost two to one, Prince Eugene attacked. Surprised, the Turks fled, leaving 30,000 casualties to the imperial army's 5,000.

Following Prince Eugene's success at Petrovaradin, Oglethorpe's next military encounter was the month-long siege of Timisoara. During the siege there occurred the only personal episode of his early campaigns that he related in Boswell's presence to Dr. Samuel Johnson's circle. The subject was insults and duels. Oglethorpe recounted the tale of how, when he was affronted by "a prince of Wirtemburg" who flipped wine in his face, he looked at his challenger and, in Boswell's words, "smiling all the time, . . . said, 'Mon Prince,'—I forget the French words he used, the purport however was, 'That's a good joke; but we do it much better in England;' and threw a whole glass of wine in the Prince's face. An old General who sat by, said, 'Il a bien fait, mon Prince, vous l'avez commencé:' and thus all ended in good humour."[8]

Another personal episode, which the general provided for Boswell's notes for the unrealized Oglethorpe biography, describes Oglethorpe's meeting with his mother's cousin, Field Marshal George Browne. In late September 1716, Oglethorpe presented himself to Browne. Oglethorpe admitted to Boswell that he appeared finely dressed. Browne, more soldier than courtier, ridiculed Oglethorpe's finery in front of German and Irish officers. The following day, Oglethorpe made his appearance plainly clad. His mother, he told Browne, had early inured him to discomfort by cutting holes in his shoes. He was, he implied, capable of soldierly deportment. Browne approved of the young man, and Oglethorpe was usually with Browne during the campaign. On October 1 when Browne was wounded, Oglethorpe helped to carry him from the field.[9]

Following the Turks' surrender on October 12, Oglethorpe "went for a hasty tour to Venice—Turin and Paris." When he returned to Vienna he was assigned to serve with Field Marshal Joseph Anton O'Dwyer, who commanded the imperial forces in Wallachia. This was a dangerous period for the young aide-de-camp, for there were frequent incursions across the Danube and infiltrations through the Eastern Gate.[10] In early summer, however, Eugene prepared his assault on Belgrade and recalled O'Dwyer from his outpost.

Of his early military campaigns Oglethorpe apparently recalled the two-month siege of Belgrade most vividly. Fifty-five years later, in 1772, responding to Dr. Johnson's request for "an account of the siege of Belgrade," "the General, pouring a little wine upon the table, described every thing with a wet finger: 'Here we were, here the Turks,' &c. &c. Johnson listened with the closest attention."[11] Early in the siege, Prince Eugene's forces seemed destined for victory. By the end of July, however, the Turkish army of relief threatened the imperial army from the south and in mid-August they were as near to the Austrian army as thirty paces. Eugene decided that he must attack, and early on August 16, 1717, Eugene's troops, under cover of fog, achieved some brief measure of surprise. The advantage, however soon shifted to the Turks. Although, as he wrote to his sister Fanny, Oglethorpe emerged unscathed, Villette, another of the young aides-de-camp, was fatally wounded at his side. Finally Prince Eugene and the imperial army put the enemy to headlong flight. But the imperial army's losses were heavy, especially in the communications corps. In addition to Villette, the German adjutant general had been killed; Oglethorpe's own adjutant general had been wounded; and Orazio Rasponi, papal emissary turned aide-de-camp, had died in a duel.[12] Thus Oglethorpe found himself senior aide-de-camp on a battlefield that lacked an active adjutant general. According to Boswell's notes, Oglethorpe then acted as adjutant general, took possession of the Turkish camp, and upon bringing Prince Eugene the casualty report, received the rank of lieutenant colonel. The following day, Eugene evidently sent him to the Court at Vienna to report details of the victory.[13]

After the surrender of Belgrade, Oglethorpe, like most of the other volunteers, took an extended winter leave. In October or early November he was in Turin with his brother Theophilus, and there he met the earl of Mar, the Pretender's secretary. Later he visited Urbino on his return trip through Italy; and there in February 1718 he made two secret visits to the Pretender, possibly as a gesture of gratitude for the recent grant to Theophilus of a Jacobite baronetcy.[14]

Apparently Oglethorpe remained with his brother longer than he had intended. In March 1718 a truce prevailed, and on May 5 a peace conference was opened at Passorowitz. After General Georg Olivier Wallis was dispatched to Naples on May 7, 1718, to oppose Spanish invaders in Sicily, Oglethorpe apparently joined him.[15] But he seems to have been unable to muster enthusiasm for a campaign against the Spaniards. Although Prince Eugene had given him a lieutenant colonelcy in the imperial army, Oglethorpe did not succumb, as did his friend Keith, to the excitement of the life of a soldier of fortune. Instead he returned to England, taking with him Eugene's recommendation to George I. On August 15, 1718, Fanny wrote, "Jemmy returns to England. We expect him every day/He'll stay here a month"; and on September 19 she wrote again that "Jemmy is here and going home."[16] Oglethorpe, however, found it impossible to obtain an English commission, partly because of his family's Jacobite activities. So on June 25, 1719, he reentered his name on the books of Corpus Christi College, Oxford, where his attendance is indicated by entries on the college buttery books beginning on July 3, 1719.[17]

Oglethorpe's next and best documented military experience came, of course, in Georgia, a score of years later. Following his Georgia experience, Oglethorpe might have led a peaceful if unexciting life. But he was to enter yet another and more mysterious military experience. In 1755 he left England, not to return before late 1760 or early 1761. Except for two letters to Keith written early in the period, these years have remained a complete blank in Oglethorpe biography. But thanks to these letters and to his friend James Boswell, the story of part of the period can now be reconstructed.

In late 1755 Oglethorpe was bored, restless, and bitterly resentful. His 1744 marriage to Elizabeth Wright had been placid enough, but the couple had no children. Although Oglethorpe was nearing sixty, he retained his energies, but their outlets were gradually becoming more restricted as he was deprived of his business, political, and military activities. Among the most depressing of these deprivations had been the loss of his seat in the House of Commons, where since 1722 he had represented Haslemere. His defeats in both the Haslemere and Westminster elections in 1754 had been cruel blows. But most galling of all to Oglethorpe was his military inactivity. In 1747 he had been promoted to the rank of lieutenant general, with expectation of continued service. But the charge of treason brought by William Augustus, duke of Cumberland, in 1745 had effectively terminated Oglethorpe's military career. In spite of his honorable acquittal, Oglethorpe failed in 1755 to gain reactivation of his Georgia regiment for service in America.[18] Because Cumberland was responsible for higher military assignments,

Oglethorpe's name did not appear on the list of commands in October 1755. So bitter was Oglethorpe that he apparently feared he would not be able to control his temper if he met Cumberland. As Oglethorpe later told Boswell, so that he "would not be killed by any of the Duke's adherents," he felt "obliged to sell a manor for little value" in order to go abroad. As he wrote to William Pitt on October 6, 1761, "The treatment I met with made me retier from a wourld that did not want men who preffered the publick to their privat intrest." [19]

In 1755 Oglethorpe followed a pattern of behavior similar to that which he had displayed in 1715. Then he had met his friend James Keith in Paris; now, nearly forty years later, war again looming on the horizon, he turned again to his friend Keith, who, following a varied career as a soldier of fortune, in 1747 had accepted from Frederick the Great the rank of field marshal. Oglethorpe left England for Rotterdam, arriving before December 9, 1755. Then from Rotterdam he wrote to Keith, reminding him of their past association and subtly asking for Keith's help. Finally Oglethorpe suggested that he wanted to meet Frederick the Great: "I am at Roterdam and hoped to have had the Happyness of Seeing your great Master whose Actions and Genius I have long admired." He concluded by urging secrecy: "As I am yet incognito my Equipage &c not being arived the Letter need not have my name to it." [20] Apparently Oglethorpe received encouragement, for after visiting his sister Fanny (Frances Charlotte, Marquise des Marches) in Piedmont, he wrote again to his friend, on May 3, 1756, again stressing the need for secrecy: "If I come it must be absolutely incognito to Prevent Cerig-mony Expense & as you rightly observe speculations. Hetherto none but those I had business to [,] know my name. . . . I desire to be entierly unknown except to the king & your self. . . . I take the name of De Hurtmore an Estate of which I am Lord of the Mannor though it being amongst others and far from London no body thincks of me under it though I have right to Carry it." [21]

The following five years are blank in Oglethorpe biographies. But we do now know where Oglethorpe was during part of that period, for Boswell recorded that Oglethorpe "went abroad in 1756 to his friend Keith," "took name of one of his manors," "fought in the army," and "was with Keith when killed."

As readers of Thomas Carlyle's *History of Friedrich the Great* doubt-less recall, Field Marshal Keith died at the Battle of Hochkirch, in the arms of an English volunteer, John Tebay.[22] Indeed, Sir Andrew Mitchell, British ambassador to Prussia, received a letter from John Tebay, describing Keith's death; and Andrew Bisset, Mitchell's biographer, printed the letter and added, "There is among his [Mitchell's] papers a certificate of respectability of Mr. Tebay's character and connexions, . . . with a receipt endorsed on the back from Messrs. Drummond, Mitchell's bankers in London, for ten guineas, which Mr. Mitchell had advanced to Mr. Tebay."[23] The certificate of respectability for "Mr. Feby" still exists. However, rather than proving the existence of a genuine Tebay it helps to reveal Oglethorpe's attempt to create a false identity—for the forty-nine signatures attesting to "Tebay's" or "Feby's" character are all written in three inks and by only three hands.[24]

De Hurtmore, Oglethorpe's avowed pseudonym, was appropriate enough for travel in France and Savoy but would have been an embarrassment in an army fighting the French. So it must have become obvious to Keith and Oglethorpe that an alternative pseudonym was essential. The name he assumed, Tebay, or Tibby, was clearly English, and if Oglethorpe still wanted the name of one of his manors, it can be considered appropriate. Although he apparently had no property in Westmorland, where there is a considerable town named Tebay, he did have a close connection with the island of Tybee in Georgia. (Oglethorpe's sisters and their families believed that he had left considerable estates in Georgia,[25] and he may have thought and written or spoken of Tybee Island as part of his own domain.) Tybee, like Tebay, has many alternate spellings, one of which is Tibi, as Boswell spelled it.

Whatever the reason, Oglethorpe as John Tebay prepared to join his friend Keith, who had been called by Frederick to return to Potsdam by July 10, 1756. Probably during the fall or winter of 1756 occurred the episode that Alexander Burnett, Mitchell's secretary, later recounted to Boswell: "He told me that during the last war Marshal Keith was one day riding out, when there came up to him an Englishman, who called himself John Tibi, Esq. His story is curious; but I find it too long for my journal, so shall mark it in another place."[26] If Boswell recorded it other than in the notes for his projected biography of Oglethorpe, the account has not been recovered.

If Oglethorpe had not already joined Keith before he established winter quarters in Dresden, surely he did so then. On April 26, 1757, Keith, accompanied by Mitchell, the British ambassador, led a col-

umn of Frederick's army against Prague.[27] Mitchell often accompanied
or visited Keith. Oglethorpe, of course, would have kept his distance
during these meetings, for Mitchell might have questioned him concerning his background and credentials. The siege of Prague began with
every expectation of Prussian victory. However, on June 18 Frederick
attacked Marshal Daun and lost about 15,000 men. His losses forced
Frederick to raise the siege and withdraw. Keith remained with the rear
guard to take charge of baggage and artillery, then joined Frederick on
the Elbe. On November 5, Frederick finally routed the enemy, inflict-
ing over 10,000 casualties while suffering only 548. After this success,
Frederick dispatched Keith upon an invasion of Bohemia, or at least
for forays into Bohemia from headquarters at Chemnitz in southeast
Saxony. Later that winter, Keith, in poor health, moved his headquarters to Dresden.

At some time during the winter, Oglethorpe evidently followed the
pattern he had established during his campaigns with Prince Eugene:
he took leave from winter quarters to visit his sisters. On June 30, 1758,
Frederick wrote to Keith: "Vous aurez appris par Jacques Rosbuf tout ce
que l'on lui a dit dans l'armee autrichienne."[28] Evidently Oglethorpe
had visited his sister the Marquise des Marches, traversing territory
held by the Austrian Empire. Frederick doubtless recalled Oglethorpe's
service in the Austrian army from 1716 to 1719, and he apparently remembered also that Oglethorpe's Christian name was Jacques, not Jean,
in spite of his alias, John Tebay. Perhaps one of the most interesting
revelations from Frederick's letter to Keith is that in the higher circles
of the Prussian army, Oglethorpe, alias John Tebay, apparently came to
be known as "RoastBeef." Joseph Yorke, envoy to Frederick and ambassador to the Hague, visited Keith and referred to Oglethorpe as "John
Tibby, alias RostBif."[29] The nickname was a tribute, for roast beef had
been declared the proper food for a brave Englishman in contrast to the
fancy dishes of the French. Henry Fielding had popularized the notion
in three musical plays, and in 1735 Philip Leveridge published his song,
later known as "The Roast Beef of Old England."[30] Thus Oglethorpe's
nickname was a compliment to an old soldier, courtier, and ally against
a common enemy, France.

In March, the spring campaign soon to begin, Keith was too ill for
duty. In the absence of other nurses, Oglethorpe occasionally attended
at his friend's bedside. Oglethorpe was, during this period, in great

danger of having his identity discovered. For two months in the spring of 1758, Joseph Yorke, special envoy to Frederick, was occasionally with Keith also. Yorke was the son of Philip Yorke, one of Oglethorpe's chief accusers at his court-martial. Now Yorke's son Joseph began to make inquiries concerning John Tebay. Yorke even wrote to Robert D'Arcy, earl of Holdernesse, then secretary of state, to obtain authentication of Tebay's reference. Finally, after he returned to the Netherlands, Yorke received and forwarded to Mitchell Holdernesse's information from Tebay's reference: " 'As to one John Tibby Esquire there is no such Person, but for one John Deaby there was. . . . He as you mention was not likely . . . to rise high in military glory, being looked on here as dull heavy Fellow, &c.' "[31] Fortunately for Oglethorpe, the "Deaby" identification apparently lulled Yorke's suspicions.

Keith's health finally improved, and on September 26 he rejoined Frederick's forces. In October, encamped at Hochkirch, Keith warned against their vulnerability to attack. Frederick, however, failed to protect the position adequately, and early on October 14 the enemy attacked. In the defeat that followed, the bravery of both Keith and Oglethorpe was evident. Excerpts from a letter from "Tebay" (Oglethorpe) written two weeks later detail the death of Keith:

> The Marschal [was] always where their was most danger and riding from right to left to make the Troups advance but all in vain. . . . the Marschel Stud Expos'd to the fier of the Enemy when we had not one single trup Prussien wetwext hus and the Enemy who Advanc'd at that time in great force; til at Last he recev'd his mortal wound not haveing disire to out Live that day he tumbld Dead from his hors into my arms. . . . his Death will give me reason to remember to see the Actions of so brave a man and after that be an Eye wittness of his Death. I did all my Indevour to get him from the Field of Battle but all in vain. I got six Solders and got him set upon the Hors again to bring him of but une Officieur came ad Drove the Soldiers away and would not let them Assist which was such babarity as I never see.

Powerless to help Keith, Oglethorpe withdrew. His letter continued with an appeal to Mitchell for a loan, which we know was granted to him as John Tebay. As Oglethorpe wrote, "So I am at present without frinds without money and in a strange place without your goodness will be so good as assist me with a Smal Trifil and a Letter of reccommendation . . . and be Assur'd that you Shal never Losse a Farthing by me and I hope you will grant me the Above favour for I have no frind at present in this Contry but you to Apply to."[32]

Thus Oglethorpe found himself with only the clothes on his back, twice wounded, friendless, moneyless, unable to speak more than halting German; he was in an ambiguous position with the Prussians and an even worse one with the British ministry, for he was abroad under an assumed name, with false credentials, and had arranged for forged credentials to be sent to Mitchell, to whom he was appealing for assistance. As we have seen, the assistance was granted. Although Mitchell knew that Tebay's credentials were forged, that there was "no such person," he had received from his bankers ten guineas. If Mitchell ever realized who "Tebay" was, he apparently kept his diplomatic silence.

Oglethorpe performed one final act for his good friend Keith. As he later told Boswell, he "begged his [Keith's] body of the French" and he may have remained in Berlin until Keith was reinterred there, on February 3, 1759. Then instead of joining the First British Contingent, as he had apparently intended,[33] he probably made a prolonged visit to his sister Fanny in Piedmont.

Only after George II died on October 25, 1760, did Oglethorpe, according to Boswell's notes, return to England; and the first reliable record of his presence there is the letter he wrote to William Pitt on October 6, 1761. Oglethorpe must have frequently returned in memory to the years he spent with Keith and to Keith's recollections of Frederick and his court, for some evidence exists of stories he told of these times. On February 16, 1783, Horace Walpole recorded one of the old general's anecdotes, an account of a meeting of Frederick, Keith, and Voltaire: "One day before the King of Prussia, Voltaire having Attacked Marshal Keith pretty freely, the King s[ai]d, 'Marshal, do you say nothing in return?' 'Oh,' s[ai]d the Marshal, 'I have nothing to say to him but that he is a Poet in history and an historian in Poetry.'"[34] Apparently Oglethorpe never told the story of his years with Keith and Frederick to anyone but Boswell and perhaps to his wife, Elizabeth, and to Keith's brother, George, the Earl Marischal. If Oglethorpe discussed his exciting adventures with Keith under Frederick the Great, his friends kept his confidence.

Oglethorpe and James Wright
A Georgia Comparison

Kenneth Coleman

The two Jameses—Oglethorpe and Wright—had more in common than just Christian names. Both men led Georgia during crucial times and each, according to Kenneth Coleman, deserves high marks for his achievements. Georgia may not have survived, as we know it, without the leadership of the former; Georgia might not have had the strength to join the revolutionary movement without the stability of the latter—an irony of which Wright must have been painfully aware.

The style and approach of these two men varied widely. Oglethorpe was more mercurial, better loved (and hated), and less down-to-earth in his approach to everyday problems. Wright proved to be more prosaic in his leadership style than Oglethorpe, but his executive impact may well have been more profound, according to Coleman, dean of Georgia historians.

In this comparative essay, the actions and aspirations of both men are assessed. Their achievements and failures are weighed, one against the other, and a tentative conclusion is made of the importance of each man to the broad mainstream of Georgian and American colonial history.—Editors

James Oglethorpe and Sir James Wright, by all counts colonial Georgia's two most outstanding leaders, both died in 1785. Wright, Georgia's last and best colonial governor, was twenty years younger than Oglethorpe and came to Georgia seventeen years after Oglethorpe left. These men differed in many respects, but both had considerable ability and both had Georgia's best interest, as they saw it, at heart. The purpose of this chapter is to compare their styles and accomplishments in Georgia.

First Oglethorpe, about whom most people know more than they do about Wright. James Oglethorpe was born in London on December 22, 1696, to Jacobites Sir Theophilus and Lady Eleanor Oglethorpe. Sir Theophilus and James made peace with the government and served it, while Lady Eleanor and the rest of the family remained Jacobites. James attended Eton, and then went on to Corpus Christi College at Oxford. He held a commission in the British army and served for a time under Prince Eugene of Savoy. In 1722 he was elected to the House of Commons for Haslemere, a constituency his father and brothers represented earlier, and held the seat until 1754.[1]

When Oglethorpe came to Georgia with the first colonists, he knew little about America, and his military career had included but minimal true command experience. Yet he was well acquainted in governmental and philanthropic circles in London, came from an important old family, believed in hard work, and trusted in his abilities to accomplish his desires in America—characteristics that helped as a leader of a new colony.[2]

It was Oglethorpe who pushed the idea of a charity colony through The Associates of Dr. Bray until they agreed to apply for a charter. He worked hardest to secure the charter, became the leading Georgia Trustee, came to Georgia with the original colonists, and oversaw the colony during its first decade.[3]

Oglethorpe could be a stern and unbending soldier, but he could also be a kind "father" to the unfortunates who made up the first settlers in Georgia. On the voyage across the Atlantic on the *Anne*, the colonists gave Oglethorpe the name "father" and celebrated his birthday with punch and mutton.[4] He saw to many things, trivial or important, on the voyage over and during the first years of the colony's life. Samuel Eveleigh, a Charles Town merchant, said after his March 1733 visit to Savannah that Oglethorpe comforted the sick, settled arguments, kept a strict discipline so that no one was drunk or swore, and saw that a great deal of work was done in laying out and building Savannah. "In short, he has done a vast deal of Work for the Time, and I think his Name justly deserves to be immortalized."[5] The Salzburger pastor

Johann Martin Boltzius quoted Jean Purry as saying "that Mr. Ogle-thorpe loved the Germans very much and, since he had no children of his own, had taken them on, in a manner of speaking, as his children."[6]

Although Oglethorpe held no title in Georgia except Trustee—he could not hold any other office and remain a Trustee—he was the real leader and source of much authority during his decade in the colony. The Trustees had not set up an adequate government; especially did Georgia lack a real executive. Apparently none of the original colonists possessed sufficient ability to make the province work. How the Trustees expected it to succeed thus is a mystery. Although they never gave Oglethorpe any executive position, they must have suspected that he would exercise such authority. Oglethorpe was never one to quibble over details when he considered that something needed doing.[7] He assumed authority, and it is lucky that he did. Many, including myself, have speculated on what would have happened in the first few years in Georgia if Oglethorpe had not come. But he did come! Oglethorpe did not err in assuming authority originally, but he kept too much of it in his hands too long.

As an administrator, Oglethorpe left a good bit to be desired. He was not systematic, he was not an adequate record keeper, and he did not keep the Trustees informed of his actions. As both a civilian and a military leader, he was good at personal leadership and inspiring others to follow him and to do what he wanted them to do. But in larger movements, like his 1740 campaign against Saint Augustine, he did not do so well. When Oglethorpe was absent from Georgia much argument occurred between individuals as to what he had authorized, but no records existed to prove it one way or another.[8]

Besides Savannah, Oglethorpe located and had laid out Augusta, Ebenezer, Frederica, Darien, and the out-settlements around Savan-nah. He saw to the surveying of land for the settlers and the formation of the Trustees' garden at Savannah from which mulberry trees, grape-vines, and exotic plants would be distributed to Georgians.

Oglethorpe immediately formed a friendship with Tomochichi, the old Yamacraw chieftain, and began to use Mary Musgrove, whose hus-band's trading post was located near the site of Savannah, as an aide and interpreter in Indian affairs. One of Oglethorpe's strongest points in Georgia was his ability to get along well with the Indians and to have Indian allies when he needed them against the Spanish. Oglethorpe saw that the Indians were treated fairly, but his main reason for Indian friendship was his ability to convince the Indians that he was their friend and would help them. He once told some visiting Chickasaws, "I am a red man, an Indian, in my heart."[9]

Oglethorpe was responsible for several of the regulations that made Georgia a "peculiar colony" and insisted on them long after they were clearly not working in Georgia. He blamed all the early deaths in Savannah on rum drinking and continued to oppose rum as a drink in Georgia, although this prohibition could never be enforced. Oglethorpe opposed any change in the amount of land to be granted to colonists or the admission of slaves as going against the Trustees' original idea of peasant proprietorships to aid the unfortunate. He refused to recommend approval of Samuel Eveleigh's desire for a monopoly of the Indian trade in Georgia, although this could well have furnished badly needed exports to aid in Georgia's trade. Oglethorpe seemed uninterested and uninformed on economic affairs and continued during his entire stay in Georgia to insist that silk production was the best way to make a living, something that almost any of the settlers could have told him was not true. Certainly these ideas held back the overall economic development of Georgia.[10]

Oglethorpe furnished the link between the Trustees and the British government in London and the colonists in Georgia. Often he told the Trustees and British officials what he had done and what they should do, rather than asking what should be done. He reported what he wanted London to know, he was successful in getting funds from Parliament for Georgia, and he represented Georgia to the British government and people. Of course, he never hesitated to do or not to do anything that he thought good for the colony.

With the founding of Georgia, Oglethorpe assumed the leadership of the English in the Spanish-English struggle for the debatable land below the Savannah River, a struggle that had been going on since the founding of Charles Town in 1670. He also assumed leadership in the French-English struggle in the Alabama country. He planned and carried out the defense structure of Georgia, including securing the first British regiment stationed permanently in America. We shall not go into his merits or demerits as a military leader but merely say that when his fighting against the Spanish ended in 1743, shortly before he left Georgia for the last time, Spain held no more territory than she had ten years earlier when Georgia was founded. There was to be no more fighting between English and Spanish in the debatable land before Spain ceded Florida to Britain in 1763. Of the three reasons for the founding of Georgia, Oglethorpe effectively carried out imperialism by securing the debatable land for the English.[11]

For the forty-two years that Oglethorpe lived after his return to England, he was to be known as the founder of Georgia, and this has been his claim to fame since. A poem dedicated to him at the time of his death said, not entirely accurately:

> A vigorous soldier, and a virtuous sage;
> He founded Georgia, gave it laws and trade;
> He saw it flourish, and he saw it fade.
> (*Gentleman's Magazine*, July 8, 1785)

From Oglethorpe's Georgia career, we turn to that of James Wright. Born in London in 1716, apparently he came to South Carolina about 1730 when his father, Robert Wright, became chief justice of South Carolina. James finished his growing up in South Carolina and became familiar with the government and economic activities of that area. He attended Gray's Inn in London in 1741 and was called to the bar there. He occupied various court offices in South Carolina and was attorney general from 1742 to 1757. For the next three years he was South Carolina's agent in London, a position he held when he was appointed lieutenant governor of Georgia in 1760.[12] The next year he became governor and retained that office until 1782.

Thus Wright came to Georgia with a thorough knowledge of colonial government, the economy of the area, the government in London, and with the personal acquaintance of the officials who worked with colonies. From this background Wright was ideally qualified to be a colonial governor—probably better qualified than most of his fellow governors.

Wright succeeded the popular Henry Ellis but did not have the personality to become popular with the mass of Georgians as Oglethorpe and Ellis had been. He never qualified as "father" of the colony. He was a reserved, somewhat formal and aloof eighteenth-century gentleman who did his duty to his king and to his colony as he saw it and who would not be diverted from this duty by neglect nor by a desire for popularity with his colonists. He considered himself the king's chief servant in Georgia, even when he did not approve of the orders he had to carry out. If he had suggestions, they were put forward most deferentially. But Wright was always a colonial as well. He thought that the welfare of the empire and of Georgia should go forward together. He tried to be loyal to two worlds and two masters—always difficult and often impossible, especially in America after 1765.[13]

Wright, unlike Oglethorpe, was an able administrator. He kept adequate records and wrote fully to his superiors in England. He offered effective leadership to his council, assembly, entire government, and other leaders in Georgia.[14] He was certainly the best governor that Georgia had had to date. Although Wright and the elected Commons House of Assembly differed frequently over colonial rights after 1765, they cooperated to the end in many governmental affairs, and they respected each other.

Once in Georgia, Wright identified himself completely with the colony and became a leader in many ways. He sometimes must have wished for the more sophisticated society of Charles Town, for Savannah was a mere village in the 1760s. But when the South Carolina governor granted land south of the Altamaha in 1763 before that area could be transferred to Georgia, Wright protested vigorously to both Charles Town and London and secured the area for Georgia.[15]

Soon after his arrival, Wright disposed of his South Carolina lands and began acquiring Georgia lands. He became one of the largest planters with 25,578 acres of land tilled by 523 slaves by the end of the colonial period. His annual crop of two to three thousand barrels of rice made him one of the wealthiest men in the colony and indicated his abilities as a planter. Although Wright's position as governor made it easy to secure land, there is no evidence that he acquired any more than he was entitled to under the laws of the colony.[16] In fact, Wright was always a conservative influence in land granting opposing grants that would be held for speculation. He knew that for protection against the Indians, Georgia needed more population and needed to be settled in a contiguous pattern.

Certainly Wright watched over his Georgia as closely and as carefully as had Oglethorpe, but after 1763 it was a different Georgia. The Spanish and French were gone, more land and slaves were available to the colonists, the population was increasing rapidly, the "peculiar regulations" of the Trustees were no more. Georgia was modeling it-self more and more on South Carolina, and no single individual could be the colony's "father" any longer. Wright was just as concerned as Oglethorpe about everything that happened in Georgia and used his in-fluence to secure the type of Georgia he wanted. His personal economic and social interests in the colony gave him a better leadership potential than many governors possessed. He hoped to grow and prosper with Georgia, and he did.

Oglethorpe had the advantage in locating towns and indicating directions of settlement because Georgia was a wilderness when he came. Wright did not have this advantage, but he was able to achieve a good deal by surveying and granting of land from two major Indian cessions made during his tenure as governor. He personally toured the 1773 cession and helped to indicate sites for mills and towns. Wright encouraged groups of settlers who came to Georgia together to settle in townships for protection and better social relationships. The two best-known township settlements were the Scotch-Irish at Queensborough, begun in 1768, and the Quakers at Wrightsborough, begun in 1767.[17] Wright was instrumental in declaring Sunbury a port of entry in 1762 and in officially creating the town of Brunswick in 1770.[18]

Like Oglethorpe, Wright worked for and achieved good Indian rela-tions. He had a great advantage after 1763 because the exit of the French and the Spanish as neighbors of Georgia left only the British as a source of Indian trade or backing. Colonists now pushed harder against the Indian frontier with their insatiable desire for land, which could have caused considerable Indian trouble. However, throughout his governorship, Wright worked with Indian Superintendent John Stuart in insisting that the Indians be given their treaty rights and that whites not settle on Indian lands or take "satisfaction" against Indians for transgressions against white life and property. Wright did not have the personal good feeling for Indians that Oglethorpe displayed and he could not inspire Indians to the same sort of friendship or loyalty, but he kept Indian peace and helped secure two sizable Indian land cessions (in 1763 and 1773) for Georgia settlers.[19]

By 1760 when Wright came to Georgia, most of the economic ideas of the Trustees had been abandoned except the production of silk. At the end of the Trustee Period about 500 pounds of raw silk were pro-duced annually in Georgia. In 1760, 1,200 pounds were produced, and the high production of 1,900 pounds came in 1767. Wright encouraged silk production by urging that a bounty continue to be paid, as otherwise silk would not be raised in any marked amount. Wright never, as Oglethorpe had, insisted that silk should be the main economic basis for Georgia, and there is no evidence that he ever produced any on his plantations.[20]

Wright was, of course, the main link between the government in London and that in Savannah. But Georgia's growth had created many other links by this time, so that he could not be "Mr. Georgia" to Englishmen as Oglethorpe had been. Wright was sure that he best understood the English government and officials, and he was probably correct.

Wright had no military career to compare with Oglethorpe's, but he frequently advised the ministry in London on Georgia's military needs. He long insisted that more troops were needed to protect the colony against the Indians, enforce the laws of trade, and overawe the revolutionaries when troubles began in the 1770s. Georgia never received the troops he thought necessary.[21]

While Oglethorpe had troubles with the malcontents during his tenure in Georgia, they were not as serious as Wright's troubles with the revolutionaries. Like many Americans who eventually sided with the king, Wright was of two minds about much of the early revolutionary activity. He was a good enough colonial to understand and even agree with the American objections to some British policies and actions. Wright told the 1775 Georgia Assembly: "You may be advocates of liberty, so am I, but in a constitutional and legal way. . . . Where there is no law there can be no liberty." Yet he was also the king's deputy in Georgia and considered that it was to him that he owed his first loyalty. So in the end he sided with the royal government. Yet Wright, because of the personal respect he commanded and because he would not allow himself to be intimidated, kept control of his government and kept his colony out of rebellion longer than other colonial governors.[22] Ironically, Wright's success in Georgia helped the colony to grow strong enough to rebel in 1776—certainly considered by Wright his greatest failure.

Both Oglethorpe and Wright left their impress on Georgia. Oglethorpe founded the colony and kept the Spaniards from destroying it. But most of the other things he advocated—peasant proprietorships, silk and wine production, no slaves or strong drink, a paternalistic government—were dead before the Trustees gave up their control of Georgia in 1752. Wright's contributions were less exciting—population growth, new settlement patterns, economic prosperity, larger farms and plantations, an efficient government—and were not abandoned when he left. They did not especially excite Georgians then nor historians since, yet they may well have been more important for Georgia's future development than Oglethorpe's better-known ideas.

Oglethorpe died June 30, 1785, at Cranham, his wife's estate, and was buried in the parish church there. Wright followed on November 21, 1785, at his house in Westminster, and was buried in the historic Abbey Church there. Perhaps the best way to sum up their feelings about Georgia and America in 1785 is seen in Oglethorpe's call upon John Adams, the first United States minister to England, just a few weeks before Oglethorpe's death. He expressed his esteem for America and regret at the recent troubles with Britain.[23] His career in America had been long enough before to prevent any bitterness about the recent separation. But for Wright such an action in 1785 was impossible. Three years was not a long enough interval to accept his beloved Georgia as a part of the United States and to hope for the welfare of both in their new independence.

The Search for Authentic Icons
of James Edward Oglethorpe

Edwin L. Jackson

*I*f portraits and other kinds of artistic or semi-artistic representations are adequate mirrors to a man's soul, then theoretically we should
know a great deal about James Edward Oglethorpe. But in spite of the many
"icons" of him that are extant today, we are not at all sure precisely what he
looked like at any given time in his life. Edwin L. Jackson undertakes, in this
unusual photo-essay, the task of tracking down engravings, prints, medals,
and portraits of Georgia's founder, authenticating the likenesses, and ascrib-
ing names to the various pieces of art that purport to re-create the true image
of Oglethorpe. Jackson uses various methods, such as eighteenth-century
fashion and time-dating techniques, to aid him in his work.

This essay is the fullest compilation to date of the various contemporary
likenesses of this appealing yet enigmatic man. The Oglethorpe that slowly
takes form through history's mists is not unlike the popular perception of
the man that has been accepted for the last century or so. Jackson's careful
research into the sources, though, and his determination to track down every
clue help document the definitive physical picture of Georgia's leader that here
gradually comes into focus.—Editors

Why include an iconography in a scholarly examination of James
Edward Oglethorpe? First, until now scant attention has been devoted
to artistic renderings of his life, despite concerns over the authenticity
of surviving portraits and other likenesses. An iconography seeks to
verify this record by distinguishing originals from copies and identi-

fying artists and the dates of their works. Second, an iconography is important because art has a useful contribution to make in the study of the past. A contemporary painting of a historical event—even when imperfectly depicted—can provide an important image of the site and characters. As will be seen with respect to William Hogarth's painting of the Gaols Committee investigating Fleet Prison, research on the artist and the story behind the painting can reveal valuable information to the historian. Features such as clothing, insignia, armor, and hairstyle may offer clues as to when an undated portrait was painted and provide insights into the subject's status in society.

Art is important for yet another reason. As British portrait historian David Piper argues, even the most poorly executed portrait offers something that words cannot: "When the faces are of those well known to history, they add a new dimension to history. Words cannot convey more than a vague impression, different in every reader, of a character's physical displacement of time and space. It is the virtue of a portrait that it offers a definition, not a final one . . . but nevertheless a positive and measurable definition; it underlines its subject's humanity, the common heritage of perishable flesh."[1]

The commemoration of Georgia's 250th birthday in 1983 and the 200th anniversary of James Oglethorpe's death in 1985 provided a timely opportunity to take a new look—both figuratively and literally —at Georgia's founder. Toward this end, a photographic record was compiled of all known portraits, engravings, sculptures, and other visual representations contained in public and private collections both in England and in the United States.[2] Additionally, to the extent possible, a history for each was established that included information about the artist, date of completion, size, subsequent ownership, current location, and other background material. For purposes of this chapter, the list of icons was limited to known, reputed, or possible contemporary likenesses of Oglethorpe; copies of originals; old engravings; and a few other noncontemporary but widely recognized works.

Had each portrait been signed and dated, the task would have been infinitely easier, with less need for conjecture. Unfortunately, many artists of Oglethorpe's era neither signed nor dated their works. Occasionally a portrait itself revealed clues that help establish it as a probable or possible contemporary likeness. In other instances, a chronology of Oglethorpe's life or a biographical account of the artist unlocked key information. Regrettably, several portraits defied all efforts to tap their secrets. In the end, however, these uncertainties created a more fascinating story than one where a definitive record was available on every image.

British art historians tend to give low marks to the quality of native portraiture during much of Oglethorpe's lifetime.[3] Even into the eighteenth century, painting was not a particularly respected occupation in England—certainly not compared to poetry or music. Portraiture particularly suffered; charges that it was not art but imitation hurt. Also, many Britons were xenophiles, convinced that with only a few exceptions true art came from the Continent. By 1760 this attitude was changing, in no small part owing to the rising popularity of English artist Sir Joshua Reynolds, who by 1759 averaged almost three portraits a week. In 1780 he counted among his sitters none other than General Oglethorpe, for a portrait subsequently destroyed and for which no engraving survives.[4] Whatever the case, the demand for portraits mushroomed in the second half of seventeenth-century England. By the time Oglethorpe and the first contingent of Georgia colonists sailed from Gravesend in 1732, it was de rigueur for an English gentleman to have a portrait of himself—and usually his wife and absent friends and relatives.[5]

Portraits were occasionally commissioned by third parties, but commonly it was the subject himself—usually motivated by vanity or a desire to impress friends and neighbors—who precipitated the arrangement. Moreover, according to W. Y. Carman, "They wished to put themselves on record in the light most becoming, not only to their physical charm but also to their social station."[6] Rather than risk unhappy clients, artists commonly erred on the side of glorification. Often, the artist sketched only the subject's head from life, later completing the portrait in the sitter's absence. Not infrequently, the final product showed the subject in a pose, dress, and setting quite unlike that of the times, such as the laurel and toga of a Roman emperor. This practice was convenient to both artist and subject, alluded to the status of the subject, and, with an eye toward posterity, suggested the subject's timelessness.[7]

Military officers were typically depicted in heroic stance in full dress, or even armor, rather than actual campaign uniform. As Carman explains, "To dress up in the family armour would make a much more convincing picture of a military career."[8] Also, field officers were often shown holding a baton, the traditional symbol of command.[9] Thus, several contemporary portraits of Oglethorpe present him in regalia that, except for the cuirass, is probably unlike anything he actually wore— particularly during the campaign against the Spanish in Georgia and Florida.

More important than military uniforms in dating anonymous eighteenth-century portraits are the wigs worn by subjects, as wig styles changed dramatically during the era of their popularity. Perukes gained popularity in England in the 1660s, although fashionable in France four decades earlier.[10] Because of premature balding, Louis XIII began wearing a full wig. Out of courtesy to the king, members of the French court followed suit and adorned their heads with long hairpieces. With the restoration of Charles II in 1660, England followed the French example, and full wigs quickly became popular with the king, court, and members of the upper classes. In defense of the artificial tresses, supporters cited their convenience, cleanliness (in that era, real hair was seldom washed, but a peruke user's hair was either closely cropped or shorn completely), and the fact that use of a wig instantly announced one's standing in society.[11] The era of the full wig—the long, heavily curled hairpiece that extended far below the shoulders to the front and back—lasted until the 1730s (except that some older men and certain professions continued wearing full wigs into the 1740s and beyond).[12] This fashion note, plus the fact that during the 1720s it was in vogue to use a gray-blonde powder on perukes, helps establish the probable date for one Oglethorpe portrait (Figure 9-4).[13]

Between 1720 and 1740, the height of wigs—which sometimes stood three or more inches off the top of the head—dropped. Their length also was shortened so that the hair no longer fell to the middle of the back.[14] While hair still might extend to the shoulders, more often the sides were shortened, curled, or pulled back into a pigtail. By the time of Oglethorpe's final return to England from Georgia, full wigs were seldom seen and by 1753 were considered out of style except for judges, doctors, and certain other professions and offices. By 1760, many men again wore their own hair, though often powdering it to look like a wig. Around 1770, wigs made a brief comeback, but the 1780s marked the beginning of the final decline of perukes. Because James Oglethorpe lived during the era of the wig and obviously wore one, knowledge of the changing styles can be important in establishing a chronology of a number of undated likenesses of Georgia's founder.

Contemporary written accounts about Oglethorpe are not lacking, but few touch on his physical appearance. This lack of description makes us heavily dependent upon artists' perceptions in surviving portraits. At a time when the average height of the English male was about five feet, five inches, it is thought that Oglethorpe was relatively tall.[15] Hogarth's sketch of the Gaols Committee (Figure 9-6) seems to confirm Oglethorpe's height, but William Verelst's painting of the Trustees' Common Council meeting (Figure 9-11) does not depict Oglethorpe as taller than any of the other standing figures. Yet as will be seen, Verelst's concern in that painting was faces, resulting in a distortion in perspective that limits our ability to make meaningful comparisons of the height of the men in the painting.

Unlike some contemporaries, Oglethorpe seems to have suffered no weight problems. Even his fuller face in later life (see Figure 9-21) more likely reflects the natural aging process than corpulence. Supporting this conclusion, several accounts written at different stages of his life suggest that he was in good physical shape. Finally, the fact that Oglethorpe lived past his eighty-eighth birthday—an age far beyond the lifetime of the typical eighteenth-century Englishman—suggests a healthy lifestyle. Oglethorpe was rather handsome, with a slim and aristocratic face in his younger years. One facial feature that most portraits document—and indeed that has become a litmus test when authenticating his portraits—is the prominent Oglethorpe family nose. Whether best described as hawkish or Roman, his nose represents a strong distinguishing feature.

Extant Portraits of James Oglethorpe

Reputed copy by Habersham of 1718 portrait of Oglethorpe as aide-de-camp to Prince Eugene

This canvas—approximately 25 × 39 inches—hangs within Solomon's Lodge No. 1 F. & A. M. in Savannah (see Figure 9-1). Unsigned, it has the following inscription painted in the upper left-hand corner, "James Oglethorpe 1718." According to Solomon's Lodge officials and historical accounts of freemasonry in Georgia during the eighteenth century, this is a copy of a 1718 portrait of Oglethorpe painted in Belgrade by an unknown artist.[16] Although not yet twenty-two years old, Oglethorpe had served as an aide-de-camp to Prince Eugene in his victorious campaign against the Turks. Oglethorpe, the story goes, later carried the original portrait to Savannah, where he gave it to James Habersham, a friend and fellow member of Solomon's Lodge, which Oglethorpe organized in 1734. Later, Richard West Habersham (1812–89) painted this copy of the original, possibly around 1830 while studying art in Paris with Samuel F. B. Morse.[17] No one knows what happened to the original, but in 1911 Mrs. Eugene Edwards, granddaughter of the painter and wife of a lodge member, presented this copy to Solomon's Lodge.

In contrast to Figure 9-4, which also portrays Oglethorpe about the time of his service with Prince Eugene, the Habersham copy shows Oglethorpe without the full wig. Figure 9-1 shows Oglethorpe wearing a shorter and darker wig or perhaps no wig at all. Evidence that he abandoned the full tresses during the European campaign has been uncovered by Rodney Baine and Mary Williams, who wrote that when Oglethorpe reported to Field Marshal George Browne "looking more like a courtier than a soldier," Browne ridiculed the young aide-de-camp; the next morning Oglethorpe reported to Brown wigless and in plain uniform.[18]

A copy in oil of the Solomon's Lodge portrait by Habersham today hangs at the Carl Vinson Institute of Government at the University of Georgia. The 25 × 39–inch canvas is unsigned and undated (see Figure 9-2). In the upper left-hand corner of the portrait has been painted an inscription, "James Oglethorpe aide to Prince Eugene."

Habersham portrait of Oglethorpe, 1885

More than fifty years after painting the portrait shown in Figure 9-1, Habersham painted a second Oglethorpe (see Figure 9-3). In the 1885 copy, Habersham made a number of changes in Oglethorpe's armor and cape and added a background scene; however, the face on the second bears a noticeable resemblance to the first. Stylistic differences

Figure 9-1. Reputed copy by Richard Habersham of an original 1718 portrait of James Oglethorpe as aide-de-camp to Prince Eugene, circa 1830. (Courtesy Solomon's Lodge No. 1, F&AM)

Figure 9-2. Oil rendering of Habersham's copy of a lost eighteenth-century Oglethorpe portrait. (Courtesy of the Carl Vinson Institute of Government, University of Georgia)

Figure 9-3. Habersham portrait of Oglethorpe, 1885. (Courtesy of The Georgia Historical Society)

Figure 9-4. Contemporary portrait of Oglethorpe, circa 1720 (?). (Courtesy of Oglethorpe University)

Figure 9-5. Portrait of Elizabeth Oglethorpe by Bartholomew Dundridge. (Courtesy of Oglethorpe University)

are apparent; Habersham painted the earlier portrait as a young art student, while the latter was painted four years before the artist's death. The 50¼ × 33¾–inch canvas is signed by Habersham and dated 1885, the year he presented it to the Georgia Historical Society in Savannah, where it is found today.

Portrait of Oglethorpe, circa 1720 (?)

Because of his armor and youthful appearance, it is assumed that this portrait (see Figure 9-4) depicts Oglethorpe during or following his service in the imperial army under Prince Eugene (1716–18). During the war, James had visited his mother and sisters, who then lived in Paris, and the portrait could have been painted in France. More likely, it was completed sometime between his return to England in the fall of 1718 and his 1722 election to the House of Commons. Certainly a heroic portrait to display at Westbrook, Oglethorpe's Godalming manor, would have befitted a new member of Parliament.

Neither signed nor dated, the portrait shows a standing three-quarter figure in military armor. The very full, gray-blonde wig came into vogue in England in the 1720s, which may be another indication that the portrait was completed following Oglethorpe's return to England.

Evidence of the portrait's authenticity comes from Surrey County attorney and antiquarian William Bray, who provided legal services to the Oglethorpes and is known to have visited in their home.[19] In his history of Surrey published in 1804, Bray reported that "A ¾ portrait of the General and another of his lady are in the family of the late Mrs. Dickinson of Tottenham who was executrix of the latter."[20] The Oglethorpes never had children. At the time of his death in 1785 and hers in 1787, there were no close heirs, so Mrs. Dickinson played an important role in disposing of the Oglethorpe estate. She joined Granville Sharp as coexecutor of her friend's will and also was named as Elizabeth's residual legatee.[21] Among the items apparently retained by Mrs. Dickinson were the two portraits.

Thornwell Jacobs, president of Oglethorpe University from 1917 to 1944, visited England in 1923 in search of Oglethorpe's grave. While there he also looked for portraits of his university's namesake. Following Bray's lead, he proceeded to Tottenham. There he found in the possession of a Mrs. Richardson a 48 × 39–inch portrait of a military officer (Figure 9-4) and a 49½ × 39½–inch portrait of a lady (Figure 9-5) mounted in identical frames.[22] Jacobs subsequently approached Mr. and Mrs. Joseph M. High, prominent Atlanta philanthropists, and convinced them to purchase the two portraits for Oglethorpe University. Since 1924 the paintings have hung in the Atlanta university's library.

Although we can only speculate on what happened, it seems plausible that following his marriage to Elizabeth, James commissioned Bartholomew Dundridge, whose name appears on her portrait, to paint a portrait of his wife to hang alongside his (see Figure 9-5). Dundridge's painting—the only known representation of Elizabeth—is not dated, but as she was thirty-six years old at the time of their marriage in 1744, her youthful appearance suggests it was probably completed fairly soon thereafter.

Hogarth sketch of the Gaols Committee at Fleet Prison, 1729

This untitled oil on paper by William Hogarth (1697–1764) was sketched on February 27, 1729, or soon thereafter. It portrays members of a House of Commons committee—commonly known as the "Gaols Committee"—investigating conditions at Fleet Prison in London (see Figure 9-6). A series of considerations led warden John Huggins of the Fleet to retire from his lifetime post in August 1728. He then sold the position to deputy Thomas Bambridge and Dougal Cuthbert; Bambridge would prove even more ruthless than Huggins.

The chain of events leading to the investigation portrayed by Hogarth in Figures 9-6 and 9-7 began in June 1728, when Robert Castell, a friend of James Oglethorpe, was sentenced to Fleet. Castell had written and published *The Villas of the Ancients Illustrated* that year, but insufficient sales had plunged him into debt. Like other Fleet inmates, Castell was required to pay fees for his room. Prisoners who could afford the payment were allowed to stay in quarters adjoining the prison known as "sponging houses," while even larger payments entitled them to live in the surrounding area known as the "Rules of the Fleet."[23] Less fortunate prisoners, however, lived under wretched conditions at Fleet. At first, Oglethorpe's friend was able to afford a sponging house—and for a brief time to live within the "Rules." When Castell exhausted his resources and refused to make further payments, Bambridge transferred him to a sponging house where smallpox had broken out. In December, Castell died of the disease.

Most Oglethorpe biographers correctly cite Castell's death as the event that triggered Oglethorpe's push in the House of Commons for an investigation of the plight of indebted prisoners.[24] James had visited Castell during his incarceration at Fleet and was so shocked over his death that he took action in Parliament. However, a more proximate event stirring the other M.P.'s to follow Oglethorpe's lead involved Bambridge's treatment of Sir William Rich, a baronet who had been sentenced to Fleet. On January 25, 1729, Bambridge and several assistants came to Rich demanding payment of a fee. Rich indicated that he had already paid, a scuffle followed, and Bambridge or one of his assistants was stabbed.[25] Subsequently, Rich was placed in irons and confined to a dark cell over the sewer in which the dead were kept before burial. The baronet's friends came to his defense, and on February 8, Bambridge had to appear in court to show "why he iron'd Sir Wm. Rich, Bart."[26]

With abuses rampant, the time was ripe for legislative action. On February 25, 1729, Oglethorpe introduced a motion in the Commons to create a committee to investigate the condition of the prisons. Two days later, the Gaols Committee visited Fleet, where they questioned Bambridge and Rich.[27] As one committee member recorded in his diary: "We then proceeded to examine Mr Bambridge, the warden . . . being asked how many were in irons, he said one for stabbing his man, viz. Sir William Rich, and for an escape; so the committee proceeded to examine Sir William Rich, having ordered the irons to be knocked off during the examination (they weighed 15 lb.), which proved a very cruel usage of him, and then Mr Erle and I went away."[28] As soon as the committee left, Bambridge not only ordered Rich back in irons but added two extra sets. Returning the next day, members of the Gaols Committee found Rich in great pain, his arms and legs swollen. Oglethorpe led the investigation that followed and gained thereby a national reputation. Two years later, in recognition of his work in prison reform, Corpus Christi College at Oxford awarded him an honorary master of arts degree.

In Hogarth's sketch, a standing prisoner (possibly Rich) in tattered rags is shown testifying. Oglethorpe is seated at the far left in outer coat,

Figure 9-6. Contemporary sketch by William Hogarth of the Gaols Committee investigating Fleet Prison, 1729. (Courtesy of the Fitzwilliam Museum, Cambridge)

Figure 9-7. Contemporary painting by William Hogarth of the Gaols Committee at Fleet Prison, circa 1729. (Courtesy of the National Portrait Gallery, London)

Figure 9-8. Detail from Hogarth's painting of the Gaols Committee at Fleet Prison. (Courtesy of the National Portrait Gallery, London)

Figure 9-9. Detail from Hogarth's painting of the Gaols Committee at Fleet Prison. (Courtesy of the National Portrait Gallery, London)

Figure 9-10. Engraving (circa 1830) by S. Bull of the Gaols Committee investigating Fleet Prison. (Courtesy of the University of Georgia Libraries)

waistcoat, and knee-length pants and has turned to warden Bambridge (standing at far left) to question him. Meanwhile, the attention of the rest of the committee is focused on the leg and neck irons, which the prison turnkey has assembled on the table for their inspection.

Years later, Horace Walpole, to whom Hogarth gave the sketch, characterized the scene in a more dramatic manner:

> The scene is the committee; on the table are the instruments of torture. A prisoner in rags, half starved, appears before them; the poor man has a good countenance that adds to the interest. On the other hand is the inhuman gaoler. It is the very figure that Salvator Rosa would have drawn for Iago in the moment of detection. Villany, fear, and conscience are mixed in yellow and livid on his countenance, his lips are contracted by tremor, his face advances as eager to lie, his legs step back as thinking to make his escape; one hand is thrust precipitately into his bosom, the fingers of the other are catching uncertainly at his button-holes. If this was a portrait, it is the most striking that ever was drawn; if it was not, it is still finer.[29]

When compared to Hogarth's later canvas of the event (Figure 9-7), a number of significant differences are immediately apparent. First, in contrast to the dungeon setting of the final canvas, the sketch shows a well-lighted, spacious room where the committee investigation is taking place. Some have explained the inconsistency by suggesting that Hogarth might not have been allowed to accompany the Gaols Committee during its Fleet visit, and thus the actual event he sketched took place somewhere else, for example, the speaker's chamber or even the home of a committee member.[30] While it is true that Commons committee meetings were not generally open to the public and were frequently conducted in the speaker's chamber, this was not an ordinary committee meeting. Also, it was sometimes possible to bribe the doorkeepers to gain entrance to legislative proceedings.[31] Moreover, at the time of the sketch, Hogarth was one month away from marrying the daughter of M.P. Sir James Thornhill, himself a noted artist, and the latter may have helped secure permission for his future son-in-law to go with the committee. It is doubtful that the members would have objected to a painting being made to recognize their humanitarian efforts. Also, the fact that Hogarth's own father earlier had been committed to Fleet because of indebtedness might have motivated him to pursue a chance to expose the evils of the prison on canvas.

As to the inconsistency in settings between sketch and painting, there is a simple explanation. In February, the bowels of Fleet Prison would have been an unpleasantly cold and foul place for a legislative committee to conduct its meeting. We know that the committee inspection of Fleet included its dungeons; however, as one committee member wrote in his diary, the stench was so terrible in many of the cells and quarters that "we were forced to hold our noses."[32] Surely there were above-ground rooms within the walls of Fleet, or within its "Rules," where the actual interrogation could have taken place. That the final canvas portrayed a dungeon setting reflects a bit of artistic license by Hogarth to dramatize the event and make it resemble what it was supposed to be—a prison investigation.

A more troublesome feature of Hogarth's sketch is a small inscription—"Huggins the Keeper"—noted under the figure at far left. John Huggins, however, had sold his wardenship to Thomas Bambridge six months earlier and was no longer at Fleet. It seems unlikely that Hogarth could have made such a mistake, although Huggins himself was under active investigation by the Gaols Committee because of the many abuses during his tenure as warden. Huggins was a friend of Sir James Thornhill, and it is not likely that Hogarth would unnecessarily risk the anger of his father-in-law by incorrectly attributing the warden. Moreover, at the time of the sketch, Huggins was seventy-four years old. The warden drawn by Hogarth is clearly a younger man. When the inscription is compared with Hogarth's signature, the "Hs" are dissimilar. Thus, the caption "Huggins the Keeper" may have been added by a subsequent owner, but however it got there, Hogarth scholars believe the sketch to be a genuine, contemporary representation.[33]

Some years later, Hogarth gave the sketch to Horace Walpole. In 1842, it was purchased from Walpole's collection by T. S. Forman. C. Fairfax Murray eventually purchased the sketch and then gave it to the Fitzwilliam Museum at Cambridge University. Today, it is found there cataloged as No. 675, "Prisoner of the Fleet being examined before a Committee of the House of Commons."

Contemporary Hogarth painting of the Gaols Committee at Fleet Prison, circa 1729

Hogarth's decision to produce an oil canvas based on his sketch (Figure 9-6) may or may not have arisen from a request by a member of the Gaols Committee. In any event, a completed painting might generate the demand for additional copies from committee members. Only one oil on canvas—that in the National Portrait Gallery in London—has been found (see Figure 9-7), but some evidence exists that a second was also produced.

On November 5, 1729, eight months after the visit to Fleet, committee member Sir Archibald Grant commissioned a copy and paid Hogarth one-half of the fee in advance.[34] Grant later suffered bankruptcy and in 1732 was expelled from the House of Commons. Grant's financial problems presumably kept him from ever obtaining the painting, inasmuch as Hogarth's account ledger in January 1731 notes Grant's commission among "ye Pictures that Remain unfinnshd."[35] Whether Hogarth ever completed Grant's copy is unknown. The National Portrait Gallery has attempted to document the history of its version—cataloged as NPG 926—but even its experts are unable to establish whether NPG 926 is the canvas initiated by Grant.

Early in 1730, engraver George Vertue indicated he had observed a "well painted" representation "of the Gentlemen of the Committee of the House of Commons, to the jayles, setting upon the examination of those malefactors."[36] This probably was not the Grant commission, because in 1731 Hogarth still listed it as unfinished, and it may be this painting that now is in the collection of the National Portrait Gallery. A second copy is possible, but no hard evidence has surfaced attesting to the fact.

Certainly, Hogarth—about to take on the added financial responsibilities of marriage—must have hoped that additional copies would be ordered. Confirming this are the many changes in the final oil from the original eye-witness account. In his sketch, attention is focused on Oglethorpe's interrogation of Bambridge. Meanwhile, an animated committee in the background is inspecting firsthand the irons brought by the prison turnkey. Except for Oglethorpe, no committee member is recognizable, and in fact, several have their backs toward the artist. Contrast that feature with the final painting, in which each of the thirteen committee members is positioned to face the viewer. Not counting the prisoner and prison staff, Hogarth's painting amounted to thirteen miniature portraits on a single canvas. Likely, Hogarth hoped each committee member would commission a personal copy.

In the final painting, Hogarth also substituted the dramatic confrontation between the prisoner and Bambridge, where the prisoner stands looking directly at the warden, with a half-clothed, dark-skinned prisoner who kneels with his back to Bambridge before one of the committee members. Also, as noted in the discussion of Figure 9-6, the setting has been switched. The cells in the background and the manacled prisoner clearly lend a more somber air to the final version.

As to the identity of the characters in the painting, the first seated figure at the left unquestionably is the thirty-four-year-old Oglethorpe (see Figure 9-8). To the left stands Fleet warden Thomas Bambridge. Seated next to Oglethorpe is a figure who could be Colonel Richard Onslow or Sir John Percival.[37] The third seated figure to Oglethorpe's left is either transcribing or taking notes and is probably Lucas Kenn, clerk of the Gaols Committee. The standing figure third from the right is thought to be Sir Archibald Grant, who in November 1729 commissioned a copy of the painting. Likely, the committee member before whom the prisoner is kneeling is William Hucks and the standing figure at the far right Sir Edward Knatchbull. It is difficult to identify the other figures in the painting because there is no official list of which committee members actually participated in the inspection of Fleet.[38] Others shown in the painting are the prison turnkey (standing behind the committee), the kneeling prisoner in the foreground, and a faintly visible figure to the far left (presumably a prison staff member). There is speculation that the prisoner in the original sketch was Sir William Rich, but the character has been changed in the final version (see Figure 9-9), perhaps to represent Portuguese inmate Jacob Mendez Solas, one of the first debtors at Fleet to be manacled with irons.[39]

The National Portrait Gallery has substantiated that its Hogarth was purchased at Christie's in May 1796 by the fifth earl of Carlisle and was later given to the NPG in November 1892 by his descendant, the ninth earl. The 20⅛ × 27–inch canvas is cataloged as NPG 926—"The 'Committy of the house of Commons' (the Gaols Committee)."

Bull engraving of the Gaols Committee at Fleet Prison, circa 1830

This work by London engraver S. Bull (see Figure 9-10) was based on the Hogarth canvas (Figure 9-7). Date of completion is unknown, but probably it was in the 1830s when the only recorded exhibition of Bull's work occurred.[40] It has been reproduced in several books, including the 1900 edition of *Life and Works of William Hogarth*.

Verelst's contemporary painting of Oglethorpe presenting the Georgia Indians to the Trustees' Common Council, circa 1734–36

In June 1734, James Oglethorpe arrived in England escorting a delegation of Georgia Indians, including Yamacraw chief Tomochichi. On July 3, the Indians appeared at the Georgia Office in London for a special meeting with the Trustees' Common Council—a meeting this painting by William (Willem) Verelst (?–1756) recaptures (see Figure 9-11).[41]

London portrait painter Verelst was the son of a Viennese painter who had immigrated to England before his child's birth. Although not a major artist, he was "esteemed in his day."[42] No record exists as to how Verelst was selected to paint the visit of the Indians to the Trustees, but apparently the Trustees themselves commissioned the work. Neither is there proof that Verelst actually witnessed the meeting, but he must have been present to sketch the relative position of the participants. We do know that the painting took at least two—and perhaps as many as five—years to complete, during which time Verelst seems to have painted each character from life at separate sittings. For instance, in his diary, the earl of Egmont reported sitting for Verelst on April 23, May 13, and July 17, 1735, followed by another sitting on April 10, 1736, "so that he might finish my face."[43] Multiple sittings were a common practice for group paintings, since full and readily identifiable faces meant the possibility of additional income when group members ordered personal copies of the painting.

Verelst had another reason to ensure that every figure was clearly visible. The Trustees had agreed to divide the cost of Verelst's fee. An entry in Egmont's diary for March 5, 1739, reveals that Verelst had asked Trustee John White "to pay his share of the Trustee's picture," to which White had responded, "Yes, if you will cut out my face." Rather than indicating displeasure at Verelst's final product, Egmont attributed White's response to "the hatred he bears to us."[44] By 1739, White had so soured in his support for the Georgia experiment that he now said,

Figure 9-11. Contemporary painting by William Verelst of Oglethorpe presenting the Georgia Indians to the Trustees' Common Council, circa 1734–36. (Courtesy of The Henry Francis du Pont Winterthur Museum)

Figure 9-12. Copy by Alfred Edmund Dyer of Oglethorpe from the Verelst painting, circa 1927. (Courtesy of the National Portrait Gallery, London)

Figure 9-13. Bust of James Oglethorpe on the "Christian Hero" Prize Medal, 1737. (Courtesy of The Trustees of the British Museum)

Figure 9-14. Contemporary mezzotint of Oglethorpe, circa 1743–45, by Thomas
Burford. (Courtesy of The Trustees of the British Museum)

Figure 9-15. Copy of the Burford mezzotint of Oglethorpe, painted in 1940 by Lewis Gregg. (Courtesy of the Atlanta Historical Society)

"if we may have a peace with Spain by giving up Georgia, it were a good thing."[45]

To ensure that each of the twenty-four Trustees' faces was visible, Verelst ignored certain laws of perspective. At first glance, it appears that some Trustees in the back are standing on raised platforms. Closer inspection, however, reveals that all are sitting or standing around a long table. That the resulting perspective in the final painting was technically impossible was less important to Verelst than his need to have each Trustee clearly portrayed. As to when it was painted, Verelst undoubtedly began preliminary portraits of the individual characters about the time of the July 3, 1734, meeting. Egmont sat for Verelst in 1735 and 1736, and as late as May 1739 White still had not paid his share of Verelst's fee, meaning completion might not have occurred until 1737 or 1738.

The painting presumably hung in the Georgia Office as late as 1752, the year the Trustees returned their charter to the Crown. In that year or shortly before, the remaining Trustees gave it to Sir Anthony Ashley Cooper, the fourth earl of Shaftesbury, a fellow Trustee noted for his hard work on behalf of the Georgia colony. A contemporary inscription on the frame states: "A Representation of the Audience given by the Trustees for Establishing the Colony of Georgia in America, to Tomo Chachi Mico of Yamacran and his Indians on the 3rd day of July in the Year of Our Lord 1734." Also listed on the frame are the names of the twenty-four Trustees who were shown in the painting, with a faint number painted on the cuff or sleeve of each Trustee to identify them. Also written on the frame is "Gift of Trustees to 4th Earl of Shaftesbury."

Verelst's rendering remained in the collection of the earl of Shaftesbury at Saint Giles House, Wimborne, Dorset, until purchased by American Henry Francis du Pont on December 10, 1931. In 1956, the painting became part of the collection of the Henry Francis du Pont Winterthur Museum in Delaware, where it is found today. The museum had minor restoration and retouching done to the $40\frac{1}{2} \times 60\frac{3}{8}$–inch canvas in 1967. Today, it is cataloged as No. 56.567, "Trustees of Georgia." In recognition of Georgia's semiquincentenary in 1983, Winterthur allowed the painting to be featured on the cover of Southern Bell telephone directories issued in Georgia in December 1982. Also, the painting was brought to the state in 1983 for public exhibition in Savannah and Atlanta.

Dyer copy of Oglethorpe from the Verelst painting, circa 1927

This likeness frequently is used to portray Oglethorpe as a young man (see Figure 9-12). Actually it is a painting done circa 1927 by London artist Alfred Edmund Dyer in which he faithfully copied the head and shoulders of Oglethorpe from Verelst's painting of the Trustees' Common Council (Figure 9-11)—at which time James would have been approaching his thirty-eighth birthday.

Although not critically acclaimed as an artist, Dyer had an active practice copying historical portraits. He may have heard of—or been contacted by—Oglethorpe University president Thornwell Jacobs, who in 1923 gained considerable notoriety in England based on his efforts to locate Oglethorpe's grave. During that visit, Jacobs also searched for Oglethorpe portraits, and Dyer capitalized on this interest by painting a head and shoulders enlargement of Oglethorpe from the Verelst original and a copy of Hogarth's Gaols Committee for Oglethorpe University. No records survive at Oglethorpe University, where the two Dyer works hang today, to verify when they were completed, but as late as 1932 Jacobs was still in contact with Dyer. The likely chronology of events was that hearing of Jacobs's interest, Dyer located the Verelst painting, then in the possession of the earl of Shaftesbury at Saint Giles. At the time, he painted the small oval portrait of Oglethorpe, now in the National Portrait Gallery's collection in London, and then painted a second, larger copy for Jacobs. Or, possibly the sequence of Dyer portraits was reversed. Although the NPG version is not dated, it was purchased from Dyer by the gallery in 1927. It is an oval oil on panel, 5½ × 4½ inches, cataloged as NPG 2153a, "James Edward Oglethorpe."

Oglethorpe's bust on the "Christian Hero" Prize Medal, 1737

The December 1735 issue of *Gentleman's Magazine* contained an announcement by editor Edward Cave (who used the nom de plume

"Sylvanus Urban") that his magazine was sponsoring a new contest. Prizes would be offered for the four best poems entitled, "The Christian Hero." Contestants had until June 11, 1736, to submit their entries. The first-place winner would be awarded a gold medal that would feature on one side a representation of the head of Lady Elizabeth Hastings, who devoted her life to charitable work; the reverse side would depict the head of James Oglethorpe (see Figure 9-13).

Between June 1734 and October 1735, Oglethorpe was back in England with a delegation of Georgia Indians. In addition to the recognition he had received for prison reform and establishing a new British colony in America, to which oppressed Salzburgers might go, it now was widely publicized that the Indians desired to be instructed in the Christian faith. Oglethorpe's likeness on a "Christian Hero" medal, therefore, was a popular choice, and indeed several of the poems entered in the contest were about, or at least made reference to, him.[46] Lady Hastings declined to be memorialized, so the likeness of Archbishop Tillotson was substituted. Because the prize medal presents a very important—but seldom seen—full frontal contemporary head and shoulders of Oglethorpe, it is important to establish when the sitting occurred.

Oglethorpe might have been sketched during his first return visit to England (June 1734–October 1735), but it seems unlikely bcause he departed London for Georgia on October 14, 1735, two months before the contest's announcement. More likely, Oglethorpe sat for the medallist shortly after his second return to London on January 6, 1737; indeed, the medal bears the date 1737. Although the contest had ended in June 1736, the winning entry was not announced until May 1738.[47] The delay in awarding the prize medal—almost two years after the contest's end—suggests that the medallist was forced to await Oglethorpe's return to complete his work. On this visit Oglethorpe remained in London until June 1738, but the sitting probably occurred before the summer of 1737. In June 1737, he was named commander-in-chief of the military forces in Georgia and South Carolina and two months later was commissioned colonel of his own regiment to defend Georgia. Yet the Oglethorpe shown on the prize medal is wearing open-collared civilian clothing instead of the uniform and armor characteristic of portraits of military officers.

The medallist portrayed James as a rather handsome figure with much more sharply defined facial features—particularly his chin—than in the earlier Verelst painting. The wig, however, is similar. Although shorter than the full wig, and confined to falling behind the shoulders, even this length wig soon would be unfashionable.

Decades later, just after Oglethorpe's death, the July 1785 issue of *Gentleman's Magazine* contained a letter asking if the Christian Hero medal had ever been struck. The editor's response was that several medals had been struck, after which the die was broken.[48]

Gold, silver, and bronze versions of the forty-two-millimeter diameter medal today are found in the British Museum. The medal is unsigned, but the museum attributes Jean Dassier as probable medallist. Dassier (1676–1763) was born in Geneva, where he worked in the mint before traveling to London in 1728. He produced a great number of medals during his career and was later characterized as "one of the greatest of eighteenth century Medallists."[49]

Burford's contemporary mezzotint of Oglethorpe, circa 1743–45

This mezzotint by Thomas Burford (1710–70) shows a three-quarter length standing portrait of Oglethorpe with the inscription, "His Excellency James Oglethorpe Esq. General & Commander in Chief of all his Majesties Forces in Carolina and Georgia, and Colonel of one of His Majesties Rigiments of Foot &c." (see Figure 9-14).

Oglethorpe's promotion from colonel to brigadier general did not occur until September 1743. In September 1745, he was ordered to take a force to the north of England to counter an invasion by the Stuart Pretender, but, because of controversy centering upon his strategy in the 1745 campaign, he was subjected to a court-martial. Although exonerated, it is doubtful that so complimentary an illustration would have been published after the fall of 1745, because his reputation as a hero was now tarnished. Therefore it is believed that the Burford mezzotint must have been completed between 1743 and 1745.[50] Possibly the work was completed earlier, for in June 1737 Oglethorpe received the appointment of general and commander-in-chief of the military forces in Georgia and South Carolina, followed by a commission as colonel of his own regiment in late August 1737.[51] Inasmuch as he remained in England until July of the next year, it would have been possible for Burford to have completed his mezzotint then. However, Oglethorpe had done nothing to distinguish himself as a military figure at that point, and in all probability the work was completed after his return to England in 1743.

Although engravings and mezzotints were commonly based on other artists' works, Burford is known to have worked from life on some occasions.[52] An engraving based on another artist's original usually would acknowledge both artist and engraver. This mezzotint lists only Burford's name, so it is likely that he worked from life. The National Portrait Gallery catalog indicates "after an unknown original." Burford may have sketched Oglethorpe and then added the battle armor and helmet to impart heroic dimensions to the portrait. Also attributed to the artist's imagination are the fortress atop the hill to the left of Oglethorpe—possibly intended to suggest Fort Frederica—and the two horsemen in the background to the right. Burford's prints were issued between 1741 and 1765, and in 1745 he published a set of plates of contemporary and historical figures, so this may have been the collection of which the Oglethorpe mezzotint was a part.[53] It is 12½ × 9¾ inches in size. Copies are found in a number of collections, including the British Museum and the Telfair Art Museum in Savannah.

Artistically, Burford's effort is not a particularly noteworthy rendering (for instance, the eyes appear disproportionately large). The armor and cape are similar to those shown in other paintings. The definition of the chin is more similar to the Christian Hero medal image. The heavily curled wig seems shorter than in prior renderings, reflecting contemporary English fashion.

What is significant about Burford's mezzotint is that it represents the first nonoil individual portrait of Oglethorpe. Mezzotint and engraved art could be reproduced in quantity, giving English citizens the first opportunity to view the hero who had so recently turned back the Spanish in Georgia. It also gave engravers an image that in turn could be used to produce their own adaptations. Thus, Burford's work became the basis for Ravenet's engraving of Oglethorpe (see Figure 9-16), which in turn was used by Greatbach (see Figure 9-17), who in turn was copied by Burt (see Figure 9-18), and so on. At the same time, Burford's original rendering has become one of the most recognized and widely utilized portraits of Oglethorpe both in the United States and in England.

Gregg copy of the Burford mezzotint of Oglethorpe, 1940

In 1940, the Trust Company of Georgia sponsored a series of illustrations of famous Georgians. Atlanta artist Lewis Gregg painted a color copy of the Burford mezzotint in oil (see Figure 9-15). That canvas is now in the possession of the Atlanta Historical Society. Interestingly, Gregg lowered the height of the hill and substituted Fort Frederica for the two riders in the Burford version.

Ravenet engraving of Oglethorpe, circa 1757

This familiar engraving was done by Simon François Ravenet (1706–74), who came to London from France in 1750 (see Figure 9-16). It first appears as a $3\frac{5}{8}$–inch diameter illustration in Tobias Smollett's original edition of his *History of England*, published in 1757.[54] It is likely Ravenet produced the engraving specifically for use in Smollett's book. Although he reversed the direction of Oglethorpe's head and placed the eyes in better proportion to the dimensions of the face, it is apparent that Burford's mezzotint was the model. Oglethorpe would have been sixty years of age at the time Ravenet produced his likeness.

Greatbach engraving of Oglethorpe, circa 1847

This widely used representation of James Oglethorpe was the work of William Greatbach (1802–ca. 1885), an English engraver active during the mid-nineteenth century (see Figure 9-17).[55] We do not yet know when and for what publication it was intended, but its first use apparently was as the frontispiece to William Bacon Stevens's *A History of Georgia*, published in 1847. Beneath the $3\frac{11}{16} \times 2\frac{7}{8}$–inch engraving in that book is the notation, "From an original Engraving in the possession of Geo. Wymberly Jones." In Jones's impressive array of Georgiana

GENERAL OGLETHORPE.

Figure 9-16. Engraving of Oglethorpe by Simon François Ravenet, circa 1757. (Courtesy of Hargrett Rare Book and Manuscript Library, University of Georgia Libraries)

Figure 9-17. Engraving of Oglethorpe by William Greatbach, circa 1847. (Courtesy of Hargrett Rare Book and Manuscript Library, University of Georgia Libraries)

Figure 9-18. Engraving of Oglethorpe by Charles K. Burt, circa 1879. (Courtesy of Hargrett Rare Book and Manuscript Library, University of Georgia Libraries)

Figure 9-19. Possible contemporary portrait of Oglethorpe, unknown date. (Courtesy of The Chatham Club, De Soto Hilton Hotel, Savannah, Georgia)

Figure 9-20. Mary Bryan and Nicholas Woloshuk with painting shown in Figure 9-19. (Courtesy of *Atlanta Journal and Constitution*)

was an original plate of Greatbach's Oglethorpe, for in the acknowledgments of *A History of Georgia*, Stevens expresses appreciation to Jones for providing the plate of Oglethorpe's bust used in the book.[56] At the University of Georgia, where Jones's collection (now designated the De Renne Collection) is housed, there is an exact duplicate of the Greatbach engraving printed alone on heavy stock with no identifying credits. The 1931 catalog of the De Renne Collection makes no reference to the original plate, although the plates of several other Oglethorpes are noted. The location of the original of the Greatbach plate is not known.

Although the direction of the head has been reversed, back to that of Burford's mezzotint, and the wig changed, there are so many similarities between the Ravenet and Greatbach as to suggest that the latter was copied from the former. Greatbach replaced the curly, shoulder-length wig portrayed by Ravenet with a shorter one, with the hair pulled back into a pigtail—a style popular after the 1740s. His attentiveness to contemporary fashion, however, may have been at the expense of Oglethorpe's actual preference, for several contemporary portraits show him wearing unstylishly long wigs. In any event, Greatbach produced a handsome countenance, helping account for its wide use.

Burt engraving of Oglethorpe, circa 1879

This likeness by American engraver Charles K. Burt (1823–92) is the third in a set of related engravings based on the Burford original or its subsequent copies (see Figure 9-18). It was prepared for use in volume 3 of William Cullen Bryant's and Sidney Howard Gay's *Popular History of the United States*, first published in 1879. In the book, Burt's work is credited as "From the contemporary engraving reprinted in Stevens' *A History of Georgia*," which, of course, is the Greatbach version.[57] Burt's engraving has been widely used since its first appearance.

Possible contemporary portrait of Oglethorpe, unknown date

Considerable mystery and intrigue surround this painting (see Figure 9-19). In fact, we are not even certain that it is a representation of

James Oglethorpe, although Salzburger scholar George Fenwick Jones at one point believed it to be a long-missing portrait of Oglethorpe painted in 1736 by the servant of Philipp Georg Friedrich von Reck.[58] Despite a lack of pronounced facial resemblance with other portraits of Georgia's founder, this painting has been included because of a possibility that it is an authentic Oglethorpe icon.

In the Salzburger *Detailed Reports* for October 13, 1736, Boltzius noted that von Reck's servant, Christian Muller, had completed a "beautifully elaborated portrait" of Oglethorpe.[59] In a subsequent entry for November 7, Boltzius recorded that the portrait had been presented to Georgia's leader by Muller.[60]

In 1972, George Fenwick Jones and Marie Hahn published their translation of the Salzburger diary for 1736, and they refer to the painting mentioned in the November 7, 1736, entry as "a portrait now lost or unknown."[61] However, Jones already suspected that a portrait for sale in Atlanta in 1963—Figure 9-19—might be the lost work of Muller. Jones had a photograph of the newly discovered painting and tried unsuccessfully to locate the owner for additional information. Nevertheless, because of similarities with other likenesses of Oglethorpe, Jones concluded that the newfound portrait probably was the long-missing work of Muller.[62]

In the early 1960s, an unsigned and undated portrait of a military officer, presumably British, was purchased in Houston, Texas, at an estate sale. The late owner had been a local interior decorator who had bought the painting while on a trip to France. In 1963, Nicholas Woloshuk, a Houston gallery owner, purchased the same painting for $1,500 from the new owner. Woloshuk believed that it was possibly a contemporary portrait of General Oglethorpe. Tests on the paint pigment plus inspection of the canvas weave convinced him that it was of eighteenth-century origin.[63] But, was it of Oglethorpe?

Woloshuk, a self-proclaimed art sleuth, studied known portraits of the General and also sent photographs of the painting to the Georgia State Archives, Oglethorpe University, the University of Georgia, and the Georgia Historical Society. Enough interest was created by these inquiries for him to bring the painting to Georgia, where he hoped it would be purchased.

In late August 1963, Woloshuk arrived in Atlanta with his new acquisition. First, he contacted Mary Bryan, then director of the Georgia State Archives. Bryan and her assistant, Carroll Hart, went to Woloshuk's motel room to inspect the painting. Also present were a newspaper reporter and photographer to record the story of how Oglethorpe's portrait had returned to Georgia (see Figure 9-20).[64] Both Bryan and Hart believed it to be an old painting, but neither felt qualified to judge whether it was an authentic Oglethorpe likeness.[65] Consulting with Secretary of State Ben Fortson (under whose jurisdiction the State Archives belonged), they decided—at least for the time being—not to buy it. Disappointed, Woloshuk contacted other potential buyers but with no success. He then decided to leave the painting on loan with the archives, an action motivated by his hope that the state would eventually purchase the portrait to hang at the new State Archives Building, then under construction.[66]

For almost four years, the canvas remained in the custody of archives officials, apparently without being publicly displayed. Exactly what happened next is unclear. For some reason the archives released the portrait on March 2, 1967, to a man who represented himself as the attorney for Dan Gibbs of Dallas, Texas.[67] No record remains at the archives as to the basis of Gibbs's claim, and former director Carroll Hart cannot recall the circumstances of the release. Recently contacted in Santa Fe, New Mexico, Woloshuk remembers selling the painting, at a token price, while it was still in the custody of the Georgia Archives. The purchaser, a friend in Dallas, had agreed that he would then donate it to the state of Georgia and take a tax write-off. He has no recollection of a Dan Gibbs but does recognize the name of the man who picked up the painting in 1967. That man was not an attorney, according to Woloshuk, but rather a dealer in carpets and rugs.[68]

Where the painting went after March 1967 is unknown. At some point thereafter, Atlanta banker Mills B. Lane was approached by a man attempting to sell a portrait of General Oglethorpe. Lane does not recall the date, nor the identity of the solicitor, but does remember that without hesitation he turned down the initial asking price of $50,000.[69] Lane was then asked to make an offer. Not expecting the man to accept, Lane offered $1,500 and suddenly found himself to be the painting's new owner. When he later retired to Savannah and organized the Chatham Club atop the De Soto Hilton Hotel, Lane presented the portrait to the club, where it hangs today.

Could Figure 9-19—with its mystery—be an authentic canvas of

Oglethorpe? It came from France instead of England, but then two of James's sisters, Eleanor and Fanny, had married Frenchmen and lived and reared their families there. Moreover, Elizabeth Oglethorpe's will bequeathed Westbrook Manor, James's large Godalming home, and its possessions to Eugene, Marquis de Bellegarde, great-nephew of James.

But, is this a portrait of Oglethorpe? The armor is similar to that in other portraits of him. There are minor differences, such as the greater number of overlapping plates between the shoulder and elbow, but these can result from the eighteenth-century practice of painting the face from life and adding such features as military armor later.[70] The baton —known as a staff or truncheon—in the subject's right hand suggests a commanding officer and can also be seen in Burford's mezzotint of Oglethorpe (Figure 9-14), but the painting is notably less animated and heroic.

Troubling aspects of the portrait are the subject's wig and facial features. The height of the wig on top, plus its length, descending over the front of the right shoulder, is more appropriate to fashion of the 1720s than of the 1740s. The wig is also much darker than that in any known contemporary rendering of Oglethorpe, although Figure 9-21 suggests that at some time after his return to England he apparently abandoned white and heavily powdered wigs.

Lack of attention to facial detail in this portrait contrasts with the more sharply delineated chin in Figures 9-13 and 9-14. Of course, the most characteristic feature in Oglethorpe portraits is his prominent nose. Here, because of the direction of the subject's head and the full light on his face (which means an absence of shadow detail around the nose), it is difficult to gauge the length of the subject's nose. In comparison, see Figure 9-21. Whether the painting depicted in Figure 9-19 is a contemporary portrait of Oglethorpe is open to debate. A recent examination by an art expert confirmed Woloshuk's findings in 1963.[71] In terms of pigment and canvas weave, it appears to be from the eighteenth century, but there is evidence of more recent touching up. The portrait likely is from Oglethorpe's era, but we simply may never be able to prove its authenticity as a likeness of the General.

As to the final question—is it Muller's long-lost portrait?—the answer has to be that most likely it is not. The subject in Figure 9-19 is a military officer of high rank; yet at the time Muller presented his portrait, Oglethorpe was a civilian. Not until 1737 did he receive dual commissions as commanding officer of the forces of Georgia and South Carolina and colonel of an infantry regiment.[72] Muller, at the very least, would not have seen Oglethorpe in all his military finery.

One possible answer to the fate of Muller's painting is provided by Hugh McCall, who in 1811 wrote that while in Georgia, Oglethorpe gave Noble Jones a gift. It was a portrait of Oglethorpe "in a neat frame, representing his Indian pupil standing by his side reading."[73] McCall, however, records that the painting was lost in December 1778 when the British captured Savannah.

If Figure 9-19 is a portrait of Oglethorpe painted from life, it likely occurred following his return to England from Georgia in 1743. The fuller face suggests a sitting sometime between the Burford mezzotint and the oval portrait (Figure 9-21) now in the possession of Oglethorpe University.

Contemporary portrait of Oglethorpe, unknown date

In the spring of 1932, Oglethorpe University president Thornwell Jacobs received a letter from a friend connected with the art business in London stating that a portrait had been brought in for cleaning and that it appeared to be a genuine contemporary portrait of Oglethorpe (see Figure 9-21). The owner was willing to sell the painting for £1,000, the letter continued, and Jacobs was to indicate immediately if he were interested. Jacobs considered it important enough to leave right away for England.[74]

In London, Jacobs had the portrait photographed and then took copies to experts at the British Museum and National Portrait Gallery, where he was assured that it did appear authentic. On July 7, 1932, he had Alfred Dyer, a London artist who had copied several paintings of Oglethorpe (see discussion of Figure 9-12), inspect the newly discovered portrait. Dyer concluded that the portrait appeared genuine, particularly because of the physical likeness to other portraits of the General. On the following day, Jacobs had two specialists in old prints and engravings also examine the work. They agreed with Dyer: it appeared to be an authentic portrait of General Oglethorpe.[75]

Jacobs contacted the portrait's owner, Captain Carstairs, in an effort

Figure 9-21. Contemporary portrait of Oglethorpe, unknown date. (Courtesy of Oglethorpe University)

Figure 9-22. United States postage stamp, 1933, showing an engraved version of the portrait shown in Figure 9-21.

Figure 9-23. New York artist Charles F. Naegele's 1933 copy in oil of portrait shown in Figure 9-21. (Courtesy of Corpus Christi College, Oxford University)

to learn more about the painting's history.[76] Carstairs submitted the following written statement:

> To Thornwell Jacobs, Esquire. With regard to the painting: I wish to put on record that to the best of my belief it is a painting of General Oglethorpe, that it came into my possession by private bequest on the death of an elderly maiden lady, my first cousin once removed, at the age of 81, and that I have always heard it referred to in the family as a portrait of Oglethorpe: I know that this portrait was left to my cousin by her mother who died at the age of 98: The only point I wish to reiterate is that to the best of my belief this painting is a genuine portrait of General Oglethorpe.[77]

In a separate note, Carstairs indicated that the recipient of the portrait was a lady of his family of whom the General was very fond.[78]

When writing his autobiography over a decade later, Jacobs recalled the owner's account a little differently: "that it had been left him by the death of a maiden aunt, that she, in turn, inherited it from her grandmother, that it had been presented to a member of his family who, as a young girl, was the sweetheart of the General whose portrait it was."[79] However, the first account quoted above should be considered more accurate, because it is found in recently discovered correspondence by Jacobs from 1932 that quotes Carstairs directly.

The only other explanation given for the history of the portrait is found in a July 2, 1934, United Press release from London quoted in the *Atlanta Constitution.* Jacobs and Amos Ettinger had just returned to London from presenting a copy of the oval portrait to Oglethorpe's alma mater, Corpus Christi College at Oxford. While in England they also visited Oglethorpe Hall, the ancestral home of the Oglethorpes in Yorkshire, and Westbrook, the Surrey boyhood home of James. According to the newspaper account, the disputed portrait was discovered in a tiny cottage in Scotland. Moreover, "Dr. Jacobs has established the fact that it was given by Oglethorpe himself to a young Scotch girl with whom he was in love and that it passed down through her family from generation to generation still hanging on the same wall until it was found by Dr. Jacobs in 1932."[80]

Had Jacobs and Ettinger, during their 1934 pilgrimage, discovered new details about Oglethorpe's romantic life, as the newspaper account might suggest? Apparently not, inasmuch as Jacobs's later account about the discovery of the portrait makes no mention of a young lady from Scotland. More conclusively, Amos Ettinger, who two years later published the standard volume on Oglethorpe's full life, makes no reference in that work to substantiate the United Press story in any way.

Almost certainly, the painting was done following Oglethorpe's final return to England from Georgia in September 1743. As represented in Figure 9-21, Oglethorpe seems to be in his mid-forties or older, given the tendency of many artists to flatter their subjects. Compare the fuller face and slight double chin of this figure with the face of the forty-year-old Oglethorpe depicted six years earlier on the Christian Hero prize medal (Figure 9-13).

How much after 1743 the portrait could have been painted is speculative. If the oval portrait were a gift to a "lady . . . of whom the general was very fond," as Carstairs wrote, it would likely have been prior to September 14, 1744, for on that day, after a very brief courtship, a marriage license was issued to James Oglethorpe and Elizabeth Wright, with the wedding ceremony held the next day. During the year between his return to England and his marriage, although extremely busy on a host of matters, Oglethorpe seems to have at last found the time for courtship after a lengthy bachelorhood. The August 1744 issue of *Gentleman's Magazine* announced his marriage to Elizabeth Sambrooke, sister of Sir Jeremy Sambrooke.[81] Obviously this reference was a mistake but suggests that Elizabeth Sambrooke could have been the young lady to whom James bestowed his portrait. Another explanation is that the recipient was not a sweetheart but rather a female friend of both James and Elizabeth. The General was something of a lady's man in his declining years, even though the Oglethorpes seem to have had a close relationship throughout their marriage.[82] Hannah Moore, almost fifty years his junior, met Oglethorpe in 1784 and apparently was somewhat taken with the old hero. In 1785, she wrote her sister, "I am going to flirt a couple of hours with my beau, General Oglethorpe."[83] After his death, Elizabeth Montagu—a prominent London social leader (and widow)—referred to him as "my old Love the General."[84]

Other romantic or friendly liaisons may have occurred prior to or during his marriage to Elizabeth Wright, but it may also be that the Carstairs family tradition was in error. If so, the oval portrait could have been painted after his 1744 marriage to hang at Cranham Hall. As they had no children, it might have passed into unknown hands

after Elizabeth's death in 1787. Or, it could have been claimed by
Mrs. Dickinson, whom Elizabeth had named as executrix and residual
legatee of her estate. A problem with the latter explanation, however,
is that William Bray, who later recorded that the three-quarter-length
portraits of James and Elizabeth were in Mrs. Dickinson's possession,
makes no mention of the half-length oval portrait. The fact that the
portrait emerges in the possession of Captain Carstairs, who cited the
family tradition linking it to Oglethorpe, presents a stronger case, particularly in the absence of any evidence to suggest an alternative story.

The 28½ × 23-inch oval portrait is unsigned, with no hint as to
whom the artist might have been. It is a very fine portrait and commonly accepted as the most important single surviving likeness of the
General. Since its purchase in 1932, the portrait has hung at Oglethorpe University, where today it is found in the president's office. The
original asking price had been £1,000, but Carstairs reduced the price
significantly when he found it would be hung at the university named
after the subject of the painting.[85] Jacobs purchased the portrait using
money willed to the university by a woman who had stipulated that her
bequeath be used for purchasing art.

To mark the bicentennial of Georgia in 1933, the United States Post
Office issued a commemorative first class stamp featuring an engraved
version of the newly acquired oval portrait (see Figure 9-22). Thornwell Jacobs then had an exact copy in oil made by New York artist
Charles F. Naegele (see Figure 9-23). As it turned out, James Oglethorpe's alma mater, Corpus Christi College at Oxford, did not have
a portrait of one of its most prominent students, and Jacobs wanted
to rectify this omission. Jacobs personally gave Naegele's copy to Corpus Christi president Richard Livingston at special ceremonies on June
12, 1934. Also in attendance were future Supreme Court Justice Felix
Frankfurter and Oglethorpe scholar Amos Ettinger.[86]

Sketch of Oglethorpe at age eighty-eight, by Ireland

The last surviving representation of Oglethorpe was sketched from
life by Samuel Ireland (?–1800) on February 18, 1785, at the auction of
the library of Oglethorpe's late friend, Dr. Samuel Johnson. Made into
an engraving by Ireland, it was published by I. Cary on September 9,
1785, just three months after Oglethorpe's death (see Figure 9-24).

Figure 9-24. Samuel Ireland's 1785 sketch of Oglethorpe at age eighty-eight. (Courtesy of Hargrett Rare Book and Manuscript Library, University of Georgia Libraries)

E.tched by J.P. &c

Genl Oglethorpe, aged 102.

Sketched at Dr Johnson's Gate June 30 1785. Vid Pennant

Published by C.G. Myer Soho

Figure 9-25. Engraving of the Samuel Ireland sketch of Oglethorpe. (Courtesy of Oglethorpe University)

Figure 9-26. Copy of engraving shown in Figure 9-25. (Courtesy of Eudora DeRenne Roebling)

Figure 9-27. Portrait of Oglethorpe by C. R. Parker, 1826. The portrait is at the Georgia Capitol.

Figure 9-28. Monument of Oglethorpe by sculptor Daniel Chester French, 1910.

Beneath the sketch is a caption: "Died 30th June 1785 Aged 102 said to be the oldest General in Europe——Sketch'd from Life at the sale of Dr Johnsons books Feby 18, 1785 where the Genl was reading a book he had purchas'd without spectacles——In 1706 he had an Ensigns commission in the Guards & remember'd to have shot snipes in Conduit mead where Conduit Street now stands."

That Ireland overstated Oglethorpe's age by fourteen years arises from the mystery then existing as to his actual age. Oglethorpe was reluctant to reveal his true date of birth, perhaps even enjoying the notoriety occasioned by the popular belief that he was approaching the century mark. The confusion arises from the fact that another James was born to Theophilus and Eleanor in 1689, but that child died within his first year. Later, they chose to use the name again for their son born in 1696. Ireland also is in error on the date of the ensign's commission: it was 1709 rather than 1706.

The 7¾ × 6½-inch sketch—found in many collections—is not an attractive rendering of the aged general, and it borders on caricature. Yet, Ireland had no reason to paint him in an unflattering light, and we may assume that he drew Oglethorpe fairly accurately. Samuel Rogers, who at age twenty-two met Oglethorpe at the sale depicted by Ireland, described him as "very, very old, the flesh of his face like parchment."[87] Perhaps, this was simply the stark contrast between youth and advanced age, for Horace Walpole the next month wrote about Oglethorpe: "His eyes, ears, articulation, limbs, and memory would suit a boy, if a boy could recollect a century backwards. His teeth are gone; he is a shadow, and a wrinkled one; but his spirits and his spirit are in full bloom."[88]

What Ireland preserved was a final look at Georgia's founder in the twilight of his life (Oglethorpe died four months later). Yet, it is a fitting one, for rather than showing a frail, invalid figure, we see a man who retained his faculties to the end. Although missing his teeth, as evidenced by the protruding chin, his eyesight still serves him without a need for glasses.

The Ireland sketch has been the basis for more copies and variations than any other version. One very early version etched by "T.P." and published by C. G. Dyer, Soho, has Oglethorpe facing the opposite direction from Ireland's original (see Figure 9-25). The 6 × 4½-inch engraving presents a somewhat more flattering and better executed rendering of the aged general. Copies of this engraving are found in the Oglethorpe University Library and in the De Renne Collection at the University of Georgia Library. Figure 9-26 shows a copy of the "T.P." engraving from an undated zinc plate currently owned by Eudora DeRenne Roebling. Numerous nineteenth-century American engravers copied Ireland's original for use in historical accounts about Georgia or American history.

Oglethorpe portrait (1826) at the Georgia Capitol

General Lafayette's triumphant visit to Georgia in the spring of 1825 concluded with a visit to Georgia's statehouse in Milledgeville. Shortly thereafter Georgia lawmakers adopted a resolution authorizing Governor George M. Troup to procure portraits of General Lafayette and George Washington to be hung in the senate chamber, portraits of Thomas Jefferson and Benjamin Franklin for the house chamber, and a portrait of General Oglethorpe for the governor's office (see Figure 9-27).[89] Consequently, artist C. R. Parker was contacted and agreed to paint the five portraits for a fee of $600 each. Although it is not known in which order they were painted, all were completed by 1826, and on December 5, 1826, $3,000 was appropriated from the state treasury to pay Parker for his efforts.[90] Following designation of Atlanta as Georgia's new capital city in 1868, the large 6 × 10–foot oil portraits were transferred from Milledgeville. Today, all five hang in the rotunda of the capitol. A comparison of Parker's work with Ireland's sketch shows Parker's indebtedness, but he did alter the setting of the portrait and placed in the General's hand a large book opened to a map of Georgia.[91]

Daniel Chester French monument of James Oglethorpe

For some time, Savannah citizens and patriotic societies had sought a monument in that city to commemorate the founder of Georgia. To that end, the Oglethorpe Monument Association was incorporated in May 1901 and a fund-raising campaign initiated. The association was successful in building support within the Georgia General Assembly, and on August 20, 1906, legislators appropriated $15,000 for the monument, half to be spent in 1907 and half in 1908, providing that the association could raise at least $5,000. Chippewa Square was designated the site for its location, "the title to said square being owned by the State."[92]

The governor appointed a seven-member commission to oversee the project. Daniel Chester French was chosen as sculptor and New York architect Henry Bacon was picked to design the pedestal and base. A few years later French and Bacon again teamed up to produce the Lincoln Memorial in Washington, D.C.

French examined the variety of existing portraits and engravings of Oglethorpe and also studied contemporary military uniforms of Oglethorpe's era. The image he chose to portray was not Oglethorpe the colonizer but Oglethorpe the military commander. Undoubtedly it is the most handsome and heroic rendering of Georgia's founder, who is depicted facing southward, looking toward the Spanish (see Figure 9-28). French accurately portrayed Oglethorpe in the military dress of the 1740s—with a cuirass (shoulder and breast plates), sword, waistcoat, high boots, and tricorn hat.[93] In contrast to the tightly curled wig portrayed by Burford (Figure 9-14), French selected a wig similar to that worn by Oglethorpe in 1737 (Figure 9-13). The nine-foot bronze statue of Georgia's founder stands atop a pedestal on which is carved a portion of the charter of the colony. A lion holding a shield is located on each corner of the base. On these shields are found Oglethorpe's coat of arms and the seals of the colony, the state, and the city of Savannah. Construction of the monument proved more expensive than anticipated, and the city of Savannah agreed to match the state's $15,000 appropriation, with an additional $10,000 raised by the Oglethorpe Monument Association, Society of Colonial Dames, Daughters of the American Revolution, and other groups. The unveiling of the monument occurred on November 23, 1910, at ceremonies to which citizens of Savannah and the state, members of patriotic societies, and a variety of officials—including the governors of South Carolina, Florida, Mississippi, and Alabama—were invited.

Nonextant Portraits of James Oglethorpe

At least three, and possibly five, portraits of Oglethorpe have been lost. The oldest is the 1718 portrait reportedly done in Belgrade and later given to James Habersham in Savannah (see discussion of Figure 9-

1). Next we know of a portrait that Oglethorpe gave his Indian friend, Tomochichi, which was seen by John Tanner, a Haslemere neighbor of Oglethorpe who visited Georgia during 1735 and 1736.[94] Two other missing portraits were identified earlier in the discussion of Figure 9-19: the 1736 portrait by Christian Muller and the pre-1743 portrait reportedly given by Oglethorpe to Noble Jones, which was later lost when the British captured Savannah.

These last two paintings could be the same, as there is no record of what happened to the 1736 work or where Oglethorpe obtained the portrait he gave Jones. There is even the possibility that the last three paintings are one and the same. We know that Muller had completed his painting prior to October 13, 1736, and that he apparently hoped to gain Oglethorpe's influence to return to London. Boltzius records that Muller "is going back to London with said Captain Thomson with the permission and help of Mr. Oglethorpe, which he hopes to attain by presenting his beautifully elaborated portrait."[95] Muller presented the gift soon after its completion, as Boltzius's entry for November 7 indicates that after giving Oglethorpe the portrait, Muller had taught children for several weeks in Purrysburg.[96] This means that the portrait was given to Oglethorpe not later than October 23, one month before Oglethorpe, Tanner, and Muller departed Georgia for England (November 23, 1736).[97] Perhaps realizing that he would be in England for an indefinite time, Oglethorpe may have presented Muller's portrait to Tomochichi. Tanner, who had spent considerable time among the Indians, likely visited Tomochichi prior to his departure, and it could have been then that he observed the portrait. Upon Tomochichi's death three years later, the portrait could have been returned to Oglethorpe, who later gave it to Jones before his final departure from Georgia in 1743. Obviously, we can never prove whether the three written records refer to the same painting, but we must recognize the possibility that this could be the case.

The most important loss is an Oglethorpe portrait completed in 1780 by Sir Joshua Reynolds (1723–92). The duke of Rutland had commissioned a painting of the eighty-three-year-old general, and sittings began in March 1780. No records survive as to whether Oglethorpe approved of the likeness. Unfortunately, it and a number of other portraits by Reynolds perished in an 1816 fire at Belvoir Castle before a copy was engraved.[98]

Conclusion

The goal of this chapter—and indeed of all the chapters in this volume—was to undertake a new look at James Edward Oglethorpe on the 200th anniversary of his death. In the case of this iconography, that goal took on literal as well as figurative import.

Initially, I was convinced that awaiting liberation from a small Surrey or Essex antique shop was an unidentified, dusty portrait of a man in cuirass—undoubtedly a genuine Oglethorpe. Although no such portrait yet has been found, the search for Oglethorpe icons has not been in vain. Located in British museums were two representations of Georgia's founder that had escaped modern-day biographers. Also, a record was compiled of all known extant and nonextant images, thereby permitting a chance to view representations of Oglethorpe that span his adult life.

In addition to using resources traditionally consulted by historians, the iconography relied on investigations of art, fashion, and customs of the day. Thus it was possible to establish why Georgia's founder often was portrayed in military armor unlike that which he actually wore. Also, by studying the artist and events behind a particular painting —such as Hogarth's two renderings of the Gaols Committee—new insights were gained into both art and history.

Yet, in the end, a variety of mysteries remain. Artists were most active in capturing Oglethorpe's image during his involvement with prison reform and in the first decade of Georgia's existence. Few likenesses of Oglethorpe were taken after 1745, reflecting his declining role in the Georgia experiment, his 1746 court-martial, the loss of his seat in Parliament in 1754, and his mysterious absence from England between 1755 and 1761 (documented by Baine and Williams in chapter 7).

Nevertheless, true to his family motto—"Nescit Cedere"—Oglethorpe was not to be counted out; he soon returned to prominence in London social and literary circles. Following the death of one of his friends, Samuel Johnson, an auction was held in February 1785 to dispose of Johnson's library. In attendance was the eighty-eight-year-old Oglethorpe, as well as occasional artist Samuel Ireland. Ireland, likely aware that this might be one of the last chances to draw the aged general from life, quickly sketched Oglethorpe as he intently reviewed the auction's catalog. In four months, Oglethorpe was dead, but Ireland's sketch survived to become the most widely used and copied representation of Georgia's founder. Today, high above the rotunda floor within Georgia's state capitol hangs a painting based on Ireland's sketch. From that vantage point, thousands of visitors pass by daily, many pausing to look up and pay their respects to Georgia's founder.

Notes

Abbreviations

A few frequently cited sources have been abbreviated in the Notes as follows:

Coll. GHS	*Collections of the Georgia Historical Society*
CRG	*Colonial Records of Georgia*
Diary of Percival	R. A. Roberts, ed., *Manuscripts of the Earl of Egmont: Diary of Viscount Percival, Afterwards First Earl of Egmont* (London, 1920–23)
Egmont Papers	Phillipps Collection of Egmont Papers, Hargrett Rare Book and Manuscript Library, University of Georgia Libraries, Athens, Georgia
Egmont's Journal	Robert G. McPherson, ed., *The Journal of the Earl of Egmont* (Athens, Ga., 1962)
GHQ	*Georgia Historical Quarterly*
Ms. CRG	Manuscript, Colonial Records of Georgia
WMQ	*William and Mary Quarterly*

1. Circles in the Sand: Perspectives on the Southern Frontier at the Arrival of James Oglethorpe (Peter H. Wood)

1. Ulrich B. Phillips (1877–1934) to George J. Baldwin, May 2, 1903. This letter in the Southern Historical Collection is quoted in W. K. Wood, "'My Dear Mr. Snowden': U. B. Phillips' Letters to Yates Snowden of South Carolina College, 1904–1932," *South Carolina Historical Magazine* 85 (October 1984): 295–96.
2. Columbus, Georgia, Sunday *Ledger-Enquirer* Magazine, November 3, 1963, p. 22.

3. Ulrich B. Phillips, *Plantation and Frontier, Documents: 1649–1863*, 2 vols. (Cleveland, 1909).

4. Crane had done impressive research on the background of the Georgia colony in British primary sources. See, for example, "The Promotion Literature of Georgia," in *Bibliographical Essays: A Tribute to Wilberforce Eames* (Cambridge, 1925), 281–98. For a profile and appreciation of Crane, see my preface to the Norton reprint of Verner W. Crane, *The Southern Frontier, 1670–1732* (New York, 1981), vii–xvi.

5. Jack P. Greene and J. R. Pole, eds., *Colonial British America: Essays in the New History of the Early Modern Era* (Baltimore, 1984), 498, 503; Clarence L. Ver Steeg, "Historians and the Southern Colonies," in Ray Allen Billington, ed., *The Reinterpretation of Early American History: Essays in Honor of John Edwin Pomfret* (San Marino, Calif., 1966), 95.

6. Francis Jennings, *The Invasion of America: Indians, Colonialism, and the Cant of Conquest* (New York, 1975); William Cronon, *Changes in the Land: Indians, Colonists, and the Ecology of New England* (New York, 1983).

7. See, for instance, J. Leitch Wright, Jr., *The Only Land They Knew: The Tragic Story of the American Indians in the Old South* (New York, 1981). Also see the early chapters of Albert E. Cowdrey, *This Land, This South: An Environmental History* (Lexington, Ky., 1983); and R. Reid Badger and Lawrence A. Clayton, eds., *Alabama and the Borderlands: From Prehistory to Statehood* (University, Ala., 1985).

8. See, for example, the useful survey by W. Stitt Robinson, *The Southern Colonial Frontier, 1607–1763* (Albuquerque, 1979).

9. William P. Cumming, *The Southeast in Early Maps* (Princeton, 1958; reprint, Chapel Hill, 1962), 202.

10. Kristian Hvidt, ed., *Von Reck's Voyage: Drawings and Journal of Philipp Georg Friedrich von Reck* (Savannah, 1980), 34–35.

11. This incident was analyzed by Delores Boisfeuillet Floyd in "The Legend of Sir Walter Raleigh at Savannah," *GHQ* 23 (1939): 103–21. She stated (p. 105) that the burial mound had been located at "a site today corresponding to Emmet Park on the Bay just east of Habersham Street."

12. Louis De Vorsey, Jr., ed., *De Brahm's Report of the General Survey in the Southern District of North America* (Columbia, S.C., 1971), 153.

13. Ibid.

14. Floyd, "Legend of Sir Walter Raleigh," 114–16. For a drawing of an "unidentified French leader answering to the description of Jean Ribault," see Charles E. Bennett, trans., *Three Voyages: René Laudonnière* (Gainesville, 1975), 33, cf. 156.

15. Samuel Eveleigh, *South Carolina Gazette*, March 17–24, 1733; De Vorsey, *De Brahm's Report*, 153.

16. European use of sites previously cleared by Indians was commonplace throughout the colonial South. For example, on his map of the area around Fort Loudoun on the Tennessee River that was ceded to the Carolinians in 1755 by the Cherokees, De Brahm indicates "Taskigee old Town[,] this place the Indians proposed for a Fort." De Vorsey, *De Brahm's Report*, map opposite p. 99.

17. Hvidt, *Von Reck's Voyage*, 35.

18. De Vorsey, *De Brahm's Report*, plan opposite p. 155. For appraisals of Tomochichi by four generations of scholars, see Charles C. Jones, *Historical Sketch of Tomo-Chi-Chi, Mico of the Yamacraws* (Albany, N.Y., 1868); Frederick W. Hodge, ed., *Handbook of American Indians North of Mexico*, 2 vols., *Bureau of American Ethnology Bulletin* 30 (Washington, D.C., 1907–10), 2:776, 986; John R. Swanton, *Early History of the Creek Indians and Their Neighbors*, *Bureau of American Ethnology Bulletin* 73 (Washington, D.C., 1922), 108–09; and David H. Corkran, *Creek Frontier, 1540–1783* (Norman, 1967), 82–83.

19. For an excellent introduction to the recent literature on this long span of contact, see James Howlett O'Donnell III, *Southeastern Frontiers: Europeans, Africans, and American Indians, 1513–1840: A Critical Bibliography* (Bloomington, 1982).

20. See Henry F. Dobyns, *Native American Historical Demography: A Critical Bibliography* (Bloomington, 1976); and Charles M. Hudson, "The Genesis of Georgia's Indians," in Harvey H. Jackson and Phinizy Spalding, eds., *Forty Years of Diversity: Essays on Colonial Georgia* (Athens, Ga., 1984), 25–45.

21. Henry F. Dobyns, *Their Number Become Thinned: Native American Population Dynamics in Eastern North America* (Knoxville, 1983), 291–95; Peter H. Wood, "La Salle: The Discovery of a Lost Explorer," *American Historical Review* 89 (April 1984): 309, n. 34.

22. John Lawson, *A New Voyage to Carolina*, ed. Hugh Talmage Lefler (Chapel Hill, 1967), 231–32.

23. Ibid., 232–33. See Peter H. Wood, "The Impact of Smallpox on the Native Population of the Eighteenth-Century South," *New York State Journal of Medicine* 87 (January 1987): 30–36.

24. Grant D. Jones, "The Ethnohistory of the Guale Coast through 1684," in David Hurst Thomas, Grant D. Jones, Roger S. Durham, and Clark Spencer Larsen, *The Anthropology of St. Catherine's Island: 1. Natural and Cultural History*, Anthropological Papers of the American Museum of Natural History, 55, pt. 2 (New York, 1978); Carolyn Stefanco-Schill, "The Gualean Revolt of 1597: Anti-Colonialism in the Old South," *Southern Exposure* 12 (November/December 1984): 4–9; Gene Waddell, *Indians*

of the South Carolina Lowcountry, 1562–1751 (Spartanburg, S.C., 1980); Daniel H. Usner, Jr., "Frontier Exchange in the Lower Mississippi Valley: Race Relations and Economic Life in Colonial Louisiana, 1699–1783" (Ph.D. diss., Duke University, 1981).

25. See, for example, the impressive researches of James H. Merrell, such as "The Indians' New World: The Catawba Experience," WMQ, 3d ser., 41 (October 1984): 537–65; and of Richard White, The Roots of Dependency: Subsistence, Environment, and Social Change among the Choctaws, Pawnees, and Navajos (Lincoln, Nebr., 1983).

26. Francis Le Jau to the secretary, June 13, 1710, in Frank J. Klingberg, ed., The Carolina Chronicle of Dr. Francis Le Jau, 1706–1717 (Berkeley and Los Angeles, 1956), 78.

27. Hvidt, Von Reck's Voyage, 46, 118, 119. Von Reck's watercolor is also reproduced in Jessie Poesch, The Art of the Old South: Painting, Sculpture, Architecture & the Products of Craftsmen, 1560–1860 (New York, 1983), p. 42.

28. See Peter H. Wood, "The Changing Population of the Eighteenth-Century South: An Overview, by Race and Subregion from 1685 to 1790," in Peter H. Wood, Gregory A. Waselkov, and M. Thomas Hatley, eds., Powhatan's Mantle: Indians in the Colonial Southeast (Lincoln, Nebr., forthcoming).

29. Speech of September 9, 1730, quoted at greater length in Peter H. Wood, Black Majority: Negroes in Colonial South Carolina from 1670 through the Stono Rebellion (New York, 1974), 262n. According to the chronicler Alexander Hewatt, Historical Account of the Rise and Progress of the Colonies of South Carolina and Georgia, 2 vols. (London, 1779), 2:22, when Tomochichi traveled to England with Oglethorpe in 1734, he was "struck with astonishment at the grandeur of the British court" and addressed King George II as follows:

> This day I see the majesty of your face, the greatness of your house, and the number of your people; I am come in my old days, though I cannot expect to see any advantage to myself—I am come for the good of the children of all the nations of the Lower and Upper Creeks, that they may be instructed in the knowledge of the English. —These are feathers of the eagle, which is the swiftest of birds, and which flieth around our nations.—These feathers are a sign of peace in our land, and we have carried them from town to town there.— We have brought them over to leave thus with you, O great King, whatever words you shall say unto me, I will faithfully tell them to all the Kings of the Creek Nations.

30. Parish Transcripts in the New-York Historical Society, New York City, "South Carolina," Box I, folder 4, p. 32a.
31. Hvidt, *Von Reck's Voyage*, 35. To acknowledge this loyalty and optimism, and to underscore the beginning of a new phase, Oglethorpe "at once . . . ordered a new church to be built at Savannah, as well as a wharf for more convenient landing of cargoes, and he had one hundred more laborers hired." Ibid.
32. Phinizy Spalding, *Oglethorpe in America* (Chicago, 1977), 85–87.
33. Ibid., 87.
34. Herbert E. Bolton, *Texas in the Middle Eighteenth Century: Studies in Spanish Colonial History and Administration* (Berkeley and Los Angeles, 1915; reprint, Austin, 1970), 4–6; Elizabeth A. H. John, *Storms Brewed in Other Men's Worlds: The Confrontation of Indians, Spanish, and French in the Southwest, 1540–1795* (College Station, Tex., 1975), 258–66.
35. Patricia Dillon Woods, *French-Indian Relations on the Southern Frontier, 1699–1762* (Ann Arbor, 1980), 123–25.
36. Ibid., 113, 119, 129; cf. n. 30 above.
37. The so-called de Batz map, dated September 7, 1737, was sent to Paris by the Frenchman Alexandre de Batz and is in the Archives Nationales, Archives des Colonies, C13A, tome 22, fol. 67. See Dunbar Rowland and A. G. Sanders, eds. and trans., *Mississippi Provincial Archives: French Dominion*, 3 vols. (Jackson, Miss., 1927–32), 1:355–56, 3:703. For a full discussion of this map and others like it, see Gregory A. Waselkov, "Indian Maps of the Colonial Southeast," in Wood, Waselkov, and Hatley, *Powhatan's Mantle*.
38. Crane, *Southern Frontier*, 132–35.
39. Patricia K. Galloway, "Henri de Tonti du village des Chacta, 1702: The Beginning of the French Alliance," in Patricia K. Galloway, ed., *La Salle and His Legacy: Frenchmen and Indians in the Lower Mississippi Valley* (Jackson, Miss., 1982), 155.
40. Francis Jennings, *The Ambiguous Iroquois Empire* (New York, 1984), 95, 112.

2. Oglethorpe and the Earliest Maps of Georgia (Louis De Vorsey, Jr.)

1. Verner W. Crane, *The Southern Frontier, 1670–1732* (Ann Arbor, 1929), 303; Kenneth Coleman, "The Southern Frontier: Georgia's Founding and the Expansion of South Carolina," *GHQ* 56 (1972): 163–74.

2. Herbert E. Bolton and Mary Ross, *The Debatable Land: A Sketch of the Anglo-Spanish Contest for the Georgia Country* (Berkeley and Los Angeles, 1925).

3. As quoted in Crane, *Southern Frontier*, 93–94.

4. For a discussion of "A Map of South Carolina Shewing the Settlements of the English, French & Indian Nations from Charles Town to the River Mississippi by Capt. Tho. Nairn," see William P. Cumming, *The Southeast in Early Maps* (Princeton, 1958; reprint, Chapel Hill, 1962), 41–42, 179–80.

5. Mattie Erma Edwards Parker, ed., *North Carolina Charters and Constitutions, 1578–1698* (Raleigh, 1963), 90–104.

6. In addition to the depictions of the Savannah, Altamaha, and Saint Johns rivers, attention should be directed to the fact that the "Ogehee" (Ogeechee) River is correctly placed between the Savannah and Altamaha. The Altamaha's principal headstream is named "Okonny" by Nairne but its valley is shown to be occupied by the "Okesee Nation 700 men." These were the Indians known to the Charles Town traders as the Ochese Creek who had migrated eastward to take advantage of the superior trading opportunities afforded by the South Carolinians. Crane has argued and John R. Swanton agreed that Ochese Creek was the early name for the Ocmulgee River. The tribal name "Creek," the same authorities agree, developed from the habitual shortening of the term "Ochese Creek Indians." See John R. Swanton, *Early History of the Creek Indians and Their Neighbors, Bureau of American Ethnology Bulletin* 73 (Washington, D.C., 1922), 215; Charles M. Hudson, "The Genesis of Georgia's Indians," in Harvey H. Jackson and Phinizy Spalding, eds., *Forty Years of Diversity: Essays on Colonial Georgia* (Athens, Ga., 1984), 39.

7. Crane, *Southern Frontier*, 162.

8. William Bartram, *Travels Through North and South Carolina, Georgia, East and West Florida*, Facsimile of the 1792 London Edition (Savannah, 1973), 53.

9. Jackson and Spalding, *Forty Years of Diversity*, 40.

10. Crane, *Southern Frontier*, 206.

11. Sir Robert Montgomery, *A Discourse Concerning the design'd Establishment of a New Colony to the South of Carolina, In the Most Delightful Country of the Universe* (London, 1717), 5. This tract is included in the collection of promotional literature edited and introduced by Trevor R. Reese and titled, *The Most Delightful Country of the Universe . . .* (Savannah, 1972).

12. Ibid., 5.

13. Ibid., 9–12.

14. Ibid., 11–12.

15. Coleman, "Southern Frontier," 166.

16. See Cumming, *Early Maps*, 185, for a list of early eighteenth-century maps that showed Azilia.

17. *A Description of the Golden Islands, With an Account of the Undertaking now on Foot for Making a Settlement there: Explaining 1st, The Nature of that Design, in general 2dly, The Measures already taken: And, 3dly, Those intended to be taken hereafter* (London, 1720), reprinted in Reese, *Most Delightful Country*.

18. Ibid., 40–41.

19. Herman Moll, "A New Map of the North Parts of America."

20. Louis De Vorsey, Jr., *The Georgia–South Carolina Boundary: A Problem in Historical Geography* (Athens, Ga., 1982), 26–27.

21. Franklin K. Van Zandt, *Boundaries of the United States and the Several States*, Geological Survey Professional Paper 909 (Washington, D.C., 1976), 85.

22. Crane, *Southern Frontier*, 229–34.

23. J. Leitch Wright, Jr., *Anglo-Spanish Rivalry in North America* (Athens, Ga., 1971), 76.

24. Crane, *Southern Frontier*, 233. Crane includes a detailed description of Fort King George derived from Barnwell's journal; see pp. 236–37.

25. *Gentleman's Magazine* 2. The August, September, and October 1732 issues included an extended description of the township plan. The article also detailed the founding of the first of the Savannah River towns, Purrysburg. In addition it included a surprisingly accurate description of the province written by Jean Purry and three of his Swiss associates. For a detailed discussion of the Purrysburg settlement, see Henry A. M. Smith, "Purrysburgh," *South Carolina Historical and Genealogical Magazine* 10 (1909): 187–219.

26. Crane, *Southern Frontier*, 294.

27. Coleman, "Southern Frontier," 170.

28. Crane, *Southern Frontier*, 318.

29. Albert B. Saye, ed., *Georgia's Charter of 1732* (Athens, Ga., 1942), 3.

30. Ibid., 39–41.

31. *Diary of Percival*, 1:289. On August 3, 1732, the Trustees ordered Martyn's tract printed. Although the date Martyn penned *Some Accounts* is not recorded, it was likely after the charter for Georgia was promulgated on June 20, 1732, inasmuch as it includes quotes from that document.

32. For a discussion, see Cumming, *Early Maps*, 197, and Louis De Vorsey, Jr., "Maps in Colonial Promotion: James Edward Oglethorpe's Use of Maps in 'Selling' the Georgia Scheme," *Imago Mundi* 38 (1986): 36–37.

33. See De Vorsey, *Georgia–South Carolina Boundary*, passim.

34. [Benjamin Martyn], *Reasons for Establishing the Colony of Georgia . . . With some Account of the Country and the Design of the Trustees* (London, 1733).

35. One prospective migrant to Georgia, Samuel Hill of "Clarendon in Jamaica," wrote of being favorably impressed by a copy of an advertisement called "Reasons for Settling Georgia," which his sister had sent him from England. In a letter dated January 10, 1735, Hill expressed his desire for "any Plans lately taken of this particular colony and the country contiguous only with relation to the situation of the Towns as intended, the Roads laid out, the River's Mouth with its forts, etc. for its defence or anything of this kind to give me a farther insight as [to] the number of people already gone, and if healthy" (quoted from CRG, 20:146–50). There is no record of whether Hill ever received the more detailed maps of Georgia he requested to verify his initial impressions.

36. Phinizy Spalding, *Oglethorpe in America* (Chicago, 1977), 24.

37. Oglethorpe to Trustees, March 12, 1733, in Mills B. Lane, ed., *General Oglethorpe's Georgia*, 2 vols. (Savannah, 1975), 1:7.

38. *Reasons*, 179–80, To anyone familiar with the true distance between the Savannah and Altamaha rivers, the estimate of "between sixty and seventy Miles" as given in *Reasons* would appear to be much more accurate than the "120 miles" Oglethorpe reported in 1733. It could be that the General was confusing the length of the circuitous boat navigation passage between the two rivers with the geographical distance that separated them. It is also possible that he was actually giving the estimated distance between the Savannah River and the Saint Johns River. As discussed later in this chapter, Oglethorpe was responsible for the preparation of maps that showed a nonexistent branch of the Altamaha River connecting with the Saint Johns River. Whether this was deliberate falsification and distortion of nature by Oglethorpe cannot be determined.

39. Hector Beaufain to Mr. Simond, January 23, 1734, in Lane, *General Oglethorpe's Georgia*, I:36. Beaufain's mention of Oglethorpe's interest in improving inland navigation by making "the great rivers . . . communicate with one another" suggests another hypothesis to explain Oglethorpe's linking of the Altamaha and Saint Johns rivers. It is possible that his map depicting a connection between these rivers was intended as a graphic demonstration of the feasibility of such a linkage rather than its existence in nature.

40. Ibid., 36–37.

41. Oglethorpe to Trustees, August 12, 1733, ibid., 22.

42. "Register of Draughts in the Drawing Room 1743," War Office 55/2281, British Public Record Office (BPRO). Researchers interested in Georgia appear to have missed this citation because it was listed under the heading "Mediterranean and America" in the "Register."

43. George Fenwick Jones, ed., *Henry Newman's Salzburger Letterbooks* (Athens, Ga., 1966), 119.
44. Ibid., 489.
45. CRG, 1:202.
46. *Egmont's Journal*, 76.
47. CRG, 2:87. The time that it took to have his original manuscript maps engraved and printed would explain the several months that intervened between Oglethorpe's return to London and the formal delivery of the "Benefaction."
48. For the period prior to the 1730s, Sarah Tyacke includes several examples of printed maps identified as "draughts" in her collection of advertisements for maps placed in the *London Gazette* 1668–1719. See her *London Map Sellers 1660–1720* (Tring, Hertfordshire, 1978).
49. A full-scale facsimile, with "Introductory Notes" by William P. Cumming and Helen Wallis, was published in 1972 by Harry Margary, Lympne Castle, Kent, England.
50. Popple's original manuscript is titled, "A Map of the English and French Possessions on the Continent of North America. 1727. H. Popple." It is filed as Additional Manuscript 23,615 f. 72 in the collection of the British Library, London. A photocopy of this map in the Library of Congress, Geography and Map Division, was used in this study. At least two early-stage Popple maps have been identified in collections in the United States. They are held by the American Philosophical Society and the Colonial Williamsburg Foundation. Both of these early impressions repeat the 1727 manuscript map coastal configurations and appear to be identical. They were both also altered by the addition of a pasted-on cancel overlay carrying a later improved depiction of the coastline. It would appear that early prints of Popple's sheet 10 were updated by later overlays containing more accurate coastal configurations.
51. It is noteworthy that no materials written by Oglethorpe were mentioned in the 1780 "List of Maps, Plans, etc. Belonging to the Right Hon.ble. the Lords Commissioners for Trade and Plantations. Under the Care of Francis Aegidus Assiotti, Draughtsman." This omission might suggest that Popple received Oglethorpe's Georgia sketches and surveys even before they became a part of the official file. Assiotti's "List" is found in the BPRO, London.
52. See Cumming, *Early Maps*, 210. An excellent facsimile print of this map is published and distributed by Historic Urban Plans, Ithaca, New York.
53. Leo Bagrow, *History of Cartography* (Cambridge, 1964), 272.
54. The "Salzburger Tracts" contain the journals, diaries, and letters of the

Lutheran pastors who ministered to the Salzburger exiles and numerous other German refugees who were settled in Georgia. For translations, see the several volumes edited by George Fenwick Jones under the title of *Detailed Reports on the Salzburger Emigrants Who Settled in America . . . Edited by Samuel Urlsperger*, 8 vols. to date (Athens, Ga., 1968–).

55. Jones, *Newman's Salzburger Letterbooks*, 163.

56. John W. Reps, *Town Planning in Frontier America* (Princeton, 1969), 242.

3. Parson and Squire: James Oglethorpe and the Role of the Anglican Church in Georgia, 1733–1736 (Harvey H. Jackson)

1. Harold E. Davis, *The Fledgling Province: Social and Cultural Life in Colonial Georgia, 1733–1776* (Chapel Hill, 1976), 193. See also Reba C. Strickland, *Religion and the State in Georgia in the Eighteenth Century* (New York, 1939). Of the ministers mentioned in this study, Samuel Quincy became a successful clergyman in South Carolina while John and Charles Wesley were major evangelists and founders of the Methodist movement. See Edgar Legare Pennington, "The Reverend Samuel Quincy, S.P.G. Missionary," *GHQ* 11 (1927): 157–65; Robert G. Tuttle, Jr., *John Wesley: His Life and Theology* (Grand Rapids, Mich., 1978); and David T. Morgan, "John Wesley's Sojourn in Georgia Revisited," *GHQ* 64 (1980): 253–62. John Wesley to James Vernon, September 11, 1736, in Mills B. Lane, ed., *General Oglethorpe's Georgia*, 2 vols. (Savannah, 1975), 1:277–78. Also performing religious duties at this time were the Reverend Edward Dyson, the Reverend Benjamin Ingham, and Charles Delamotte.

2. The Georgia charter may be found in CRG, 1:1–13. See also "Some Account of the Designs of the Trustees for establishing the Colony of *Georgia in America*," and Benjamin Martyn, "Reasons for Establishing the *Colony of Georgia*," in Trevor R. Reese, ed., *The Most Delightful Country of the Universe: Promotional Literature of the Colony of Georgia, 1717–1734* (Savannah, 1972), 69, 183–86; and Phinizy Spalding, "Some Sermons Before the Trustees of Colonial Georgia," *GHQ* 57 (1973): 337.

3. Strickland, *Religion in Georgia*, 44–46; Davis, *Fledgling Province*, 193; Leslie F. Church, *Oglethorpe: A Study of Philanthropy in England and Georgia* (London, 1932), 191–92. Donna Rabec, "Economy and Society in Early Georgia: A Functional Analysis of the Colony's Origins and Evolution" (Ph.D. diss., University of Michigan, 1978), 64, indicates that in the years under discussion in this chapter over 70 percent of the charity colonists were British; however, after 1734 a significant number of these were Highland Scots, a change that affected Anglican efforts. For an analysis of the

role of the Anglican church, see G. E. Mingay, *English Landed Society in the Eighteenth Century* (London, 1963), 248–50. See also Richard Allestree, *The Whole Duty of Man* (London, 1658), which was often reprinted.

4. Mingay, *English Landed Society*, 148.

5. Amos Aschbach Ettinger, *James Edward Oglethorpe: Imperial Idealist* (Oxford, 1936), 158–59; James Oglethorpe to the Trustees, December 1733, in Lane, *General Oglethorpe's Georgia*, 1:27; Strickland, *Religion in Georgia*, 35. For insight into the Oglethorpe family's Catholic ties, see Patricia Kneas Hill, *The Oglethorpe Ladies and the Jacobite Conspiracies* (Atlanta, 1977). Boltzius's statement is quoted in Ettinger, *Oglethorpe*, 158–59.

6. James Oglethorpe, *A New and Accurate Account of the Provinces of South-Carolina and Georgia*, reprinted in Reese, *Most Delightful Country*, 138–39. James Oglethorpe to Samuel Wesley, December 25, 1734, in George Fenwick Jones, ed., *Henry Newman's Salzburger Letterbooks* (Athens, Ga., 1966), 521.

7. Mingay, *English Landed Society*, 148.

8. Joseph Addison, "No. 112," in Donald F. Bond, ed., *The Spectator* (Oxford, 1965), 460. For insight into Oglethorpe's early life, see Ettinger, *Oglethorpe*.

9. Thomas Christie, "The Voyage of the *Anne*—A Daily Record," ed. Robert G. McPherson, *GHQ* 44 (1960): 220–30; and Peter Gordon, "Journal of Peter Gordon," in Trevor R. Reese, ed., *Our First Visit to America: Early Reports from the Colony of Georgia, 1732–1740* (Savannah, 1974), 8.

10. Trustees Journal, *CRG*, 1:84–85; Oglethorpe to the Trustees, January 13, 1732–33, ibid., 20:5; Christie, "Voyage of the *Anne*," 223–29; Gordon, "Journal," 7–9.

11. Gordon, "Journal," 12–14, 15, 19, 21; Oglethorpe to the Trustees, February 10, March 12, and May 14, 1733, in Lane, *General Oglethorpe's Georgia*, 1:5, 7, 15; *CRG*, 20:18–19.

12. Trustees Journal, *CRG*, 1:16; Oglethorpe to the Trustees, May 14, August 12, and September 17, 1733, in Lane, *General Oglethorpe's Georgia*, 1:16, 19–21, 23.

13. *Diary of Percival*, 1:302–03. Oglethorpe to the Trustees, August 12, 1733, in Lane, *General Oglethorpe's Georgia*, 1:21–22.

14. Hector Beaufain to Mr. Simond, January 23, 1734, and an Extract of an Anonymous Letter, January 26, 1734, both in Lane, *General Oglethorpe's Georgia*, 1:36, 39.

15. Extract of an Anonymous Letter, January 26, 1734, ibid., 1:39.

16. *Diary of Percival*, 2:36; Samuel Quincy to Mr. Copping, March 29, 1734, in Jones, *Newman's Salzburger Letterbooks*, 468–70; "A New Voyage to Georgia," in *Coll. GHS*, 2:40; "An Extract of the Journals of Mr. Commissary Von Reck . . . and of the Reverend Mr. Boltzius, 1734," in Reese,

Our First Visit, 59, 65. For information on population growth in Georgia, see Rabec, "Economy and Society," 43–74.

17. Pennington, "Samuel Quincy," 162; *Egmont's Journal*, 207–08.
18. Trustees Journal, CRG, 1:195; Quincy to Newman, January 15, 1735, in Jones, *Newman's Salzburger Letterbooks*, 528–30; Elisha Dobree to the Trustees, February 10 and 13, 1734–35, Thomas Causton to Oglethorpe, March 24, 1734–35, Quincy to Harman Verelst, June 18, 1735, Quincy to Newman, July 4, 1735, all in CRG, 20:227–28, 230, 284–85, 405–07, 418–19; *Diary of Percival*, 2:195.
19. Quincy to Newman, July 4, 1735, CRG, 20:419; Oglethorpe to the Trustees, April 24, 1736, *Coll. GHS*, 3:31–32; Samuel Eveleigh to Oglethorpe, October 19, 1734, in Lane, *General Oglethorpe's Georgia*, 1:60.
20. Quincy to Peter Gordon, March 3, 1735, and Causton to Oglethorpe, in Lane, *General Oglethorpe's Georgia*, 1:129, 141; Quincy to Verelst, August 18, 1735, CRG, 20:462–63; Benjamin Martyn to Quincy, October 10, 1735, and Verelst to Oglethorpe, December 6, 1735, Ms. CRG, 29:165, 202–03; Quincy to Edmund Quincy, June 15, 1735, in *Collections of the Massachusetts Historical Society*, 2d ser., ii (Boston, 1814), 188–89; *Diary of Percival*, 2:184, 303–04; *Egmont's Journal*, 96, 103; Church, *Oglethorpe*, 193–94.
21. Ettinger, *Oglethorpe*, 161; *Diary of Percival*, 2:196; *Egmont's Journal*, 107; Tuttle, *John Wesley*, 129; John Telford, ed., *The Letters of the Reverend John Wesley, A.M.*, 8 vols. (London, 1931), 1:187; "Journal of Benjamin Ingham," in Reese, *Our First Visit*, 165.
22. John Wesley to Dr. John Burton, October 10, 1735, in Telford, *Letters of John Wesley*, 1:188–91; Tuttle, *John Wesley*, 129–30; "Journal of Ingham," 159–64; Trustees' Journal, CRG, 1:234–35.
23. Ettinger, *Oglethorpe*, 153; E. Merton Coulter, *Georgia: A Short History* (Chapel Hill, 1933), 35; Francis Moore, "A Voyage to Georgia, Begun in the Year 1735," 87–90, "An Extract of the Reverend Mr. John Wesley's Journal," 185–91, "Journal of Ingham," 165–66, all in Reese, *Our First Visit*; Telford, *Letters of John Wesley*, 1:193–94. For the composition of the passengers and the purposes for which they were brought over, see Rabec, "Economy and Society," 61, 65–66.
24. Moore, "Voyage to Georgia," 89–90; "Journal of Ingham," 166, 167, 169; Nehemiah Curnock, ed., *The Journal of the Reverend John Wesley, A.M.*, 8 vols. (London, 1909), 1:114, 123–24, 131, 136–37.
25. "Journal of Ingham," 171–72.
26. John Wesley to Dr. Burton, January 20, 1736, in Telford, *Letters of John Wesley*, 1:193–94.
27. "Journal of Ingham," 174–76; "Extract of Wesley's Journal," 191–92. For information on the surplice and the controversy surrounding it, see H. J.

Clayton, *Cassock and Gown* (London, 1929), 10–14; and Charles J. Abbey and John H. Overton, *The English Church in the Eighteenth Century*, 2 vols. (London, 1878), 1:467–73. I would like to thank Father Peter Gorday of Saint Luke's Episcopal Church, Atlanta, Georgia, for pointing out to me the political significance of the surplice.

28. Oglethorpe to Trustees, April 2, 1734, Captain Dunbar to Oglethorpe, January 23, 1735, Thomas Causton to Trustees, April 2, 1735, Eveleigh to Oglethorpe, May 16, 1735, all in Lane, *General Oglethorpe's Georgia*, 1:41, 110, 156–57, 159; "Extract of the Journals of Von Reck and Boltzius," 62; Moore, "Voyage to Georgia," 112; Causton to Trustees, November 20, 1735, *CRG*, 21:56–57; Oglethorpe to Trustees, February 13, 1735–36, *Coll. GHS*, 3:13. See also Elijah Hoole, *Oglethorpe and the Wesleys in America* (London, 1863).

29. "Extract of Wesley's Journal," 194; "Journal of Ingham," 177.

30. "Journal of Ingham," 177–78.

31. Ibid., 178–79.

32. Ibid., 179; John Telford, ed., *The Journal of the Reverend Charles Wesley, M.A.* (London, 1909), 7–8; Church, *Oglethorpe*, 215.

33. Telford, *Journal of Charles Wesley*, 9–10, 35–37, 59–62; "Journal of Ingham," 179.

34. Telford, *Journal of Charles Wesley*, 17–26.

35. Ibid., 29–32, 59–62.

36. Ibid., 26–27, 32–35, 37–39; John Wesley to Charles Wesley, March 22, 1736, in Telford, *Letters of John Wesley*, 1:198–99; Curnock, *Journal of John Wesley*, 1:195; "Journal of Ingham," 179–80; Church, *Oglethorpe*, 216; Peggy Robbins, "God, Man, Woman, and the Wesleys," *American Heritage* (April/May 1984): 96–103.

37. Telford, *Journal of Charles Wesley*, 39–40; John Wesley to Oglethorpe, April 20, 1736, in Telford, *Letters of John Wesley*, 1:200–201; Church, *Oglethorpe*, 216.

38. Telford, *Journal of Charles Wesley*, 42–45.

39. Ibid., 45, 49–51, 59; Larry E. Ivers, *British Drums on the Southern Frontier: The Military Colonization of Georgia, 1733–1749* (Chapel Hill, 1974), 61.

40. Telford, *Journal of Charles Wesley*, 11, 51–52, 64, 66–67; "Extract of John Wesley's Journal," 200; Church, *Oglethorpe*, 216; Ettinger, *Oglethorpe*, 163.

41. Telford, *Journal of Charles Wesley*, 65–67; Church, *Oglethorpe*, 217.

42. Oglethorpe to Trustees, [July 26, 1736], *Coll. GHS*, 3:41–42; "Extract of Wesley's Journal," 200, 204–05; Church, *Oglethorpe*, 202.

43. Telford, *Journal of Charles Wesley*, 59–60; Ettinger, *Oglethorpe*, 164–65.

44. *Diary of Percival*, 2:371; Telford, *Journal of Charles Wesley*, 59–60, 64–65; John Wesley to Archibald Hutchinson, July 23, 1736, John Wesley to Oglethorpe, August 23, 1736, both in Telford, *Letters of John Wesley*, 1:201,

203–04; Oglethorpe to Trustees, June 1736, in Lane, *General Oglethorpe's Georgia*, 1:275; "Extract of Wesley's Journal," 205–06, 210–11.

45. "Extract of Wesley's Journal," 212–13; John Wesley to Trustees, March 4, 1737, in Telford, *Letters of John Wesley*, 1:215–16; John Wesley to Verelst, November 10, 1736, quoted in Church, *Oglethorpe*, 203–04; "Journal of William Stephens," CRG, 4:18–19, 41; William Stephens to Trustees, December 20, 1737, CRG, 22, pt. 1, 32–40.

46. Telford, *Journal of Charles Wesley*, 59–60.

47. Quincy to Newman, January 15, 1735, in Jones, *Newman's Salzburger Letterbooks*, 528–30; Moore, "Voyage to Georgia," 96–102, 103; Peter Gordon's 1734 Map of Savannah is in Mills B. Lane, *Savannah Revisited* (Savannah, 1969), 10. See also Reba C. Strickland, "Building a Colonial Church," *GHQ* 17 (1933): 276–85.

48. Ivers, *British Drums*, 55–64, 78–79; "Extract of Wesley's Journal," 204–05, 212–13.

49. Oglethorpe to Trustees, August 12, 1733, John Wesley to James Vernon, September 11, 1736, both in Lane, *General Oglethorpe's Georgia*, 1:21–22, 277–78; Strickland, *Religion in Georgia*, 46–50.

50. For the diversity of colonial immigration, see Rabec, "Economy and Society," 61–71; John Wesley to Dr. Burton, January 20, 1736, in Telford, *Letters of John Wesley*, 1:193–94.

51. Patrick Tailfer et al., "A True and Historical Narrative of the Colony of Georgia in America," in Trevor R. Reese, ed., *The Clamorous Malcontents: Criticisms and Defenses of the Colony of Georgia, 1741–1743* (Savannah, 1973), 66; John Wesley to James Vernon, September 11, 1736, in Lane, *General Oglethorpe's Georgia*, 1:277–78; "Journal of Ingham," 178; Daniel J. Boorstin, *The Americans: The Colonial Experience* (New York, 1958), 84–88.

4. James Edward Oglethorpe, Race, and Slavery: A Reassessment (Betty Wood)

1. See especially Henry Bruce, *Life of General Oglethorpe* (New York, 1890); Austin Dobson, *A Paladin of Philanthropy* (London, 1899); Leslie F. Church, *Oglethorpe: A Study of Philanthropy in England and Georgia* (London, 1932); and Amos Aschbach Ettinger, *James Edward Oglethorpe: Imperial Idealist* (Oxford, 1936). For more sober accounts, see Phinizy Spalding, *Oglethorpe in America* (Chicago, 1977); and idem, "James Edward Oglethorpe's Quest for an American Zion," in Harvey H. Jackson and Phinizy Spalding, eds., *Forty Years of Diversity: Essays on Colonial Georgia* (Athens, Ga., 1984), 60–79.

2. Several works deal with the relationship between Oglethorpe and the malcontents. See Spalding, *Oglethorpe in America*; Paul S. Taylor, *Georgia Plan, 1732–1752* (Berkeley, 1972); and Betty Wood, *Slavery in Colonial Georgia, 1730–1775* (Athens, Ga., 1984). See also idem, "Thomas Stephens and the Introduction of Black Slavery in Georgia," *GHQ* 58 (1974): 24–40; and Milton L. Ready, "The Trustees and the Malcontents: The Politics of Philanthropy," *GHQ* 60 (1976): 264–81.

3. Wood, *Slavery in Colonial Georgia*, 26–27; E. Merton Coulter, ed., *The Journal of William Stephens, 1741–1745*, 2 vols. (Athens, Ga., 1958, 1959), 1:xiv, xv; Thomas Stephens, *The Castle-Builders; or, The History of William Stephens, of the Isle of Wight, Esq.; lately deceased* (London, 1759).

4. Wood, *Slavery in Colonial Georgia*, 26–27; Kenneth Coleman, *Colonial Georgia: A History* (New York, 1976), 91–95, 100–102.

5. Wood, *Slavery in Colonial Georgia*, 29, 30, 42, 59–73; Harvey H. Jackson, "The Darien Anti-Slavery Petition of 1739 and the Georgia Plan," *WMQ*, 3d ser., 34 (1977): 618–31.

6. Slave labor at any price was the "constant toast" of the malcontents in Savannah. Alexander Heron to the Trustees, May 11, 1748, CRG, 25:294–95.

7. James Walvin, *The Black Presence* (London, 1971), 7–11; idem, *Black and White: The Negro and British Society, 1555–1945* (London, 1973); Richard Sheridan, *Sugar and Slavery: An Economic History of the British West Indies, 1623–1775* (Baltimore, 1974); Geraldine Meroney, "The London Entrepôt Merchants and the Georgia Colony," *WMQ*, 3d ser., 25 (1968): 230–44.

8. For the relevant portion of Bishop Gibson's statement, see Lorenzo J. Greene, *The Negro in Colonial New England, 1620–1776* (New York, 1942), 261.

9. Talbot's and Yorke's ruling was overturned in 1772 in the Somerset case, arguably the most important legal decision in the history of British race relations. Walvin, *Black and White*, 110–12; idem, *Black Presence*, 94–114.

10. Ruth Scarborough, *The Opposition to Slavery in Georgia prior to 1861* (Nashville, 1933), 62.

11. Oglethorpe, Egmont, and others of the original Trustees actively supported the work of the Society for the Propagation of the Gospel and the Society for the Promotion of Christian Knowledge as well as that undertaken by The Associates of Dr. Bray. Betty Wood, "The Earl of Egmont and the Georgia Colony," in Jackson and Spalding, *Forty Years of Diversity*, 82; Spalding, "Oglethorpe's Quest," 68–69; Ettinger, *Oglethorpe*, 110–12; Verner W. Crane, "Dr. Thomas Bray and the Charitable Colony Project," *WMQ*, 3d ser., 19 (1962): 49–63.

12. Ettinger, *Oglethorpe*, 147–48.

13. Wood, *Slavery in Colonial Georgia*, 2–10.

14. Ettinger, *Oglethorpe*, 84–96; Milton L. Ready, "Philanthropy and the Origins of Georgia," in Jackson and Spalding, *Forty Years of Diversity*, 46–59; Spalding, "Oglethorpe's Quest," 63–71.

15. For earlier proposals to colonize the borderlands, see Verner W. Crane, *The Southern Frontier, 1670–1732* (Ann Arbor, 1929); and Trevor R. Reese, ed., *The Most Delightful Country of the Universe: Promotional Literature of the Colony of Georgia, 1717–1734* (Savannah, 1972).

16. Sir Robert Montgomery, A *Discourse Concerning the design'd Establishment of a New Colony to the South of Carolina, in the Most delightful Country of the Universe* [London, 1717], ed. J. Max Patrick, reprinted in Emory University Publications, Sources and Reprints, ser. 4, no. 3 (Atlanta, 1948), 22.

17. Wood, *Slavery in Colonial Georgia*, 5–8; J. E. Crowley, *This Sheba, Self: The Conceptualization of Economic Life in Eighteenth-Century America* (Baltimore, 1974), 20–23, 34; Spalding, "Oglethorpe's Quest."

18. Wood, "Earl of Egmont," 83–84.

19. Wood, *Slavery in Colonial Georgia*, 5–8.

20. Benjamin Martyn to Governor Robert Johnson, October 18, 1732, Ms. CRG, 29:1–2; Oglethorpe to the Trustees, ca. December 1733, Egmont Papers, 14200, pt. 1, 51–52; George Fenwick Jones, ed., *Detailed Reports on the Salzburger Emigrants Who Settled in America . . . Edited by Samuel Urlsperger*, 8 vols. to date (Athens, Ga., 1968–), 1:56–106.

21. For relations between Georgia and South Carolina during the first decade of Georgia's settlement, see Phinizy Spalding, "Georgia and South Carolina during the Oglethorpe Period, 1732–1743" (Ph.D. diss., University of North Carolina, 1963).

22. Oglethorpe to the Trustees, August 12, 1733, Egmont Papers, 14200, pt. 1, 37–39; Oglethorpe to Samuel Wesley, November 19, 1734, in George Fenwick Jones, ed., *Henry Newman's Salzburger Letterbooks* (Athens, Ga., 1966), 514; Benjamin Martyn to Oglethorpe, November 22, 1733, Egmont Papers, 14207, 57.

23. Wood, *Slavery in Colonial Georgia*, 8–9. For a discussion of Spanish policy, see John J. TePaske, "The Fugitive Slave: Intercolonial Rivalry and Spanish Slave Policy, 1687–1764," in Samuel Proctor, ed., *Eighteenth-Century Florida and Its Borderlands* (Gainesville, 1975), 1–12.

24. Wood, *Slavery in Colonial Georgia*, 24–35. For the malcontents' most important published works, see Trevor R. Reese, ed., *The Clamorous Malcontents: Criticisms and Defenses of the Colony of Georgia, 1741–1743* (Savannah, 1973). See also Patrick Tailfer and others to the Trustees, received August 27, 1735, Egmont Papers, 14201, 108–12; and Memorial to the Trustees, December 9, 1738, ibid., 14203, 230–35. For Thomas Stephens's works see n. 26 below.

25. Wood, "Thomas Stephens," 24–40.

26. Clarence L. Ver Steeg, ed., *A True and Historical Narrative of the Colony of Georgia. By Pat. Tailfer and Others. With Comments by the Earl of Egmont* (Athens, Ga., 1960). Thomas Stephens was the malcontents' most prolific author. His works include: "Thoughts on ye Colony of Georgia, and the Trustees Measures, 24 Nov. 1739," Egmont Papers, 14210, 95–110; "Comparison between the profit and labour of Negroes with that of white men," ibid., 154–62; *The Hard Case of the Distressed People of Georgia* (London, 1742); and *A Brief Account of the Causes that have Retarded the Progress of the Colony of Georgia* (London, 1743).

27. Wood, "Earl of Egmont," 88; idem, *Slavery in Colonial Georgia*, 33–34, 37.

28. Ralph Gray and Betty Wood, "The Transition from Indentured to Involuntary Servitude in Colonial Georgia," *Explorations in Economic History* 13 (1976): 353–70.

29. Wood, *Slavery in Colonial Georgia*, 80–87, 90–109.

30. Ibid., 51, 77–78.

31. Ibid., 32–58.

32. Ibid., 59–73; Jackson, "Darien Petition," 618–31.

33. Ver Steeg, *True and Historical Narrative*, 98.

34. Jackson, "Darien Petition," 630.

35. David Brion Davis, *The Problem of Slavery in Western Culture* (Ithaca, 1966; reprint, 1970), 169.

36. Johann Martin Boltzius to George Whitefield, December 24, 1745, CRG, 24:434–39.

37. Oglethorpe to the Trustees, January 16 and 17, 1739, Egmont Papers, 14203, pt. 2, 185–88.

38. Ettinger, *Oglethorpe*, 147–48. See also Arthur Pierce Middleton, "The Strange Case of Job Ben Solomon," *WMQ*, 3d ser., 5 (1948): 342–50.

39. Wood, *Slavery in Colonial Georgia*, 53–56, 77–78; idem, "Earl of Egmont," 92–93.

40. Wood, *Slavery in Colonial Georgia*, 74–87.

41. Ettinger, *Oglethorpe*, 252–82.

42. Spalding, "Oglethorpe's Quest," 76.

5. Oglethorpe, William Stephens, and the Origin of Georgia Politics (Phinizy Spalding)

1. For more than adequate treatment on all of these aspects of Georgia's early history, see E. Merton Coulter, ed., *The Journal of Peter Gordon* (Athens, Ga., 1963); *Egmont's Journal*; *Diary of Percival*; and other primary sources. Good secondary accounts appear in Phinizy Spalding, *Oglethorpe in America* (Chicago, 1977); Kenneth Coleman, *Colonial Georgia:*

A History (New York, 1976); and Amos Aschbach Ettinger, *James Edward Oglethorpe: Imperial Idealist* (Oxford, 1936).

2. Thomas Causton to his Wife, March 12, 1733, Egmont Papers, 14200, 55.

3. Samuel Eveleigh to the Trustees, April 6, 1733, ibid., 61.

4. *South Carolina Gazette,* October 19, 1734.

5. CRG, 1:44–48, 49–52, for texts of the Rum and Negro acts.

6. Elizabeth Bland to Oglethorpe, June 14, 1735, ibid., 20:394–95.

7. Ettinger, *Oglethorpe,* 185–86.

8. *Egmont's Journal,* 230.

9. *Dictionary of National Biography,* 17:1069–70; Romney Sedgwick, ed., *The History of Parliament: The House of Commons, 1715–1754,* 2 vols. (London, 1970), 2:445.

10. See David Murray, *The York Buildings Company: A Chapter in Scotch History* (Glasgow, 1883); and A. J. Graham Cummings, "The York Buildings Company: A Case Study in Eighteenth-Century Corporation Management," 2 vols. (Ph.D. diss., University of Strathclyde, Scotland, 1980).

11. For the fullest account of William Stephens in print to date, see his son Thomas Stephens's unusual book, *The Castle-Builders; or, The History of William Stephens, of the Isle of Wight, Esq.; lately deceased* (London, 1759). The best recent scholarly article dealing with William Stephens is Carole Watterson Troxler, "William Stephens and the Georgia 'Malcontents': Conciliation, Conflict, and Capitulation," *GHQ* 67 (1983): 1–34.

12. The journal written for Horsey is printed as app. A in E. Merton Coulter, ed., *The Journal of William Stephens, 1741–1745,* 2 vols. (Athens, Ga., 1958–59), 1:235–60.

13. Horsey Journal, in ibid., 1:254.

14. *Egmont's Journal,* 260, 264.

15. Ibid., 294; Benjamin Martyn to Causton, August 3, 1737, Egmont Papers, 14209, 27; Harman Verelst to Causton, August 11, 1737, ibid., 49.

16. For his instructions, see Coulter, *Journal of William Stephens,* 1:261–63.

17. James Ross McCain, *Georgia as a Proprietary Province . . .* (Boston, 1917), 152.

18. *Egmont's Journal,* 294.

19. Martyn to Causton, August 3, 1737, Egmont Papers, 14209, 27; Verelst to Causton, August 11, 1737, ibid., 49; CRG, 4:7–11.

20. John Brownfield to the Trustees, February 10, 1737, in Mills B. Lane, ed., *General Oglethorpe's Georgia,* 2 vols. (Savannah, 1975), 1:293.

21. Brownfield to the Trustees, May 2, 1737, ibid., 306–08.

22. Ibid., 308.

23. CRG, 4:11–12.

24. Ibid., 12, 14, 15–17, 44–45, 52–53.

25. Ibid., 46.
26. Ibid., 55.
27. Ibid., 111.
28. Ibid., 129.
29. *Diary of Percival*, 2:472–74.
30. CRG, 4:140.
31. *Egmont's Journal*, 344, 345–47, 361; Benjamin Martyn to William Stephens, May 19, 1738, CRG, 29:259–60; *Diary of Percival*, 2:478–79. See also Troxler, "William Stephens," 6–7. Martyn wrote that "a second Reflection" would prove to Stephens how "impracticable" an heirs general system would be in such a diffuse province.
32. CRG, 4:157; Hugh Anderson to Adam Anderson, June 15, 1738, in Lane, *General Oglethorpe's Georgia*, 2:338.
33. CRG, 4:206.
34. Ibid., 213.
35. Ibid., 217–18. Oglethorpe was harsher on Causton than the Trustees intended. Egmont, in fact, interpreted Oglethorpe's hard-line approach as being a ploy to seek popularity from the Georgians at the expense of the Trust in London. See Sarah Gober Temple and Kenneth Coleman, *Georgia Journeys, 1732–1754* (Athens, Ga., 1961), 105–06; *Diary of Percival*, 2:516–17.
36. CRG, 4:224.
37. Ibid., 226–27.
38. Ibid., 226, 233, 239, 231, 243.
39. Ibid., 243–44.
40. For the text of the representation, see Lane, *General Oglethorpe's Georgia*, 2:371–75, or Egmont Papers, 14203, pt. 2, 330–35.
41. James Oglethorpe to the Trustees, March 12, 1739, *Coll. GHS*, 3:70–71. For additional Oglethorpe reactions, see his earlier letters of January 16 and 17, 1739, to the Trustees, in Lane, *General Oglethorpe's Georgia*, 2:387–90. Negroes bred idleness in whites, he said, and there was no effective way to limit the number of slaves permitted in the colony. This suggestion had been one of the proposals contained in the representation.
42. Anderson's letter of January 6, 1739, to Oglethorpe is found in Lane, *General Oglethorpe's Georgia*, 2:379–87, and his letter of March 3, 1739, to Egmont is reprinted in CRG, 22, pt. 2, 93–105. For an excellent account of the discontent that followed this representation, see Betty Wood, *Slavery in Colonial Georgia, 1730–1775* (Athens, Ga., 1984), 29 and passim; and idem, "Thomas Stephens and the Introduction of Black Slavery in Georgia," *GHQ* 58 (1974): 24–40.
43. Both Darien and Ebenezer finally did issue counterpetitions. For a superb

treatment of the former see Harvey H. Jackson, "The Darien Antislavery Petition of 1739 and the Georgia Plan," *WMQ*, 3d ser., 34 (1977): 618–31.

44. *CRG*, 4:273–74, 298.

45. See Verelst to Oglethorpe, June 11, 1738, ibid., 30:47–48; Martyn to the Magistrates of Savannah, June 20, 1739, Ms. *CRG*, 32:38–40; and Egmont Papers, 14210, 157–59. Two hundred copies of the Trustees' answer were ordered printed to be sent to Georgia. See *CRG*, 2:290.

46. *CRG*, 4:276; and Stephens to Verelst, January 3, 1739, ibid., 22, pt. 2, 6.

47. For the fullest account of this pamphlet war, waged on both sides of the Atlantic, see Phinizy Spalding, "Georgia and South Carolina during the Oglethorpe Period, 1732–1743" (Ph.D. diss., University of North Carolina, 1963), 137–202, and Milton L. Ready, "The Georgia Trustees and the Malcontents: The Politics of Philanthropy," *GHQ* 60 (1976): 264–81.

6. Oglethorpe's Contest for the Backcountry, 1733–1749 (Edward J. Cashin)

1. William P. Cumming, *The Southeast in Early Maps* (Princeton, 1958; reprint, Chapel Hill, 1962), 39.

2. Charles Gayarré, *History of Louisiana*, 4 vols. (New Orleans, 1879), 1:456–60; Richard Paul Sonderegger, "The Southern Frontier from the Founding of Georgia to the End of King George's War" (Ph.D. diss., University of Michigan, 1964), 55–61.

3. Oglethorpe to Trustees, March 12, 1733, *CRG*, 20:13–14.

4. *Egmont's Journal*, 193–95; for a description of the Carolina trade, see Verner W. Crane, *The Southern Frontier, 1670–1732* (Ann Arbor, 1929); M. Eugene Sirmans, *Colonial South Carolina* (Chapel Hill, 1966); William L. McDowell, ed., *Colonial Records of South Carolina: Documents Relating to Indian Affairs*, 3 vols. (Columbia, S.C., 1955, 1958, 1970).

5. Oglethorpe to the Trustees, June 9, 1733, *CRG*, 20:23–25; ibid., 4, supplement, 85–87. Colonel George Chicken tried to persuade Squirrel King to move across to the Georgia side in 1725; Newton D. Mereness, ed., *Travels in the American Colonies* (New York, 1916), 168–72; Robert L. Meriwether attempts to follow the elusive Fort Moore Chickasaws and Uchees in *The Expansion of South Carolina* (Kingsport, Tenn., 1940; reprint, Philadelphia, 1974), 70–74.

6. Samuel Eveleigh to Oglethorpe, November 20, 1734, *CRG*, 20:105–08; Crane, *Southern Frontier*, 121.

7. Sonderegger, "Southern Frontier," 61–62; Extract of a letter from South Carolina, February 1734, Oglethorpe to Trustees, April 2, 1734, Extract

of a memorial of the South Carolina Assembly to the King, April 9, 1734, all in *CRG*, 20:49–50, 52–53, 55.

8. Patrick Mackay to Thomas Causton, July 8, 1734, *CRG*, 20:60–61.

9. Mary Musgrove to Oglethorpe, July 17, 1734, ibid., 63–64.

10. Patrick Mackay to [Thomas Causton], March 27, 1735, ibid., 290–91; Phinizy Spalding, "Georgia and South Carolina during the Oglethorpe Period, 1732–1743" (Ph.D. diss., University of North Carolina, 1963), 61–82.

11. Spalding, "Georgia and South Carolina," 71; Sonderegger, "Southern Frontier," 128; John Fenwicke to Oglethorpe, April 3, 1735, *CRG*, 20:310–11.

12. Humble Memorial and Representation of the State and Condition of Your Majesty's Province of South Carolina . . . to the King's Most Excellent Majesty, April 9, 1735, *CRG*, 3:413–19; Samuel Eveleigh to William Jeffreys, July 4, 1735, ibid., 20:420–22.

13. Magistrates of Georgia to Lieutenant Governor Thomas Broughton of South Carolina, July 21, 1735, Lieutenant Governor Thomas Broughton to the Magistrates of Georgia, July 29, 1735, both in ibid., 20:488–93.

14. An Act for maintaining the Peace with the Indians in the Province of Georgia, March 21, 1733, approved by the Privy Council, April 3, 1735; An Act to prevent the Importation and Use of Rum and Brandies in the Province of Georgia, January 9, 1734, approved by Privy Council, April 3, 1735, both in ibid., 1:31–49.

15. Oglethorpe to Trustees, June 1736, in Mills B. Lane, ed., *General Oglethorpe's Georgia*, 2 vols. (Savannah, 1975), 1:268–76; Eveleigh to Verelst, July 20, 1736, *CRG*, 21:179; William Bacon Stevens, *A History of Georgia*, 2 vols. (New York, 1847), 1:95. Phinizy Spalding, *Oglethorpe in America* (Chicago, 1977), 79.

16. Oglethorpe to Noble Jones, June 14, 1736, Instructions for Mr. Lacy, June 11, 1736, Egmont Papers, 14202; *Egmont's Journal*, 272–73; *South Carolina Gazette*, October 16–23, 1736.

17. Lieutenant Anthony Willy was the ranger who escorted Tanner; see Thomas Causton to Mr. Alex Wood, January 12, 1737, *CRG*, 21:303; for an account of Tanner's brash conduct, see Thomas John's Journal or Narrative on Oath, December 2, 1736, in J. H. Easterby, ed., *The Journal of the Commons House of Assembly* 9 vols. (Columbia, S.C., 1951–62), 1:138–40.

18. *Egmont's Journal*, 193–95.

19. Eveleigh to Verelst, October 13, 1736, *CRG*, 21:211–12; Spalding, *Oglethorpe in America*, 8. Tanner is identified here as Richard, but in the *South Carolina Gazette*, October 16–23, 1736, and in the testimony in the Journal of the South Carolina Assembly, the name is John. Presumably they are references to the same person.

20. Gayarré, *History of Louisiana*, 1:481–82.
21. Causton to Trustees, April 25, 1737, CRG, 21:400–403; ibid., 4:46–47; Private Conference with the King, next Head Warriour, and the two principal Old Headmen and beloved Man of the Savano River Chicasaws, held by his Majesty's Agent in Augusta, November 14, 1758, in William H. Lyttelton Papers, William L. Clements Library, Ann Arbor, Michigan. William Gray's cloudy title to New Savannah is mentioned in Minutes of Meeting of President and Assistants, May 4, 1749, CRG, 6:245–47. See also ibid., 4:47.
22. CRG, 4:47. The Trustees Minutes of November 8, 1732, reveal that Mr. Richard Kent donated the sum of twenty pounds to the Georgia project; ibid., 1:84. Oglethorpe mentioned that Lieutenant Kent's father was Parliament member from Reading and "has a good Estate"; Oglethorpe to Verelst, October 19, 1739, ibid., 22, pt. 2, 244–49.
23. Samuel Cole Williams, ed., *Adair's History of the American Indians* (New York, 1974), 443.
24. CRG, 4:179; Causton to Trustees, August 26, 1738, ibid., 22, pt. 1, 230–34; for Lacy's contributions to Augusta, see Theophilus Hetherington to Trustees, December 1, 1739, ibid., pt. 2, 275–78.
25. Thomas Jones to William Verelst, February 17, 1739, ibid., pt. 2, 79–87; Sonderegger, "Southern Frontier," 87–88.
26. Oglethorpe to Verelst, June 15, 1739, in Lane, *General Oglethorpe's Georgia*, 2:406–07.
27. Sonderegger, "Southern Frontier," 88–91.
28. "An Abstract from my Journals . . . ," in Thomas Eyre to Robert Eyre, December 4, 1740, in Lane, *General Oglethorpe's Georgia*, 2:499–510.
29. Oglethorpe to Verelst, October 19, 1739, CRG, 22, pt. 2, 244–53; Letter from Thomas Jones, October 23, 1741, ibid., 23:116–30.
30. Oglethorpe to Trustees, March 8, 1739, and April 10, 1740, *Coll. GHS*, 3:68, 111–12.
31. Thomas Eyre to Robert Eyre, December 4, 1740, in Lane, *General Oglethorpe's Georgia*, 2:499–510.
32. Sonderegger, "Southern Frontier," 91; Gayarré, *History of Louisiana*, 1:507; Oglethorpe to Trustees, November 16, 1739, in Lane, *General Oglethorpe's Georgia*, 2:420–22.
33. Gayarré, *History of Louisiana*, 1:513.
34. Oglethorpe to Egmont, January 25, 1741, in Lane, *General Oglethorpe's Georgia*, 2:535–39.
35. Gayarré, *History of Louisiana*, 1:523–24.
36. Hugh Anderson and others to the Trustees, December 2, 1740, in Lane, *General Oglethorpe's Georgia*, 2:491–96.

37. For an example of Kent's problems, see Stephens Journal, June 3 and 30, 1740, CRG, 4:585–86, 608; for Kent's mediation efforts, see ibid., supplement, 103 (mistakenly numbered 106)–104; for the augmentation of the Augusta garrison, see ibid., 126. According to Larry E. Ivers, Sergeant Ambrose Morrison and two rangers from Fort Augusta were stationed in Fort Oakfuskee; Ivers, "The Soldiers of Fort Augusta," in Edward J. Cashin, ed., *Colonial Augusta "Key of the Indian Countrey"* (Macon, 1986), 91. For examples of Kent's dispatches, see Stephens Journal, CRG 4, supplement, 81–82.

38. *South Carolina Gazette*, August 15, 1743; the *London Magazine*, September 1760, 443–45; Knox Mellon, Jr., "Christian Priber's Cherokee Kingdom of Paradise," GHQ 57 (1973): 319–31.

39. William Horton to Mary Bosomworth, received March 30, 1736, CRG, 27:268; John Dobell to Trustees, n.d., ibid., 25:42–48.

40. William Stephens to Benjamin Martyn, March 17, 1746, ibid., 25:25–29.

41. Stephens Journal, June 30, 1740, ibid., 4:608–09; Brown, Rae and Company to the Trustees, February 13, 1750, ibid., 26:152–55. Patrick Brown and John Rae were partners in the company.

42. Minutes of Meeting of President and Assistants, June 10, 1749, ibid., 6:249–51; Minutes of Meeting of President and Assistants, May 4, 1749, ibid., 6:245–47; Minutes of Meeting of President and Assistants, July 26, 1749, ibid., 6:255–56.

43. Cumming, *Early Maps*, 47–49.

44. Extract from Report by Benjamin Martyn, CRG, 3:402.

7. James Oglethorpe in Europe: Recent Findings in His Military Life (Rodney M. Baine and Mary E. Williams)

1. This chapter draws extensively upon our "Oglethorpe's Missing Years," which appeared in the spring 1985 issue of *GHQ*, and upon our "Oglethorpe's Early Military Campaigns," in the *Yale University Library Gazette* 60 (1985). We are especially indebted to these journals for permission to quote; to the Yale University Library, the Editorial Committee of the Boswell Papers, and McGraw Hill, owner of the copyright, for permission to cite and quote the Boswell Papers; to James Alexander Elphinstone, Baron Elphinstone, for permission to quote Oglethorpe's letters to Keith; and to Phinizy Spalding, for the generous loan of his photocopy of Boswell's notes.

2. See Leslie F. Church, *Oglethorpe: A Study of Philanthropy in England and*

Georgia (London, 1932), 4, and Amos Aschbach Ettinger, *James Edward Oglethorpe: Imperial Idealist* (Oxford, 1936), 67–68.

3. Thaddeus Mason Harris, *Biographical Memorials of James Oglethorpe, Founder of the Colony of Georgia* (Boston, 1841), 4–9; Robert Wright, *A Memoir of General James Oglethorpe* (London, 1867), 5–11; and Henry Bruce, *Life of General Oglethorpe* (New York, 1890), 6, 20–22.

4. Boswell Papers, 208:1, also source of all subsequent undocumented Boswell references; Oglethorpe to Keith, December 9, 1755, from a microfilm of the original in the Scottish Record Office, Edinburgh.

5. Charles Dalton, *English Army Lists and Commission Registers*, 6 vols. (London, 1892–1904), 6:51, 53; Ettinger, *Oglethorpe*, 58, 67.

6. Boswell Papers, 208:1.

7. Ibid.

8. James Boswell, *Life of Dr. Johnson*, ed. G. B. Hill and L. F. Powell, 6 vols. (Oxford, 1934), 2:180–81.

9. Boswell Papers, 208:1.

10. Austro-Hungarian Empire, Kriegsarchiv, *Feldzüge des Prinzen Eugen von Savoyen*, 39 vols. (Vienna, 1876–92), 16:290–91; Boswell Papers, 208:1.

11. Boswell, *Johnson*, 2:181.

12. Fanny Oglethorpe to the Earl of Mar, August 28, 1717, in Great Britain, Historical Manuscripts Commission, *Calendar of the Stuart Papers . . . preserved at Windsor Castle*, 6 vols. (London, 1902–23), 4:540; Boswell Papers, 208:1; P. D. Pasolini, *Memoiria Storiche della Famiglia Rasponi* (Imola, Italy, 1876), 171; Andreas Thürheim, *Feldmarshall Otto Ferdinand Graf von Abensperg und Traun* (Vienna, 1877), 374.

13. Oglethorpe's service as adjutant general is confirmed by Thürheim, *Feldmarshall Ferdinand*, 372; *Wiennerisches Diarium*, August 18–20, 1717.

14. The Earl of Mar to Fanny Oglethorpe, February 19, 1718, in *Stuart Papers*, 5:494.

15. Oglethorpe to Keith, December 9, 1755; Thürheim, *Feldmarshall Ferdinand*, 372.

16. Fanny Oglethorpe to the Earl of Mar, in *Stuart Papers*, 7:157.

17. Sir Kenneth Dover, President, Corpus Christi College, Oxford, to Rodney M. Baine, May 23, 1983, in author's possession.

18. Oglethorpe's requests for assistance are in the British Library, Egerton MSS 3444, ff. 61–62 and Add. MSS 32859, ff. 185–87.

19. Ettinger, *Oglethorpe*, 286.

20. Deposited by James Alexander Elphinstone, Baron Elphinstone, at the Scottish Record Office.

21. Ibid. Although Oglethorpe did not own the manor of Hurtmore, he held the right of tithes and other rights in all of the manors of Godalming

Parish. See P. Woods, "The Parsonage, or Rectory manor of Godalming," *Surrey Archeological Collections* 22 (1909): 123.

22. Thomas Carlyle, *The History of Friedrich the Second, called Frederick the Great*, 6 vols. (New York, 1874–80), 5:293.

23. Andrew Bisset, ed., *Memoirs and Papers of Sir Andrew Mitchell*, 2 vols. (London, 1850), 2:501.

24. British Library, Add. MSS 6861, f. 302.

25. Ettinger, *Oglethorpe*, 328, n. 3.

26. Frederick A. Pottle, ed., *Boswell on the Grand Tour: Germany, Switzerland, 1764* (New York, 1953), 73.

27. Mitchell Papers, British Library, Add. MSS 6867.

28. *Politsche Correspondenz Friedrichs des Grossen*, 39 vols. (Berlin, 1879–1925), 17:83.

29. Mitchell Papers, BL Add. MSS 6836, f. 109, recto.

30. See Arthur H. Scouten, ed., *The London Stage, 1660–1800*, pt. 3, *1729–1747*, 2 vols. (Carbondale, 1961), 1:479; and Edgar V. Roberts, "The Ballad Operas of Henry Fielding, 1730–1732," 2 vols. (Ph.D. diss., University of Minnesota, 1960), 2:530–41.

31. Yorke to Mitchell, August 7, 1758, Mitchell Papers, BL Add. MSS 6836, f. 105, recto.

32. "Tebay" (Oglethorpe) to Mitchell, October 29, 1758, Mitchell Papers, BL Add. MSS 6836, ff. 50–51.

33. So he wrote in his letter to Mitchell.

34. Ettinger, *Oglethorpe*, 317, citing *A Note Book of Horace Walpole*, ed. W. S. Lewis (New York, 1927), 48. The brackets are Ettinger's.

8. Oglethorpe and James Wright: A Georgia Comparison (Kenneth Coleman)

1. On Oglethorpe's pre-Georgia career, see Amos Aschbach Ettinger, *James Edward Oglethorpe: Imperial Idealist* (Oxford, 1936), 47–86, and chap. 7 of this volume.

2. See Phinizy Spalding, *Oglethorpe in America* (Chicago, 1977), 2–3.

3. See Kenneth Coleman, "The Founding of Georgia," in Harvey H. Jackson and Phinizy Spalding, eds., *Forty Years of Diversity: Essays on Colonial Georgia* (Athens, Ga., 1984), 4–20, and any life of Oglethorpe or history of early Georgia.

4. Thomas Christie, "The Voyage of the *Anne*—A Daily Record," ed. Robert G. McPherson, *GHQ* 44 (1960): 220–30.

5. CRG, 3:405–09. See also Hector de Beaufain to Peter Simond and J. C. Simond, January 23, 1733/4, ibid., 20:45–46.

6. George Fenwick Jones, ed., *Detailed Reports on the Salzburger Emigrants Who Settled in America . . . Edited by Samuel Urlsperger*, 9 vols. to date (Athens, Ga., 1968–), 1:35.

7. On Trustee government, see James Ross McCain, *Georgia as a Proprietary Province . . .* (Boston, 1917), 137–225. On Oglethorpe's position, see ibid., 57–97; Spalding, *Oglethorpe in America*, passim.

8. See McCain, *Proprietary Province*, 69; Spalding, *Oglethorpe in America*, 16–17, 41–42, 72–75; Oglethorpe's correspondence from America is in CRG, vols. 20–24 (especially 20), and the Egmont Papers.

9. On Oglethorpe and Indians, see Spalding, *Oglethorpe in America*, 76–97; Ettinger, *Oglethorpe*, passim (quotation from p. 182); John Pitts Corry, *Indian Affairs in Georgia, 1732–1756* (Philadelphia, 1936).

10. Spalding, *Oglethorpe in America*; Ettinger, *Oglethorpe*; McCain, *Proprietary Province*; Oglethorpe correspondence in CRG.

11. Spalding, *Oglethorpe in America*; Ettinger, *Oglethorpe*; Herbert E. Bolton and Mary Ross, *The Debatable Land . . .* (Berkeley and Los Angeles, 1925); John Tate Lanning, *The Diplomatic History of Georgia* (Chapel Hill, 1936); Larry E. Ivers, *British Drums on the Southern Frontier: The Military Colonization of Georgia, 1733–1749* (Chapel Hill, 1974).

12. On Wright's pre-Georgia career, see E. Irving Carlyle, "Sir James Wright," in *Dictionary of National Biography*, 63:107–09; and Kenneth Coleman, "James Wright," in Kenneth Coleman and Charles Stephen Gurr, eds., *Dictionary of Georgia Biography* (Athens, Ga., 1983), 1097–98.

13. On Wright's governorship, see Kenneth Coleman, "James Wright," in Horace Montgomery, ed., *Georgians in Profile* (Athens, Ga., 1958), 40–60; Kenneth Coleman, *Colonial Georgia: A History* (New York, 1976); W. W. Abbot, *The Royal Governors of Georgia* (Chapel Hill, 1959). Wright's correspondence is in CRG, vol. 28, pts. 1 and 2; Ms. CRG, vols. 37 and 38; and *Coll. GHS*, vol. 3.

14. Besides Wright's correspondence, see the council and assembly records in CRG, vols. 7–17.

15. Abbot, *Royal Governors*, 100–102; Coleman, *Colonial Georgia*, 198–200.

16. Coleman, "James Wright," 41; *Coll. GHS*, 6:102.

17. On land granting, see Coleman, *Colonial Georgia*, 205–09.

18. Wright to Board of Trade, October 1, 1762, CRG, 28, pt. 1, 383; CRG, 11:155.

19. Coleman, *Colonial Georgia*, 195–96; Abbot, *Royal Governors*, 89–94.

20. Coleman, *Colonial Georgia*, 209; Wright to Board of Trade, CRG, 28, pt. 2, 106–08, 377–78, 382–83.

21. Coleman, *Colonial Georgia*, 263–68; Abbot, *Royal Governors*, passim.
22. Kenneth Coleman, *The American Revolution in Georgia, 1763–1789* (Athens, Ga., 1958); idem, "James Wright and the Origins of the Revolution in Georgia," in James Kirby Martin, *The Human Dimensions of Nation Making* (Madison, Wis., 1976), 105–20.
23. John Adams to Abiel Holmes, November 14, 1807, in Abiel Holmes, *The Annals of America*, 2d ed., 2 vols. (Cambridge, 1829), 2:530, n. xii; Ettinger, *Oglethorpe*, 326.

9. The Search for Authentic Icons of James Edward Oglethorpe (Edwin L. Jackson)

1. David Piper, *The English Face* (London, 1957), 329.
2. To compile this record and establish the background of each portrait, visits to England took place in 1982, 1983, and 1985. The undertaking originated from efforts to determine whether a portrait of James Oglethorpe in the possession of the Carl Vinson Institute of Government was, in fact, authentic.
3. Ellis Waterhouse, *Painting in Britain: 1530 to 1790* (Harmondsworth, England, 1962), 98; John Kerslake, *National Portrait Gallery Early Georgian Portraits*, 2 vols. (London, 1977), 1:vii; Piper, *English Face*, 156–63.
4. Waterhouse, *Painting in Britain*, 156; Charles R. Leslie and Tom Taylor, *Life and Times of Sir Joshua Reynolds*, 2 vols. (London, 1865), 2:285.
5. Ronald Paulson, *Hogarth: His Life, Art, and Times*, 2 vols. (New Haven, 1971), 1:430; Donald Garstang, ed., *The British Face: A View of Portraiture 1625–1850* (London, 1986), 12. Seventeenth-century etiquette even prescribed where portraits might hang—a restriction that broke down in the 1700s. Piper, *English Face*, 136, 139.
6. Piper, *English Face*, 139.
7. Garstang, *British Face*, 20–21.
8. W. Y. Carman, *British Military Uniforms* (London, 1957), xvi.
9. Ibid., 22.
10. Piper, *English Face*, 133; Penelope Byrde, *The Male Image: Men's Fashion in Britain: 1300–1970* (London, 1979), 163.
11. Piper, *English Face*, 134; Byrde, *Male Image*, 163. However, by mid-eighteenth century, wigs were being worn by men of all social classes.
12. Piper, *English Face*, 135; R. Turner Wilcox, *The Mode in Hats and Headdress* (New York, 1959), 141; Iris Brooke, *Dress and Undress: The Restoration and Eighteenth Century* (London, 1958), 76; Byrde, *Male Image*, 165; C. Willett

Cunnington and Phillis Cunnington, *Handbook of English Costume in the Eighteenth Century* (London, 1972), 89.

13. Piper, *English Face*, 190.
14. Cunnington and Cunnington, *English Costume*, 89; Byrde, *Male Image*, 165; Marion Sichel, *Costume Reference: The Eighteenth Century* (Boston, 1977), 23; Piper, *English Face*, 163–64.
15. Herman W. Liebert, "Portraits of the Author: Lifetime Likenesses of Samuel Johnson," in J. Douglas Stewart and Herman W. Liebert, *English Portraits of the Seventeenth and Eighteenth Centuries* (Los Angeles, 1974), 50. The tradition of his height is recorded in Phinizy Spalding, *Oglethorpe in America* (Chicago, 1977), 153; Robert Wright, *A Memoir of General James Oglethorpe* (London, 1867), 56.
16. William B. Clarke, *Early and Historic Freemasonry of Georgia: 1733/4–1800* (Savannah, 1924), 109–10.
17. Oliver Larkin, *Samuel F. B. Morse and American Democratic Art* (Boston, 1954), 102, 110.
18. Rodney M. Baine and Mary E. Williams, "Oglethorpe's Early Military Campaigns," *Yale University Library Gazette* 60 (1985): 69.
19. Bray was present in the Oglethorpe home the day before the aged general died. The following year, Elizabeth had Bray draw up her will. See Phinizy Spalding, "The Death of James Edward Oglethorpe," *GHQ* 57 (1973): 227–34.
20. Owen Manning and William Bray, *The History and Antiquities of the County of Surrey*, 3 vols. (London, 1804, 1809, 1814), 1:613. For many years, Manning had compiled extensive notes on the history of Surrey but had never published the effort. After Manning's death, Bray continued the work, three years later publishing the first of a three-volume history of Surrey.
21. Wright, *Memoir of Oglethorpe*, 405–06; Thaddeus Mason Harris, *Biographical Memorials of James Oglethorpe . . .* (Boston, 1841), 309.
22. Information sheet on the two portraits prepared by Oglethorpe University. That sheet lists 1924 as the date of Jacobs's trip to England. Actually, he was there in the fall of 1923. The Highs purchased the paintings and presented them to Oglethorpe University in February 1924.
23. "The Rules extended south from the prison on the east side of Fleet Canal to Ludgate Hill, east to Cock Alley, north on Old Bailey as far as Fleet Lane, west on Fleet Lane to the Canal, and from thence south to the prison again" (Paulson, *Hogarth*, 1:33).
24. The most extensive examination of Castell and Oglethorpe is found in Rodney M. Baine, "The Prison Death of Robert Castell and Its Effect on the Founding of Georgia," scheduled for publication in *GHQ* in 1988. Also

see Amos Aschbach Ettinger, *James Edward Oglethorpe: Imperial Idealist* (Oxford, 1936), 90; Wright, *Memoir of Oglethorpe*, 17; Leslie F. Church, *Oglethorpe: A Study of Philanthropy in England and Georgia* (London, 1932), 12; Webb Garrison, *Oglethorpe's Folly: The Birth of Georgia* (Lakemont, Ga., 1982), 24–25; Harriet C. Cooper, *James Oglethorpe: The Founder of Georgia* (New York, 1904), 9.

25. An account in London's *Daily Post* of January 29 indicated Bambridge was wounded (Paulson, *Hogarth*, 1:197–98). Gaols Committee member Sir Edward Knatchbull, however, recorded in his diary, "We then proceeded to examine Mr. Bambridge, the warden . . . being asked how many were in irons he said one for stabbing his man," indicating it was not Bambridge but one of his jailers. A. N. Newman, ed., *The Parliamentary Diary of Sir Edward Knatchbull* (London, 1963), 88.

26. Paulson, *Hogarth*, 1:198.

27. Ibid. Paulson indicates that the date of the committee interrogation of Bambridge—and hence the occasion of the sketch—was March 8. Although the committee met with Bambridge on that and several other days, Sir Edward Knatchbull's diary supports February 27 as the true date for the incident portrayed by Hogarth.

28. *Diary of Knatchbull*, February 27, 1729, 88–89.

29. Horace Walpole, *Anecdotes of Painting in England* (London, 1876; reprint, 1969), 4.

30. Kerslake, *Early Georgian Portraits*, 1:335; Paulson, *Hogarth*, 1:200.

31. Kerslake, *Early Georgian Portraits*, 1:335.

32. *Diary of Knatchbull*, February 27, 1729, 88.

33. Ibid., 79–81; Kerslake, *Early Georgian Portraits*, 1:335; David Bindman, *Hogarth* (New York, 1981), 49–51. Interestingly, Kerslake thinks the handwriting is probably Walpole's. Derek Jarrett, however, checked with Walpole expert John Brooke, who concluded the inscription was not in Walpole's handwriting. See Derek Jarrett, *The Ingenious Mr. Hogarth* (London, 1976), 206, n. 19.

34. Kerslake, *Early Georgian Portraits*, 1:332.

35. Ibid.

36. Ibid.

37. Ibid., 334. Kerslake identifies the figure as possibly Colonel Onslow. A comparison with the Thornhill and Hogarth painting of the House of Commons in 1730 includes Colonel Onslow's face, and there is a resemblance. However, the figure next to Oglethorpe has an equally compelling likeness to the Hans Hysing portrait of Sir John Percival, later earl of Egmont.

38. In all, ninety-six M.P.'s were named to the Gaols Committee on February 25 (*Commons Journals*, 21:237–38), but only a dozen participated in the

Fleet investigation. Hogarth depicts thirteen members, but one of these is a Commons clerk assigned to the committee. In addition to those already identified, we know that Giles Earle was present on February 27, probably joined by Major Charles Selwyn, who was definitely at Fleet the following day (*Diary of Knatchbull*, 88–89).

39. Kerslake, *Early Georgian Portraits*, 1:335; Paulson, *Hogarth*, 1:198–200.
40. Algernon Graves, *A Dictionary of Artists* (Bath, 1969), 41.
41. For an account of what was said at the meeting portrayed in this painting, see *Diary of Percival*, 2:113–14.
42. Samuel Redgrave, *A Dictionary of Artists of the English School* (Bath, 1970), 449.
43. *Diary of Percival*, 2:171, 175, 187, 258.
44. Ibid., 3:119.
45. Ettinger, *Oglethorpe*, 226.
46. See *Gentleman's Magazine* 6 (1736): 414–15.
47. The poems submitted in the contest had been published two years earlier. The prizewinning entry is found in *Gentleman's Magazine* 6 (1736): 477.
48. Ibid. 55 (1785): 517.
49. Leonard Forrer, *Biographical Dictionary of Medallists*, 8 vols. (New York, 1904; reprint, 1970), 1:339.
50. Kerslake, *Early Georgian Portraits*, 2:plate 572.
51. That Oglethorpe was first named general, followed by a commission several months later as a lower-ranking colonel, is explained by the fact that the first commission—general and commander-in-chief of British forces in Georgia and South Carolina—was not a military rank but rather a title that applied only in the area designated. The subsequent promotion to the rank of colonel, however, was a military rank entitling him to command his own regiment. Later, in 1743, Oglethorpe became an official general in the British army when he was promoted to brigadier general. Between 1737 and 1743, he is sometimes referred to as "General Oglethorpe" and sometimes as "Colonel Oglethorpe." After his September 1743 promotion, however, he is always addressed as "General," a rank he technically retained until his death. Wright, *Memoir of Oglethorpe*, 325. For a discussion of military rank and special relationship of a colonel to his regiment, see Colonel H. C. B. Rogers, *The British Army of the Eighteenth Century* (New York, 1977), and Alan J. Guy, *Oeconomy and Discipline: Officership and administration in the British army, 1714–63* (Manchester, England, 1985).
52. Redgrave, *Dictionary of Artists*, 62.
53. *Dictionary of National Biography*, 3:301; Daniel Mallett, *Mallett's Index of Artists* (New York, 1935), 60.
54. Freeman O'Donoghue, *Catalogue of Engraved British Portraits*, 6 vols. (London, 1908–25), 3:368.

55. The only major exhibition of Greatbach's work was in 1859 at the Royal Academy. Algernon Graves, *A Dictionary of Artists Who Have Exhibited Works in the Principal London Exhibitions from 1760 to 1893* (Bath, 1969), 117.

56. William Bacon Stevens, *A History of Georgia*, 2 vols. (New York, 1847), 1:xiii.

57. William Cullen Bryant and Sidney Howard Gay, *A Popular History of the United States*, 4 vols. (New York, 1879, 1891), 3:143.

58. George Fenwick Jones, *The Salzburger Saga* (Athens, Ga., 1984), 32.

59. George Fenwick Jones, ed. and trans., *Detailed Reports on the Salzburger Emigrants Who Settled in America . . . Edited by Samuel Urlsperger*, 8 vols. to date (Athens, Ga., 1972), 3:227.

60. Ibid., 239.

61. Ibid., 331, n. 250.

62. On October 12, 1971, Jones wrote Carroll Hart, then director of the Georgia State Archives, asking for information about the owner and indicating his desire to inspect the painting. Two years later, Jones wrote again requesting help and noting that he thought he knew who the artist might be. Jones, however, was never able to contact the owner. Appreciation is expressed to Marion Hemperley at the Georgia State Archives for locating this correspondence.

63. Telephone interview with Nicholas Woloshuk, Sante Fe, New Mexico, September 18, 1985.

64. The story ran in the *Atlanta Journal and Constitution*, September 1, 1963.

65. Telephone interview with Carroll Hart, Madison, Georgia, September 18, 1985.

66. Interview with Woloshuk.

67. Letter from Carroll Hart to George Fenwick Jones, October 29, 1971, on file at the Georgia State Archives.

68. Interview with Woloshuk.

69. Information supplied to author from Lane through B. H. Levy, Savannah, September 1985.

70. Carman, *British Military Uniforms*, xvi.

71. On May 1, 1985, at the author's request, David Robb, then director of the Telfair Art Museum in Savannah, inspected the painting. He concluded that it appeared to be from the eighteenth century, but he could make no determination as to whether it was an authentic Oglethorpe.

72. Almost all officers in the British military came from landed gentry and other members of the upper class. During Oglethorpe's era, it was a common practice to purchase one's first and subsequent commissions from retiring officers or senior officers who were buying their own promotion. This practice extended up to colonel and lieutenant colonel ranks, although

appointment to colonel increasingly was made by the king. See Rogers, *British Army*, 53–55, and Guy, *Oeconomy and Discipline*, 88–91.

73. Hugh McCall, *The History of Georgia*, 2 vols. (Savannah, 1811–16; reprint, 2 vols. in 1, Atlanta, 1909), 225.

74. Thornwell Jacobs, *Step Down, Dr. Jacobs: The Autobiography of an Autocrat* (Atlanta, 1945), 865.

75. Letter from Jacobs to A. M. Hind of the British Museum, dated May 10, 1932, on file in the Department of Prints and Drawings, British Museum.

76. In his May 10, 1932, letter to the British Museum, Jacobs referred to the portrait in question as Pape 40152, offered by A. G. Pape, c/o Midland Bank, 166 Old Broad Street, London. In a subsequent September 9 letter, however, Jacobs identified the painting's owner as Captain Carstairs, suggesting that Pape may have been Carstairs's agent. Letters on file in the collection of Oglethorpe engravings in the Department of Prints and Drawings.

77. Letter from Jacobs to the British Museum, September 9, 1932.

78. Ibid.

79. Jacobs, *Step Down*, 865.

80. *Atlanta Constitution*, July 3, 1934.

81. *Gentleman's Magazine* 14 (1744): 451. Ettinger, *Oglethorpe*, 256, describes Elizabeth as "the sister and heiress of the late Sir Jeremy Sambrooke, Baronet, for many years Oglethorpe's colleague in Parliament." According to the *Gentleman's Magazine* announcement, the wedding was supposed to have taken place on July 30, and no mention is made of Elizabeth as an heiress. Indeed, an announcement of her brother's death does not come until 1754. One author attributes the story of their marriage to financial dealings Oglethorpe had with Elizabeth Sambrooke. Garrison, *Oglethorpe's Folly*, 196, 243 n.

82. A hint of marital problems earlier in their marriage is found in an obituary notice for Elizabeth Oglethorpe published in the May 1787 issue of *Gentleman's Magazine*, 1015. Signed by "S" (perhaps Granville Sharp, coexecutor of her will), the announcement notes: "the evening of their lives was tranquil and pleasant after a stormy noon." A variety of other accounts portray a close relationship in their later years, and it is possible the "stormy noon" referred to Oglethorpe's court-martial in 1746 and other disappointments in the 1740s and 1750s.

83. Ettinger, *Oglethorpe*, 322.

84. Letter to Elizabeth Carter dated September 9, 1785, contained in Reginald Blunt, ed., *Mrs. Montagu, "Queen of the Blues,"* 2 vols. (Boston, 1923), 2:193.

85. Jacobs, *Step Down*, 866.

86. Ibid., 863.
87. Ettinger, *Oglethorpe*, 324.
88. Ibid., 324–25.
89. Georgia Laws 1825, Extraordinary Session, 34.
90. Georgia Laws 1826, 35.
91. Several years after the painting was completed, Thomas Hamilton from England recorded in his notes, "I visited the State House. . . . There is a portrait of General Oglethorpe, who first received a grant of the settlement from the British Crown. He is a fine-looking old martinet, with a countenance full of talent, and an air of high breeding." Thomas Hamilton, *Men and Manners in America* (Edinburgh, 1834), 272–73. Presumably, his description is of the Parker portrait, as no other Oglethorpe portrait is known to have hung at the statehouse.
92. Georgia Laws 1906, 1139.
93. For a description with illustrations of British military uniforms of the 1740s and 1750s, see Richard Simkin, *Uniforms of the British Army* (Exeter, England, 1982).
94. *Diary of Percival*, 2:406. During a dinner attended by Oglethorpe, Tanner, Vernon, and Egmont, Tanner, who had returned from Georgia with Oglethorpe four months earlier, reported on his visit to Tomochichi's home. One of the three rooms was a locked parlor, "wherein is the picture of the lion we gave him, as also Mr. Oglethorpe's picture, in whose arms, he said (when he was ill last year) he wished he might die."
95. Jones, *Detailed Reports*, 3:227.
96. Ibid., 239.
97. Ettinger, *Oglethorpe*, 186.
98. Leslie and Taylor, *Life and Times*, 2:285.

Selected Bibliography

What follows is a listing of the principal published works relating to James Oglethorpe and early Georgia, most of which are cited in the endnotes. It is not a comprehensive list and readers are encouraged to consult the endnotes for other books, articles, and monographs that may have pertinence.

Published Primary Sources

Bartram, William. *Travels Through North and South Carolina, Georgia, and West Florida.* Facsimile of the 1792 London Edition. Savannah, 1973.

Candler, Allen D., and Lucian L. Knight, eds. *The Colonial Records of the State of Georgia.* 26 vols. Atlanta, 1904–16.

Coleman, Kenneth, and Milton L. Ready, eds. *The Colonial Records of the State of Georgia.* 7 vols. Athens, Ga., 1968–.

Coulter, E. Merton, ed. *The Journal of Peter Gordon.* Athens, Ga., 1963.

———, ed. *The Journal of William Stephens, 1741–1745.* 2 vols. Athens, Ga., 1958, 1959.

Curnock, Nehemiah, ed. *The Journal of the Reverend John Wesley, A.M.* 8 vols. London, 1909.

De Vorsey, Louis, Jr., ed. *De Brahm's Report of the General Survey in the Southern District of North America.* Columbia, S.C., 1971.

Easterby, J. H., ed. *The Journal of the Commons House of Assembly.* 9 vols. Columbia, S.C., 1951–62.

Hvidt, Kristian, ed. *Von Reck's Voyage: Drawings and Journal of Philipp Georg Friedrich von Reck.* Savannah, 1980.

Jones, George Fenwick, ed. *Detailed Reports on the Salzburger Emigrants Who Settled in America . . . Edited by Samuel Urlsperger.* 8 vols. to date. Athens, Ga., 1968–.

———, ed. *Henry Newman's Salzburger Letterbooks.* Athens, Ga., 1966.

Lane, Mills B., ed. *General Oglethorpe's Georgia.* 2 vols. Savannah, 1975.

McDowell, William L., ed. *Colonial Records of South Carolina: Documents Relating to Indian Affairs.* 3 vols. Columbia, S.C., 1955, 1958, 1970.

McPherson, Robert G., ed. *The Journal of the Earl of Egmont.* Athens, Ga., 1962.

Mereness, Newton D., ed. *Travels in the American Colonies.* New York, 1916.

Oglethorpe, James Edward. "A Latin Poem by James Edward Oglethorpe," contributed by Rudolf Kirk, *GHQ* 32 (1948): 29–31.

————. *A New and Accurate Account of the Provinces of South-Carolina and Georgia.* London, 1733.

"Oglethorpe's Treaty with Lower Creek Indians, *GHQ* 4 (1920): 3–16.

Reese, Trevor R., ed. *The Clamorous Malcontents: Criticisms and Defenses of the Colony of Georgia, 1741–1743.* Savannah, 1973.

————, ed. *The Most Delightful Country of the Universe: Promotional Literature of the Colony of Georgia, 1717–1734.* Savannah, 1972.

————, ed. *Our First Visit to America: Early Reports from the Colony of Georgia, 1732–1740.* Savannah, 1974.

Roberts, R. A., ed. *Manuscripts of the Earl of Egmont: Diary of Viscount Percival, Afterwards First Earl of Egmont.* 3 Vols. London, 1920–23.

Telford, John, ed. *The Journal of the Reverend Charles Wesley, M.A.* London, 1909.

————, ed. *The Letters of the Reverend John Wesley, A.M.* 8 vols. London, 1931.

Ver Steeg, Clarence L., ed. *A True and Historical Narrative of the Colony of Georgia. By Pat. Tailfer and Others. With Comments by the Earl of Egmont.* Athens, Ga., 1960.

Secondary Sources

Books

Bolton, Herbert E., and Mary Ross. *The Debatable Land: A Sketch of the Anglo-Spanish Contest for the Georgia Country.* Berkeley and Los Angeles, 1925.

Bonner, James C. *A History of Georgia Agriculture, 1732–1860.* Athens, Ga., 1964.

Bruce, Henry. *Life of General Oglethorpe.* New York, 1890.

Cashin, Edward J., ed. *Colonial Augusta "Key of the Indian Countrey."* Macon, 1986.

Church, Leslie F. *Oglethorpe: A Study of Philanthropy in England and Georgia.* London, 1932.

Coleman, Kenneth. *Colonial Georgia: A History.* New York, 1976.

Middleton, Arthur Pierce. "The Strange Case of Job Ben Solomon," *WMQ*, 3d ser., 5 (1948): 342–50.

Morgan, David T. "John Wesley's Sojourn in Georgia Revisited," *GHQ* 64 (1980): 253–62.

———. "Judaism in Eighteenth-Century Georgia," *GHQ* 58 (1974): 41–54.

Pennington, Edgar Legare. "The Reverend Samuel Quincy, S.P.G. Missionary," *GHQ* 11 (1927): 157–65.

Ready, Milton L. "The Trustees and the Malcontents: The Politics of Philanthropy," *GHQ* 60 (1976): 264–81.

Saye, Albert B. "Was Georgia a Debtor Colony?" *GHQ* 24 (1940): 323–52.

Sirmans, M. Eugene. "The South Carolina Royal Council, 1720–1762," *WMQ*, 3d ser., 18 (1961): 373–92.

Spalding, Phinizy. "The Death of James Edward Oglethorpe," *GHQ* 57 (1973): 227–34.

———. "James Edward Oglethorpe: A Biographical Survey," *GHQ* 56 (1972): 241–51.

———. "James Oglethorpe and the American Revolution," *Journal of Imperial and Commonwealth History* 3 (May 1975 [1976]): 396–407.

———. "Myths and the Man: James Edward Oglethorpe," *Georgia Review* 28 (1974): 52–57.

———"Oglethorpe and Johnson: A Cordial Connection," *Johnson Society Transactions*, 1974 (1975): 52–61.

———. "Profile of an Old Independent: Oglethorpe as Seen in the Papers of James Boswell," *Yale University Library Gazette* 53 (1979): 140–49.

———. "Some Sermons Before the Trustees of Colonial Georgia," *GHQ* 57 (1973): 332–46.

———. "South Carolina and Georgia: The Early Days," *South Carolina Historical Magazine* 69 (1968): 241–51.

TePaske, John J. "The Fugitive Slave: Intercolonial Rivalry and Spanish Slave Policy, 1687–1764," in Samuel Proctor, ed., *Eighteenth-Century Florida and Its Borderlands*. Gainesville, 1975, 1–12.

Troxler, Carole Watterson. "William Stephens and the Georgia 'Malcontents': Conciliation, Conflict, and Capitulation," *GHQ* 67 (1983): 1–34.

Wood, Betty. "Thomas Stephens and the Introduction of Black Slavery in Georgia," *GHQ* 58 (1974): 24–40.

Many of the other articles cited in these essays may be found in Jackson and Spalding, *Forty Years of Diversity*.

Contributors

Born in Koscuisko, Mississippi, RODNEY M. BAINE graduated from Rhodes College, received three degrees from Oxford University, and his doctorate from Harvard. He has taught at the University of Missouri, M.I.T., the University of Alabama at Montevallo, and the University of Georgia, where he is Franklin Professor of English, Emeritus. He has published numerous scholarly articles and four books, including a critical biography of America's first comic dramatist—Robert Munford. Phinizy Spalding and he are editing the writings of General Oglethorpe.

EDWARD J. CASHIN is chairman of the Department of History, Political Science and Philosophy at Augusta College. He is the author of many articles on Georgia history (one of which won the Georgia Historical Society's E. Merton Coulter Award), and his books include *Augusta and the American Revolution* (with Heard Robertson), *The Story of Augusta*, and *Colonial Augusta: "Key of the Indian Country."* Professor Cashin recently received the Governor's Award in the Humanities from the Georgia Endowment for the Humanities for his efforts to acquaint Augustans with the history and heritage of their community.

KENNETH COLEMAN was born in Devereux, Georgia, and grew up there and in Atlanta where he attended Boys' High School. He received his A.B. and M.A. degrees from the University of Georgia and his Ph.D. from the University of Wisconsin. He was a member of the history faculty of the University of Georgia, where he is now professor emeritus. His specialty is Georgia history. Among his books are *The American Revolution in Georgia*, *Colonial Georgia: A History*, *A History of Georgia* (general editor and coauthor), *Dictionary of Georgia Biography* (coeditor and contributor), and seven volumes in the series *The Colonial Records of the State of Georgia* (coeditor).

Louis De Vorsey, Jr. holds degrees from Montclair State College, Indiana University, and the University of London and is professor emeritus of geography at the University of Georgia. His many honors include the Association of American Geographers Citation and Medallion for Meritorious Contributions to the Field of Geography (1975) and the Association of American Geographers Honor Award in Applied Geography (1983). Among his books are *The Indian Boundary in the Southern District of North America, De Brahm's Report of the General Survey in the Southern District of North America,* and *The Georgia–South Carolina Boundary: A Problem in Historical Geography.*

Edwin L. Jackson is a state government associate at the University of Georgia's Carl Vinson Institute of Government. He is author of the *Handbook of Georgia State Agencies,* the *Handbook for Georgia Legislators,* and a variety of other publications and audiovisual documentaries on Georgia history and government. Additionally, he serves as executive director of the Friends of Oglethorpe, an organization that seeks to promote scholarship and understanding of the life of James Edward Oglethorpe.

Harvey H. Jackson grew up in Grove Hill, Alabama, attended Marion Institute, Birmingham Southern College, The University of Alabama, and received his Ph.D. from the University of Georgia. He is currently professor of history at Clayton State College. His books include *Lachlan McIntosh and the Politics of Revolutionary Georgia, Forty Years of Diversity: Essays on Colonial Georgia* (coeditor and contributor), and *Georgia Signers and the Declaration of Independence* (coauthor). His articles have appeared in the *William and Mary Quarterly, Georgia Historical Quarterly, Atlanta Historical Journal,* and *Southern Studies.*

A native of Atlanta, Georgia, Phinizy Spalding attended school there and in Maryland, received his A.B. and M.A. degrees from the University of Georgia, and his Ph.D. from the University of North Carolina. His first teaching assignment was at the College of Charleston. He is now professor of history at the University of Georgia in Athens. In addition to editing the *Georgia Historical Quarterly* from 1974 to 1980, Spalding has published *Oglethorpe in America*, *The History of the Medical College of Georgia*, *A History of Georgia* (coauthor), and *Forty Years of Diversity: Essays on Colonial Georgia* (coeditor and contributor).

MARY E. WILLIAMS is a native of Savannah. She earned the A.B. at Georgia Southern College, the M.A. at Western Carolina University, and the Ph.D. in eighteenth-century British literature at the University of Georgia. Under the direction of Rodney M. Baine, her dissertation explored the relationship of James Oglethorpe, Samuel Johnson, and James Boswell. After receiving her doctorate, she taught for four years in Alabama. She is now assistant professor of humanities at Embry-Riddle Aeronautical University in Daytona Beach, Florida.

BETTY WOOD is a Fellow of Girton College and a Lecturer in the Faculty of History, University of Cambridge. She has published scholarly articles and essays in the *Historical Journal*, *Explorations in Economic History*, and the *Georgia Historical Quarterly* (one of which won the E. Merton Coulter Award from the Georgia Historical Society) and is the author of *Slavery in Colonial Georgia, 1730–1775*.

PETER WOOD is an associate professor of history at Duke University. He is the author of *Black Majority* (1974), a prizewinning study of slavery in colonial South Carolina, and, with Elizabeth Fenn, *Natives and Newcomers* (1983), a general introduction to early North Carolina history. Wood is coeditor of *Powhatan's Mantle*, a book of original essays about Indians in the Colonial Southeast (forthcoming). He is currently working on a survey of the eighteenth-century South from 1689 to 1763 for the LSU Press *History of the South* series.

Index